ROUTE SUMMARY TABLE

Stage number	Start/finish					Page No.
1	Canterbury to Shepherdswell					39
2	Shepherdswell to Dover to Calais by ferry					45
3	Calais to Wissant					55
4	Wissant to Guînes	23.4km	332m	335m	6¼hr	60
5	Guînes to Licques	16.3km	233m	172m	4½hr	64
6	Licques to Tournehem-sur-la-Hem	15.0km	233m	282m	4hr	67
7	Tournehem-sur-la-Hem to Wisques	19.8km	375m	293m	5½hr	70
8	Wisques to Delettes	18.0km	201m	278m	4½hr	74
9	Delettes to Amettes	22.8km	263m	221m	6hr	77
10	Amettes to Bruay-la-Buissière	21.1km	270m	292m	5¾hr	82
11	Bruay-la-Buissière to Ablain-Saint-Nazaire	24.7km	406m	378m	7hr	86
12	Ablain-Saint-Nazaire to Arras	22.5km	258m	275m	6hr	90
13	Arras to Bapaume	26.4km	242m	191m	6¾hr	96
14	Bapaume to Péronne	28.7km	238m	307m	7¾hr	100
15	Péronne to Trefcon	17.7km	135m	92m	4½hr	104
16	Trefcon to Seraucourt-le-Grand	28.2km	174m	200m	7¼hr	108
17	Seraucourt-le-Grand to Tergnier	18.8km	97m	112m	4¾hr	113
18	Tergnier to Laon	39.5km	478m	348m	10¼hr	116
19	Laon to Corbeny	29.6km	298m	381m	7¾hr	123
20	Corbeny to Berry-au-Bac	11.1km	42m	78m	2¾hr	127
21	Berry-au-Bac to Reims	28.5km	286m	256m	7½hr	133
22	Reims to Verzy	20.1km	197m	73m	5¼hr	140
23	Verzy to Condé-sur-Marne	19.9km	100m	226m	5hr	143
24	Condé-sur-Marne to Châlons-en-Champagne	17.0km	34m	31m	4¼hr	146
25	Châlons-en-Champagne to St-Germain-la-Ville	12.4km	22m	18m	3hr	149
26	St-Germain-la-Ville to Saint-Amand-sur-Fion	17.1km	75m	54m	4¼hr	152

Stage number	Start/finish	Distance	Total ascent	Total descent	Duration	Page No.
27	Saint-Amand-sur-Fion to Vitry-le-François	14.9km	146m	160m	4hr	156
28	Vitry-le-François to Saint-Remy-en-Bouzemont	21.1km	213m	201m	5½hr	159
29	Saint-Remy-en-Bouzemont to Outines	11.9km	86m	63m	3hr	163
30	Outines to Montmorency-Beaufort	16.5km	81m	90m	4¼hr	166
31	Montmorency-Beaufort to Précy-Saint-Martin	20.6km	178m	180m	5¼hr	169
32	Précy-Saint-Martin to Dienville	13.4km	137m	138m	3½hr	173
33	Dienville to Dolancourt	20.4km	222m	194m	5½hr	178
34	Dolancourt to Baroville	18.5km	458m	393m	5hr	182
35	Baroville to Orges	26.9km	473m	478m	7hr	186
36	Orges to Richebourg	18.8km	212m	83m	5hr	192
37	Richebourg to Faverolles	17.8km	258m	233m	4¾hr	196
38	Faverolles to Langres	21.0km	367m	267m	5½hr	200
39	Langres to Chalindrey	24.8km	161m	300m	6¼hr	205
40	Chalindrey to Coublanc	23.7km	372m	448m	6¼hr	210
41	Coublanc to Champlitte	11.7km	151m	156m	3hr	218
42	Champlitte to Dampierre-sur-Salon	19.5km	227m	275m	5hr	221
43	Dampierre-sur-Salon to Bucey-lès-Gy	33.9km	382m	368m	8¾hr	224
44	Bucey-lès-Gy to Cussey-sur-l'Ognon	14.6km	278m	250m	4hr	229
45	Cussey-sur-l'Ognon to Besançon	17.8km	256m	254m	4¾hr	233
46	Besançon to Foucherans	25.7km	696m	380m	7hr	238
47	Foucherans to Mouthier-Haute-Pierre	25.5km	297m	423m	6¾hr	243
48	Mouthier-Haute-Pierre to Pontarlier	23.7km	679m	279m	6½hr	249
49	Pontarlier to Jougne	23.1km	641m	494m	6¼hr	254
50	Jougne to Orbe	19.0km	208m	696m	5hr	263
51	Orbe to Cossonay	25.6km	520m	439m	6¾hr	271
52	Cossonay to Lausanne	24.9km	153m	331m	6½hr	277
Total	**Canterbury to Lausanne**	**1089.8km**	**13,500m**	**13,119m**	**286¼hr**	

WALKING THE VIA FRANCIGENA

PART 1

CANTERBURY TO LAUSANNE

by Sandy Brown

JUNIPER HOUSE, MURLEY MOSS,
OXENHOLME ROAD, KENDAL, CUMBRIA LA9 7RL
www.cicerone.co.uk

© Sandy Brown 2023
First edition 2023
ISBN: 978 1 85284 884 2

Printed in Singapore by KHL Printing on responsibly sourced paper
A catalogue record for this book is available from the British Library.

Route mapping by Lovell Johns www.lovelljohns.com
© Crown copyright 2023 OS PU100012932. NASA relief data courtesy of ESRI.
Contains OpenStreetMap.org data © OpenStreetMap contributors, CC-BY-SA. NASA
relief data courtesy of ESRI
The routes of the GR®, PR® and GRP® paths in this guide have been reproduced
with the permission of the Fédération Française de la Randonnée Pédestre holder of
the exclusive rights of the routes. The names GR®, PR® and GRP® are registered
trademarks. © FFRP 2023 for all GR®, PR® and GRP® paths appearing in this work.
All photographs are by the author unless otherwise stated.

Updates to this guide

While every effort is made by our authors to ensure the accuracy of guidebooks as
they go to print, changes can occur during the lifetime of an edition. This guidebook was researched and written during the COVID-19 pandemic. While we are
not aware of any significant changes to routes or facilities at the time of printing, it
is likely that the current situation will give rise to more changes than would usually
be expected. Any updates that we know of for this guide will be on the Cicerone
website (www.cicerone.co.uk/884/updates), so please check before planning your
trip. We also advise that you check information about such things as transport,
accommodation and shops locally. Even rights of way can be altered over time.

We are always grateful for information about any discrepancies between
a guidebook and the facts on the ground, sent by email to updates@cicerone.
co.uk or by post to Cicerone, Juniper House, Murley Moss, Oxenholme Road,
Kendal, LA9 7RL.

Register your book: To sign up to receive free updates, special offers and
GPX files where available, register your book at www.cicerone.co.uk.

Front cover: The 19th-century Paul Dubois statue of Joan of Arc outside Reims
Cathedral commemorates her victorious entry into the city in 1429

Symbols used on maps

main route	international boundary	castle
alternative route	regional boundary	viewpoint
bike route	station/railway	point of interest
(S) start point	ferry route	church/cathedral
(F) finish point	▲ summit	† cross
11.1 distance marker	✈ airport/airfield	cemetery
3.2 alt distance marker	= footbridge	lighthouse
■◉ bus stop/bus station	≍ bridge	windmill
■◉ railway station	)==(tunnel	water feature
M metro station	■ building	• other feature

FACILITIES

- 🏠 Accommodation
  - hostel
  - hotel
  - chambres d'hôtes (guest rooms)
  - B&B
  - ▲ camping
- groceries
- public toilets
- ATM
- petrol station
- drinking water tap
- rest/picnic area
- pharmacy
- (H) hospital
- medical clinic
- tourist/pilgrim information
- launderette

Catering
- bar
- restaurant
- café
- bakery

Relief
in meters

| 1000–1200 |
| 800–1000 |
| 600–800 |
| 400–600 |
| 200–400 |
| 0–200 |

MAP SCALES
Route maps at 1:100,000
Town maps at 1:40,000 unless otherwise stated (see scale bar)

SCALE: 1:100,000
0 kilometres 1 2
0 miles 1

SCALE: 1:40,000
0 kilometres 0.5 1
0 miles 0.5

5

Dedication

From the day of his birth I have never stopped being amazed by him. Even as a child, his confidence and poise taught me to relax and trust. Now that he is a dad, I watch his devotion to his children and stand back with wonder and love. To my son, Matt Brown McQuaid.

Acknowledgements

I quickly said 'yes' when Jonathan Williams of Cicerone Press offered to save me the quarantine days required to enter the UK and research the first two stages himself. The results are brilliant walking directions from Canterbury to Dover. In truth, Jonathan and Joe Williams committed early to this itinerary – first with pilgrim author Alison Raju a decade ago – and without them this series would never have seen the light of day.

Under Massimo Tedeschi and Luca Bruschi's leadership, the European Association of the Via Francigena ways (EAVF) offered key support for each of the three volumes. It's hard to imagine how the Via Francigena would exist today without Massimo's unfailing dedication to this grand, historic route. EAVF staff members who played a key role include Sami Tawfik, Myra Stals, Luca Faravelli, and especially Jacques Chevin, who oversees the French portion of the route. Jacques was the one I called when I wondered about a variant or an accommodation. The EAVF's accommodation listing and that of the Fédération Française Via Francigena were both of huge help to this volume.

I'm deeply indebted to the County of Kent and its many partners for their support in this volume, particularly Pete Morris and Catherine Bradley.

A talented team of Cicerone editors and designers turned my scribblings into a book. Chief among them were Natalie Simpson, Senior Editor; Georgia Laval, who edited the manuscript; and John Bingley, who designed the beautiful maps and the entire book. Then its production was ably overseen by Madeline Williams.

Among my travel companions, Bill Plunkett stands out. Whenever we set off for the day he would proclaim, 'Off to Vegas, baby!' and he greeted every obstacle with the same cheery attitude.

No one offered more support than my favorite walking partner, my wife Theresa Elliott. Even though research for this book took me away from home for months, she only thought about my safety and well-being, and made every homecoming a celebration.

CONTENTS

Note on mapping

The route maps in this guide are derived from publicly available data, databases and crowd-sourced data. As such they have not been through the detailed checking procedures that would generally be applied to a published map from an official mapping agency. However, we have reviewed them closely in the light of local knowledge as part of the preparation of this guide.

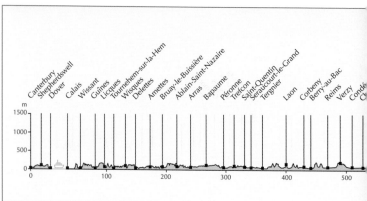

The village of Baroville is tucked into a vineyard covered valley (Stage 34)

The village of Baroville is tucked into a vineyard covered valley (Stage 34)

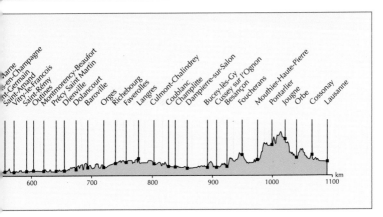

A farm road emerges from the trees near Difques (Stage 7)

FOREWORD

The Via Francigena – the Road to Rome – is a 'Cultural Route of the Council of Europe.' The European Association of the Via Francigena ways (EAVF) is a voluntary association of regions and local authorities of England, France, Switzerland and Italy, which currently accounts for more than 200 members. It was established on April 7, 2001 in Fidenza (Emilia-Romagna, Italy) to promote the Via Francigena, which stretches 3200 kilometers (2000 miles) from Canterbury to Santa Maria di Leuca.

The route travels from Canterbury through France and Switzerland to Rome, and continues to the south of Italy, heading towards Jerusalem. It passes through 16 European Regions (Kent, Hauts-de-France, Grand Est, Bourgogne-Franche-Comté, Vaud, Valais, Valle d'Aosta, Piedmont, Lombardy, Emilia-Romagna, Liguria, Tuscany, Lazio, Campania, Basilicata, and Apulia) in five countries (England, France, Switzerland, Italy and Vatican City). The Association carries out activities to enhance and promote the route at all institutional levels: local, regional, national and European.

In 2007 the Council of Europe declared the Association the 'carrier network' of the Via Francigena, assigning it the role of official reference point for safeguarding, protecting, promoting and developing the Via in Europe.

This guide to the Via from Canterbury to Lausanne is the result of collaboration between EAVF, Kent County Council, Cicerone Press and local associations.

The guide is aimed at walkers and pilgrims who want to discover the beauty of the English, French, and Swiss sections of this historic European route between the rolling farmlands of England and France, through the Jura Mountains, and ending at beautiful Lac Léman. The route is a way to discover a fascinating stretch of Europe, its traditions, cultural heritage and art treasures while getting to know its people.

This is a journey into the heart of the Via Francigena, which was defined as a 'bridge of cultures between Anglo-Saxon Europe and Latin Europe' by the famous medievalist Jacques Le Goff; a path of peace, tolerance and dialogue between cultures, religions and countries.

We wish you all a good journey! *Buon cammino!*

Massimo Tedeschi

President, European Association of the Via Francigena ways (EAVF)

For all information, visit www.viefrancigene.org, or follow us on our social media:

Facebook: @ViaFrancigenaEU

Instagram: @viafrancigena_eu, @viafrancigenasuisse

*Road to Rome community: https://www.facebook.com/groups/viafrancigena.
roadtorome*

A gravel road descends into Bar-sur-Aube (Stage 34)

INTRODUCTION: THE VIA FRANCIGENA FROM CANTERBURY TO LAUSANNE

Walkers descend a long stairway toward the bluffs after Cap Blanc-Nez (Stage 3)

In all the world there is nothing quite like the Via Francigena. Some countries host pilgrimage journeys that travel many kilometers over many days and weeks, that cross regions and mountain ranges to visit landmarks and shrines, that offer simple accommodations and memorable sights to welcome people to their nation. The Via Francigena is different. It is an international pilgrimage journey. It is founded on an ideal – that a walk across borders can transform many people into one.

The borders crossed on the Via Francigena are of nation (Britain, France, Switzerland, Italy), and language (English, French, Italian), and faith (Anglican, Catholic, Reformed). The method of the crossing is as old as the human foot: the slow-travel mode of walking that puts the scents of a new land into your nostrils, the tastes of an unfamiliar countryside onto your tongue, and the relationships built with strangers over many dinners and days into your heart.

The Via Francigena is also an itinerary of natural wonder. Two unforgettable sights frame this first portion – the **English Channel** and the **Jura Mountains**. The Channel experience begins at Dover, where the white cliffs are background for the scenic voyage to the French Côte d'Opale, colored like a dream in soft shades of turquoise and grey. The Jura Mountains, near the end of the journey, offer cascades of water falling among forested paths in high valleys, with picture-perfect villages sprung from Gustave Courbet landscapes.

Between the Channel and the Jura Mountains is a vast French countryside whose five themes are repeated with variations for 900km – fields, pastures, forests, rivers, and villages. In the northern stretches the five themes are punctuated by memorials to the last century's wars. Here the Via Francigena shines, because the itinerary crosses a once war-ravished land where the starry flag of the European Union proves that enemies can become friends. This part of the Via Francigena has human-made wonders, too. Intricate cathedrals built in the Middle Ages stand tall at **Canterbury**, **Laon**, and **Reims** and are so full of light that you might wonder how anybody called the Middle Ages dark.

But throughout the English, French or Swiss countryside the best part of the route is meeting the people, especially in their homes as they host you on your adventure. No matter their language or nationality, the people whose homes are in the quiet valleys or along the busy streets are people of great warmth. They are proud of their homeland, and they welcome you to their country with open arms.

A BRIEF HISTORY OF THE VIA FRANCIGENA

In its eight centuries of expansion, Rome as a republic and empire joined Europe, Asia Minor, and North Africa in ways they had never been connected before. As Rome's strength began to ebb it transitioned from a temporal capital to a spiritual one, and travelers made their way to and from the city on the Tiber for new reasons.

The ascendancy of Rome as premier among the spiritual capitals of Western Christianity, and the presence of the tombs of saints Peter and Paul, made it a pilgrimage destination from the earliest days of Christianity. With the evangelization of the British Isles by Saint Patrick in the fifth century and Saint Augustine of Canterbury in the late sixth, a stream of clerics and lay pilgrims began to flow between the British Isles and the capital of Western Christianity.

By the seventh century, fervent Christian missionaries like St Fredianus – an Irish priest who became bishop of Lucca – were traveling from Ireland to convert pagans and non-orthodox Christians on the Italian peninsula. A community of Anglo-Saxons – the Schola Anglorum – flourished in Rome in this era. Pilgrims who traveled overland to Rome on the most convenient route through France used what has come to be called the Via Francigena – the way of the French people. They would visit Rome and often not stop there but continue on to southerly ports for travel by sea to the Holy Land, for pilgrimage or for conquest.

Our knowledge of the overland route to Rome comes from the opportune survival of one bishop's Roman pilgrimage itinerary. In 990, the newly consecrated Archbishop of Canterbury, Sigeric of Ramsbury, traveled to Rome and back for the purpose of receiving his pallium, an item of liturgical wear meant for bishops and given only by the Pope. He listed pilgrimage churches there and key religious sites along the way. His itineraries in and from Rome to the English Channel were recorded and safely tucked away for centuries in the Canterbury Cathedral library (see Appendix D).

The itineraries made their way to the British Library, where scholars discovered them for what they are – first-hand evidence of the important geographic, economic and cultural interconnections within medieval Europe. For the 1000th-year celebration of Sigeric's journey, historian Giovanni Caselli mapped his original route with the help of Italian surveyors. Before long, leaders in Italy, like Fidenza mayor Massimo Tedeschi, realized that a modern connection among municipalities on the Via Francigena route would build international community and express the emerging idea of a united Europe. In April 2001,

the European Association of the Via Francigena ways (EAVF) was established to develop infrastructure, and the Francigena soon was designated an official Council of Europe Cultural Route. To enhance the French portion of the itinerary, the EAVF joined with the Fédération Française de la Randonnée Pédestre (FFRandonnée) who incorporated it into the French Grand Randonnée network as the GR145/Via Francigena.

Today, over 200 municipalities, 80 non-profit organizations and 500 private stakeholders underpin this pilgrimage route with resources, communication materials, and infrastructure, making it one of the world's premier walking pilgrimage itineraries.

The 11th-century manuscript containing Sigeric's itinerary in Rome and from Rome to the English Channel (courtesy of the British Library)

PLANNING YOUR WALK

Camino de Santiago pilgrims may antici-pate that they could just arrive on the Via Francigena between Canterbury and Lausanne and have everything they need for their journey, as on the Camino. Instead, in France and Switzerland it's very important to plan for your over-nights and food in advance. Experienced Francigena pilgrims will confirm this portion is more of an adventure, where smarts and planning are required to solve the route's inherent challenges, especially in France.

The route officially begins at this monument outside Canterbury Cathedral

WHERE TO BEGIN AND HOW TO GET THERE

Canterbury Cathedral is the official starting point of the Via Francigena, and if you want to get your feet under you before your Francigena, consider starting your walk from **Winchester** or **London** on the historic Pilgrim's Way

(www.pilgrimswaycanterbury.org; see *Walking the Pilgrim's Way*, published by Cicerone). A new route is being devel-oped from London to Canterbury called the Via Francigena Britannica (https:// pilgrimstorome.org.uk) that also holds promise as a walking itinerary prior to the official start in Canterbury. If you pre-fer the convenience of modern transport, a flight into London Heathrow (LHR) fol-lowed by the London Underground to St Pancras and a train to West Canterbury station is the easiest and quickest option to begin at the beginning.

Calais, Arras, Reims, Langres, and Besançon: These are also excellent start-ing points, and most of these options use Paris as their transportation connection. The Paris Metro makes transfer from the airports quite easy. Just download a Paris Metro map to orient yourself and choose your route to get from the airport to France's excellent train system. To start in Calais, fly into Paris Charles de Gaulle (CDG) and transfer to Paris Gare du Nord station. From there, it's about 2hr to the Calais Ville station. To start in Arras, follow the same basic route, and the Arras train station is right on the Via Francigena. To begin in Reims, transfer to the Gare Paris Est for the 45min jour-ney. To begin in Langres, use Gare Paris Est as well and plan on 3hr. To begin at Besançon, use Gare de Lyon and plan on 2½hr minimum to Besançon-Viotte. France's trains are clean and economi-cal; for reservations and tickets go to www.sncf.com/en or ticket apps like Trainline (www.trainline.com).

HOW TO GET BACK

Finishing at Lausanne: A good international airport at Geneva and a quick train connection from Lausanne make it an excellent place to finish. It's about a 50min train ride (CHF13.50) from Lausanne Gare (which is just 1km from this book's end point) to the Geneva International 'Cointrin' Airport (GVA). From there you can access many major European airports as well as many off the continent.

Continuing on the Via Francigena: Of course, the Francigena continues from Lausanne over the Alps to Italy and on to Rome. Check out the other volumes in this series to learn more.

WHEN TO WALK

People walking only the stages between Canterbury and Besançon can be assured that late spring through early fall are good choices for the route, with all the usual warnings about rain in the spring and fall and hot temperatures in the high summer. Over the Jura Mountains after Besançon temperatures are cooler, and cold weather comes earlier in the fall and lingers later into the spring. Fall brings hunters into the woods of France, and people unnerved by the sound of firearms will be uncomfortable in the autumn months. Those who do walk then are wise to include some kind of high-visibility clothing to avoid the unlikely scenario of not being seen by a hunter.

While in France the route crosses vast agricultural lands with crops like grain, as in this photo, and grapes, as well as livestock

19

To walk beyond Lausanne across the Great Saint Bernard Pass (GSB) requires some calculations on the calendar. Those wishing to begin in Canterbury and cross the GSB when the snow is cleared from the roadway should begin 45–60 days before the common June 1 road opening. For those wishing to cross when the GSB walking path is clear, a July–September crossing is optimal and again the 45–60 day advance start in Canterbury should be considered. The disadvantage of waiting for passable conditions on GSB is that a summer crossing puts you into Italy just in time for high-summer temperatures. You can also cross the snowy heights of the GSB by bus, which opens up spring and fall for your walk.

CYCLING AND THE 'UN-OFFICIAL BIKE OPTION'

While the Via Francigena in France is a walking itinerary, much of the terrain is perfectly suited to bicycles, and people who don't have time to walk or who just prefer to cycle may enjoy this route on two wheels. A time-friendly option is to rent a bicycle in Calais, ride it to Besançon, and return it there to continue on foot through the more mountainous terrain that follows. One bike rental agency that offers this service is www.cyrpeo.com. This compresses 900km into about 14 cycling days, which takes about three weeks off the journey.

Time and distance also enter into the equation given the design of the track itself. The GR145/Via Francigena route through France often intentionally diverts from direct asphalt roads and onto occasionally muddy dirt roads and trails so it can offer a green, pleasant, and nature-centric walking experience. The practical result is that walking pilgrims who want to preserve days and kilometers often go 'off-route' to shorten their day, sometimes even choosing to walk on a busy highway instead of a more circuitous route.

To meet the needs of both cyclists and time-conscious walkers, the author of this guide has mapped out an unofficial blue-line 'bike option' that is usually a shorter, more direct track between the villages and towns visited on the official route. This unofficial bike route assumes a mountain bike or hybrid mountain/road bike that can handle the occasional gravel road or single-track dirt path. It is not intended for narrow-tire road bikes.

Due to space concerns and the nature of its unofficial status, only the walking route is described in this book, while the bike option is shown on the maps but not described. GPX tracks for both routes are available for download at the book's website (www.cicerone.co.uk/884/GPX).

WHERE TO STAY

The greatest Via Francigena resource in France is a system of *chambres d'hôtes* – guest rooms in private homes – that specifically welcome pilgrims. While pilgrims may be accustomed to more commercial or institutional hostels, hotels or *albergues* on other pilgrimage routes, the Francigena's infrastructure of private hosts creates a unique and rewarding cross-cultural experience that should not be missed. The *chambres d'hôtes* also provide an essential resource for food when no restaurants or

Gîtes, like this one at Thérouanne, are one of many accommodation options along the way

Some pilgrims assume that tent camping is requisite in France, and some expect they'll need a tent in case they have to sleep rough. However, tent camping doesn't solve the problem of finding food when there are no restaurants or grocery stores – for this, nothing compares with the *chambres d'hôtes* system. Before planning to camp, consider the need to find and carry food, consider the weight and inconvenience of carrying a tent and cooking gear, and then also consider that even camping pilgrims generally send their camping gear back home once they are beyond Lausanne and the Great St Bernard Pass into Italy, where the Francigena offers a much better-developed network of pilgrim hostels. For more information, see www.viefrancigene.org/en/accommodations-facilities/.

grocery stores are nearby. Campgrounds in Switzerland and France often have bungalows or mobile homes available as well as tent sites, so campgrounds should not be crossed off the list for pilgrims not carrying tents. Some cities have youth hostels that welcome people of all ages. *Gîtes* (guest cottages, apartments or renovated barns) are an option as well, as are commercial hotels when available.

The most comprehensive listing of lodging is produced by the Fédération Française Via Francigena (https://ffvf.fr) and its €7 cost is money well spent. Several major online accommodation resources (www.booking.com, www.airbnb.com) are easy and familiar for English speakers, but French resources like www.chambres-hotes.fr and www.gites-de-france.com – which both have built-in English translations – will actually be more helpful in rural France.

WHAT AND WHERE TO EAT

Pilgrims on the Via Francigena will find an assortment of grocery stores, restaurants, and bars in all the medium and large metropolitan areas of England, France, and Switzerland. Be aware that restaurant and shop owners often close one day each week, and often (but not always) this is Sunday afternoon through Monday night. Because their regular customers already know this schedule, the closures may or may not be posted on the door of the establishment.

Pilgrims will find that in France's hamlets and villages there are very scarce options for purchasing food. **Sometimes there may be two or three stages between grocery stores.** Again, this is one of the benefits of the *chambre d'hôtes* system because 99% of the time you can reserve a demi-pension (dinner and breakfast) that will be provided by your host. On request, your host will usually prepare a snack lunch for you as well, for a small additional fee. Even so, it's not unwise to carry 1–2 days' worth of dehydrated hiking meals or light-weight groceries in your pack in case you find yourself without food options at stage end.

Drinking-water faucets in pub-lic places are common in Italy and Switzerland, but uncommon in France. Plan to have 1.5–3 liters capacity and fill up at your lodging in the morning, since options to refill through the day will be scarce. Look for water faucets at cemeteries and don't hesitate to ask local residents for a refill along the way if you run out. Also consider download-ing a drinking-water locator app such as Water-Map™ or DrinkStop™.

French cuisine is one of the highlights of the Francigena

SHOULD I MAKE RESERVATIONS AHEAD?

Except in commercial accommodations, on the entire Via Francigena your hosts are likely to have a full-time job some-where else and are fitting you into their often busy schedules. Don't assume they're at the door, waiting in case a pilgrim might appear. Make reservations at least 1–2 days ahead so they know you're coming and can be there when you arrive.

For non-French speakers who want to make reservations in France and Switzerland it may be tempting to use translation software and write an email, but, sadly, email responses are often not up to expectations and a phone call is required anyway. If you're uncomfortable conversing in French, ask your overnight host to help you make a few reservations in advance. They're usually very happy to help and may already know your next host.

HOW MUCH MONEY SHOULD I BUDGET?

With different currencies and different networks of accommodations, costs vary on the Via Francigena between the UK, France and Switzerland. Exchange rates among currencies vary as well, so check to see how currency conversions affect your budget. Here are some examples of daily costs (at the time of writing) in the three countries based on a single accommodation:

Expense category	UK (single cost in single accommodation, B&B or hotel)	France (single cost per person in family hosted room)	Switzerland (single accommodation in B&B or hotel)
Lodging	£80*	€25	CHF100*
Breakfast	£10	€5	CHF10
Sack lunch	£10	€5	CHF10
Afternoon snack	£5	€5	CHF5
Dinner	£20	€15	CHF25
Incidentals	£5	€5	CHF5
Total	**£130**	**€60**	**CHF155**

*divide by two if room is shared by two people

WHAT IS A PILGRIM CREDENTIAL AND HOW DO I GET ONE?

The pilgrim credential is a document that certifies that the bearer is a pilgrim who is walking, cycling, or riding the route on horseback. It allows pilgrims to stay overnight in pilgrim lodging and, if stamped for at least the last 100km before Rome, it qualifies the bearer to receive a testimonium completion certificate at Vatican City.

It's best to order a credential in advance from the European Association of the Via Francigena, which offers official credentials through its partner, SloWays (www.viefrancigene.org/en, €5 plus shipping, allow 1–2 months). Appendix B includes a list of locations on the Via Francigena between Canterbury and Lausanne where you can collect a credential in person.

Plan to hunt down one stamp corresponding to each overnight along the way. A stamp (tampon in French, pronounced 'tom-PONE') is usually available at lodgings, but also at many tourist information centers, bars, churches, museums, tourist offices and city halls.

A Via Francigena pilgrim credential

The highest of its altars hints at Canterbury Cathedral's Romanesque roots (Stage 1)

A basic understanding of the terrain and the cultures helps a Via Francigena pilgrim get the most out of his or her walk.

The two most significant topographical features of this portion of the Via Francigena are the English Channel and the Jura Mountains. Although the Channel Tunnel makes train travel simple, for most pilgrims England is still a boat ride away from France. The Jura (as in Jurassic) Mountains are the tall wall between France and Switzerland. Although their foothills begin after Langres, they become a key feature immediately after Besançon and make for a bumpy walk to Orbe and Lausanne, Switzerland. The Juras provide a few days of mountain hiking, and the walk up and out of Besançon (Stage 46) and the hikes before and after Pontarlier (Stages 48–49) are the most memorably steep.

On the English side of the Channel, walkers in Kent – the county that holds both Canterbury and Dover – quickly learn the meaning of the word 'downs.' These are low, rolling hills with thin soil covering a chalk base. The route from Canterbury to Dover descends on downs toward sea level, where the chalk produces the famous 'White Cliffs of Dover.' This whitish substrata less famously continues on the French side, where it was used as a building material as far south as Arras. From Calais to Arras the rolling hills of the downs are more exaggerated into steeper valleys and ridges, but generally of no more than about 100m in elevation.

Contrary to its reputation, everything between Calais and Besançon is not exactly flat. 'Flat-ish' may be more precise. River valleys and ridges provide downs and ups, as well as a few climbs – up into Bruay-la-Buissière, up after Bar-sur-Aube and up after Montmorency-Beaufort. These are the exceptions that prove the quasi-flat rule. The region is drainage for many notable rivers, and the walk through France until Besançon could accurately be described as crossing over successive low ridges from one river valley to the next.

The rivers – and their ingenious 16th–19th-century canals – are the primary topographical feature of the 900km between Calais and Besançon, and the Francigena touches more than 35 of them. WWI battlefields made some of them world-famous, like the Marne, Aisne, and Somme. Here the presence of the Jura Mountains is felt, since basically all rivers north of their foothills feed into the Seine which flows north into the English Channel. In the Jura foothills after Langres the route moves from the drainage of the Marne, a Seine tributary that feeds into the Atlantic, to the drainage of the Salon and Saône, tributaries of the Rhône, which feed into the Mediterranean. In over 1000 kilometers of the Via Francigena in France and Switzerland you are always in the drainages of either the mighty Seine or Rhône Rivers.

UNDERSTANDING LOCAL CULTURES

The Via Francigena spans four countries, not to mention the Vatican, and innumerable cultures. From Canterbury to Lausanne it is at its most diverse. Here are some thoughts on what to expect.

England: To English-speakers from outside the British Isles, Canterbury and Kent will feel like an older, quainter, and more charming version of home. Most will have to learn that the British drive on the left side of the road, and 'Look Right' is often emblazoned at crosswalks as a reminder.

Bread machines often fill the gap when a bakery is not nearby

Canterbury's pubs are clearly an institution. They are all named 'The [Something],' and starting in the early afternoon the narrow streets of the old city have the pleasant smells of pints being dispensed and consumed, usually with the sounds of a sports match coming from the TV to the groans or cheers of happy, anxious or weeping fans.

France: Pilgrims will almost universally discover the French to be friendly, helpful, polite, and hospitable. People will also find French villages and hamlets to be surprisingly empty and devoid of services like bars or cafés. The center of French rural gastronomy is the local bakery, and there may be no retail establishment in a town other than the stop-by-for-bread place (without chairs on which you might sit to enjoy your treat). If there's no bakery there will be a bakery delivery truck, or a vending machine designed to dispense the most basic French food commodity – the baguette.

Although English is compulsory in French schools, in the countryside most people do not speak it with confidence and prefer to use their native language, so having a smartphone app ready for translations is very helpful. Studies show that about 40% of the French population does speak some English – about double the number of English who speak French.

Switzerland: Given centuries of proximity to France and much common history, people in the Vaud region of Switzerland speak French as their primary language. Swiss also learn either German or Italian in school, and surveys suggest that about two-thirds of Swiss citizens speak at least some English.

Switzerland operates with a Helvetic efficiency and trains are clean and on time, gardens are neat and orderly, and taxes are steep and put to work on effective public services. The cost of living is also high, but so is the standard of living. The biggest surprise of walking in Switzerland is most likely to be the scale of the wine industry, which is seldom recognized internationally. These tasty wines are mostly consumed by the Swiss rather than exported, it seems, which makes it wise to sample some while in the country.

TRAINING FOR YOUR WALK

While anyone who is of average or better fitness can complete a walk of this kind, the experience is much more pleasant with some advance training. Training prepares the muscles and tendons of your legs and feet for the daily regime of long walks, and gives you time to fix any shoe or sock problems that might lead to painful blisters.

Local supporters often provide rest areas for pilgrim walkers and cyclists

A training program should include walks of increasing distance over varied terrain for 2–3 months in advance of your trip, building toward at least two successive walks of around 20–25km during the week prior to your departure.

If blisters develop in training walks, adjust your socks and shoes, sandals or boots until you find the right combination. Blisters occur especially when skin is damp, so carefully consider whether you want waterproof shoes or boots that often have little or no ventilation. Try to duplicate the conditions of your pilgrimage by walking with a loaded pack on varied terrain during training, which benefits your cardio conditioning and duplicates the stresses your feet will undergo as you walk the Via Francigena.

WHAT AND HOW TO PACK

Via Francigena pilgrims often have at least one Camino de Santiago in their past, giving them an appreciation of the benefits of packing light.

A good packing list includes:
- Backpack: 35–50L
- Clothes: layers, maximum 2–3 pants and shirts
- Rain gear: poncho, rain jacket and/or trekking umbrella, waterproof or quick-dry trousers
- Sun gear: sun hat, sunscreen, sunglasses
- Bedding: hostels are generally equipped with wool blankets, so a sleeping bag liner in summer is wise and a lightweight sleeping bag otherwise
- Walking boots/shoes and camp shoes

- Hydration system: reusable bottles or bladder
- Basic first-aid and blister kit
- Toiletries
- Hiking towel
- Smartphone/camera and charger
- Travel and identity documents
- Debit and credit cards
- Toilet paper and a few plastic bags
- Trekking poles as needed
- Miscellaneous: zippered mesh bags are helpful for keeping your items organized inside your pack. Some like to bring along a small clothes-line and clothespins for drying just-washed items, as well as earplugs for a restful sleep.

A common rule of thumb is to pack no more than 10% of your body weight – including food and water – although of course that breaks down with people who are either very large or very small. Extra food is a very wise idea, so pack 1–2 days' worth of dehydrated hiking meals at the bottom of your pack (see 'What and where to eat,' above).

BAGGAGE TRANSPORT AND STORAGE

There is a baggage transport agency in Burgundy that transports your baggage from Champlitte to Jougne/Sainte-Croix. The agency is called Roule ma Poule. You need to book it at least two or three weeks in advance. See https://www.agence-roulemapoule.fr/navettes-via-francigena-via-salina.

There is also a baggage transport agency in Switzerland named Eurotrek. See https://www.eurotrek.ch/en/travel-info/during-your-trip/luggage-transport.

Additionally, overnight accommodations are sometimes willing for a fee to make transfer arrangements for you, particularly if you're staying in a tourist-oriented hotel. Sometimes this involves a taxi trip, so the cost may be high (think €20–50 per stage). Most Via Francigena pilgrims will carry their own gear on this portion of the route, which of course recommends packing light.

TELEPHONES

SIM cards and international plans
Pilgrims from outside the EU may find it expensive to use their cell provider's international calling plan. If you anticipate heavy usage of voice calls, data, or messaging you may want to purchase a UK or EU SIM card for your unlocked smartphone when you arrive in Europe. Rather than switching out a SIM chip, it's now possible to purchase e-SIM cards for use in the UK and/or EU. One of the largest providers is www.airalo.com, which offers prepaid data plans for unlocked devices usable in over 190 countries.

The UK's big four providers are EE (https://ee.co.uk), O2 (www.o2.co.uk), 3 (www.three.co.uk), and Vodafone (www.vodafone.co.uk). France's largest providers are Orange (https://boutique.orange.fr/mobile), SFR (www.sfr.fr), Free (www.free.fr), and Buoygues (www.bouyguestelecom.fr). Switzerland's largest providers are Swisscom (www.swisscom.ch) and Sunrise (www.sunrise.ch). Italy's largest providers are Vodaphone (www.vodaphone.it), TIM (www.tim.it), and Wind Tre (www.windtre.it).

If you're beginning in Canterbury and ending in Italy it's very easy and economical to buy a Vodaphone SIM card in Canterbury and use it the entire route, since Vodaphone is also a major Italian carrier. It's also nice for English-only speakers to receive texts, web links, and phone calls from a provider that communicates in English.

Country prefixes and dialing '0'

If you're calling from a cell phone and your SIM card is from a country other than the one you're in, always dial the country code before the number – in the UK '+44,' France '+33,' Switzerland '+41.' If you're calling from the same country as your SIM card, you do not need to dial the country code, but you instead dial '0'. So, when a French number is listed in this guidebook as +33 (0)1 23 45 67 89, a British SIM card holder will need to dial +33 1 23 45 67 89. Somebody with a French SIM card in France would dial 01 23 45 67 89. Because this portion of the Via Francigena spans three countries, this guidebook specifies each phone number's respective country code.

Emergency health and safety phone numbers

Europe's continent-wide emergency number is 112 and it's a wise idea to keep that number in mind at all times. Each country has other numbers that are also useful (see table below).

Pharmacies

If you become sick or injured and don't feel it's an emergency, a good starting place for help is the local pharmacy – these are marked throughout Europe with the sign of a green cross. If the pharmacist can't help you, he or she will recommend a nearby clinic or hospital.

Service	England	France	Switzerland
General emergency	999, 112	112, 17	112
Police (non-emergency)	101	17	117
Fire department	999, 112	18	-
Medical emergencies	999, 112	15	-
Non-emergency medical	111	15, 116, 117	144
Fires, wildfires	-	18	118
Wilderness rescue	-	-	1414, 1415

The Via Francigena is also signed as the North Downs Way in the UK, the GR145 in France, and Route 70 in Switzerland

HOW TO USE THIS GUIDE

ROUTE DESCRIPTIONS

As part of Cicerone's pilgrimage series, this guide is loaded with helpful information for your walk.

Each stage is laid out in the following format:

Route summary information
Information included at the start of each stage provides the specific starting and ending point, statistics about the stage, as well as information summarizing the walk.

Total distance: Unless otherwise specified, the number given is always based on the official route with all extraneous waypoints carefully edited out and the tracks smoothed to one waypoint for each 30 meters in distance. Expect the unedited tracks from your recreational GPS, smartphone app or step counter to add about 10–15% to the total.

Total ascent and descent: These figures record the ups and downs that occur as you gain and lose elevation through the day. Elevation figures for GPS tracks in this book are provided through www.gpsvisualizer.com using the best of either ODP1, ASTER or NASA altitude data.

Difficulty: Using a formula that balances total distance, steepness and ascent/descent totals, all stages are awarded one of four designations: 'Easy,' 'Moderate,' 'Moderately hard,' or 'Hard.'

Duration: This book uses an algorithm that calculates duration based on 4km/hr with an additional five minutes added for every 100m of ascent,

rounding the result to the nearest ¼hr. Rest stops and sightseeing are not included in the duration total.

Percentage paved: This percentage shows how much of the walk is on hard surfaces like concrete, tarmac, asphalt, and cobblestones rather than softer surfaces like gravel, dirt roads, and dirt paths. Percentages in this book are derived from the website https://ridewithgps.com which bases its estimates on user data.

Lodging: Distances to settlements with lodgings between the starting and ending points are included in order to help you plan your stages.

Overview: This paragraph summarizes the stage and shares any special tips, recommendations or warnings walkers should know before beginning the walk.

Walking directions, distances and municipality information headings
Since the Via Francigena between Canterbury and Lausanne is moderately well marked, only moderately detailed walking descriptions are given for each stage. Care has been taken to provide directions when the signage was insufficient during the research walks that led to this text. Bold type is used when a landmark is also called out on the map, and intermediate distances are provided in the text between municipalities. Because underlying distance calculations are based on 100ths of a kilometer while intermediate distances are shown at 10ths of a kilometer, some minor decimal rounding discrepancies naturally result

Figure 1: Example of stage description and municipal information

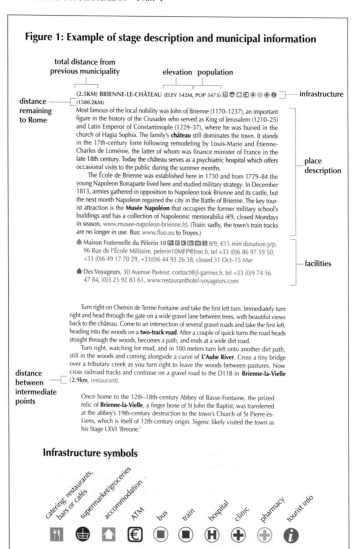

total distance from previous municipality

elevation population

(2.5KM) BRIENNE-LE-CHÂTEAU (ELEV 142M, POP 3473) — infrastructure

distance remaining to Rome
(1580.2KM)

Most famous of the local nobility was John of Brienne (1170–1237), an important figure in the history of the Crusades who served as King of Jerusalem (1210–25) and Latin Emperor of Constantinople (1229–37), where he was buried in the church of Hagia Sophia. The family's **château** still dominates the town. It stands in the 17th-century form following remodeling by Louis-Marie and Étienne-Charles de Loménie, the latter of whom was finance minister of France in the late 18th century. Today the château serves as a psychiatric hospital which offers occasional visits to the public during the summer months.

The École de Brienne was established here in 1730 and from 1779–84 the young Napoleon Bonaparte lived here and studied military strategy. In December 1813, armies gathered in opposition to Napoleon took Brienne and its castle, but the next month Napoleon regained the city in the Battle of Brienne. The key tourist attraction is the **Musée Napoléon** that occupies the former military school's buildings and has a collection of Napoleonic memorabilia (€9, closed Mondays in season, www.musee-napoleon-brienne.fr). (Train: sadly, the town's train tracks are no longer in use. Bus: www.fluo.eu to Troyes.)

place description

Maison Fraternelle du Pèlerin 10 Py R K Br W S 8/9, €15 min donation p/p, 96 Rue de l'École Militaire, pelerin10MFP@free.fr, tel +33 (0)6 86 97 59 50, +33 (0)6 49 17 70 29, +33(0)6 44 93 26 38, closed 31 Oct–15 Mar

Des Voyageurs, 30 Avenue Pasteur, contact@jl-garnier.fr, tel +33 (0)9 74 56 47 84, (0)3 25 92 83 61, www.restauranthotel-voyageurs.com

facilities

Turn right on Chemin de Terme Fontaine and take the first left turn. Immediately turn right and head through the gate on a wide gravel lane between trees, with beautiful views back to the château. Come to an intersection of several gravel roads and take the first left, heading into the woods on a **two-track road**. After a couple of quick turns the road heads straight through the woods, becomes a path, and ends at a wide dirt road.

Turn right, watching for mud, and in 100 meters turn left onto another dirt path, still in the woods and coming alongside a curve of **L'Aube River**. Cross a tiny bridge over a tributary creek as you turn right to leave the woods between pastures. Now cross railroad tracks and continue on a gravel road to the D11B in **Brienne-la-Vielle (2.9km**, restaurant).

distance between intermediate points

Once home to the 12th–18th-century Abbey of Basse-Fontaine, the prized relic of **Brienne-la-Vielle**, a finger bone of St John the Baptist, was transferred at the abbey's 19th-century destruction to the town's Church of St Pierre-ès-Liens, which is itself of 12th-century origin. Sigeric likely visited the town as his Stage LXVI 'Breone.'

Infrastructure symbols

catering: restaurants, bars or cafés | supermarket/groceries | accommodation | ATM | bus | train | hospital | clinic | pharmacy | tourist info

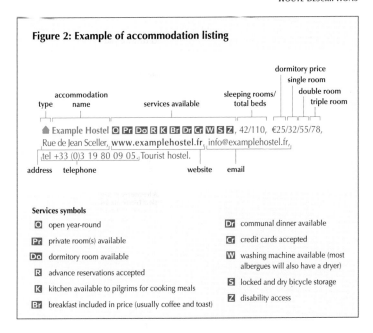

Figure 2: Example of accommodation listing

when intermediate distances are added together. Municipalities with lodgings have their own headings within the route description and on maps with 11 codes that indicate services available in those places, a key to which is given in the diagram below.

Accommodation listings

The European Association of the Via Francigena ways (EAVF) has done an excellent job of creating a network of pilgrim-specific lodgings located in churches, monasteries, convents, municipal facilities, church retreat houses, and private homes that are not included in typical tourist resources like Booking.com. Through the author's

research as well as collaboration with the EAVF, the Confraternity of Pilgrims to Rome (https://pilgrimstorome.org. uk) and the Fédération Française Via Francigena (www.ffvf.fr), the names, contact information, cost, and symbols for 10 important infrastructure elements are given, when available, for these lodgings to help you make your choice. The listings give priority to low-cost options, but also occasionally show less economical historic or scenic properties that are near the route.

Elevation profiles

Elevation profiles are included for every regional section and for stages with significant elevation changes to provide a

The Phare de Verzenay (Stage 22) was constructed to draw people toward the area's wineries

graphical representation of the distance, ascents, and descents. To save space, the profiles are provided by section in places where the route is relatively flat, but otherwise are shown by individual stage. Individual profiles for all stages can be downloaded from www.cicerone. co.uk/884.

Maps

All Cicerone guidebook maps are 'north up' and show the entire stage route at 1:100,000 resolution. Seven cities – Canterbury, Calais, Arras, Reims, Langres, Besançon, and Lausanne – are shown at 1:40,000. Routes are always depicted by a solid red line, with optional route lines in dotted red and the bike option in solid blue. Where the bike option and walking route are the

same, they are shown in red. Check the map key at the start of the book for more details about map symbols.

GPX TRACKS AND ACCOMMODATION DOWNLOADS

A printout of the accommodation listings can be downloaded from www.cicerone.co.uk/884. Always remember to visit the book's Cicerone website to find the latest book updates.

GPX tracks for the routes in this guidebook are available to download free at www.cicerone.co.uk/884/GPX. GPX files are provided in good faith, but neither the author nor the publisher accepts responsibility for their accuracy.

SECTION 1: KENT

Canterbury Cathedral towers over nearby shops and restaurants (Stage 1)

Dover Castle has stood guard over the port for centuries (Stage 2)

Section 1 overview

While much of Kent is within commuting distance of London, the county has a rural character and is proud of its nickname, the 'Garden of England.' Rolling hills over a chalk substratum are the primary topographical feature, and these 'downs' are crossed by the gently hilly North Downs Way National Trail. The Via Francigena in Kent follows exactly the path of the North Downs Way and the trail markers from Canterbury to Dover are dual signed for both the Via Francigena and the North Downs Way.

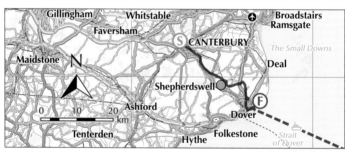

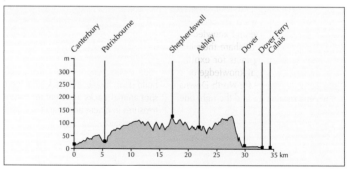

KENT COUNTY

Co-financed by the European Union and the European Regional Development Fund

UNESCO WORLD HERITAGE SITE

Canterbury is home to three UNESCO World Heritage Sites: Canterbury Cathedral, with its stunning mixture of Romanesque and Perpendicular Gothic architecture; the modest Church of St Martin (the oldest church in the English-speaking world); and the ruins of St Augustine's Abbey, once a burial place for the Anglo-Saxon kings of Kent.

Follow in the footsteps of Queen Bertha with a 1½-mile self-led walk connecting all three World Heritage Sites.

NORTH DOWNS WAY AMBASSADORS

Whether you're into history, photography, mythology, flora, fauna or folklore, the North Downs Way Ambassadors are extremely passionate and knowledgeable, and are keen to share their top tips and fascinating facts for exploring the trail. For local knowledge or a guided walk, search for North Downs Way Ambassadors to find the right one for you.

https://kentdowns.org.uk/north-downs-way/find-a-north-downs-way-ambassador

YOUR GREAT ESCAPE – EXPLORE KENT'S BEST-KEPT SECRETS

Create new memories as you immerse yourself in nature and heritage and discover unique new experiences in the Kent Downs Area of Outstanding Natural Beauty (AONB).

Tickle your tastebuds – from picturesque vineyards and orchards, to rich, rural farmlands and the wild and plentiful coast, Kent's landscape offers a bountiful crop of home-grown products, dishes and experiences, making it one of the UK's most popular foodie destinations.

Nurtured by nature – make some time to relax, refresh and breathe in the fresh air of the beautiful Kent countryside and you will soon enjoy incredible health and wellbeing experiences surrounded by nature.

Family favorites – reconnect with your favorite people. Book a llama walk, build dens, forage and cook local foods, spot animal tracks and hunt for nature's treasures in places and spaces you never knew existed.

ARTS TRAIL

Launched in the winter of 2021, the Via Francigena Arts Trail created three installations providing pilgrims with creative and beautiful places to rest and contemplate. The installations promote the special characteristics of the Via Francigena and its pilgrimage heritage as a route for reflection, renewal, and inspiration. The sculptures are located at Barham Downs and Woolage Village on the Canterbury to Shepherdswell section, with a third installation within the grounds of Waldershare Park on the Shepherdswell to Dover section. For more information, search online for North Downs Way Arts Trail.

RURAL CHURCHES

Between the celebrated pilgrim locations of Canterbury Cathedral and Maison Dieu, Dover there are several smaller but significant churches on route, each with its own story to tell. At four of these churches you will find information panels telling these stories and providing further local information about the route and things to look out for on your journey. These can be found at St Martin's Church, Canterbury; St Mary's, Patrixbourne; St Margaret's, Womenswold; and St Andrew's, Shepherdswell.

CYCLING THE VIA FRANCIGENA IN KENT

Cycling UK, in partnership with the North Downs Way National Trail have been working hard to improve cycling access on the Via Francigena. The North Downs Way Riders' Route provides an alternative cycling route that runs alongside the walking Francigena route, and there are dedicated cycle hubs in Canterbury and Dover offering shorter routes and cycling-friendly businesses. For more information, search online for the North Downs Way Riders' Route.

FOOD AND DRINK IN THE GARDEN OF ENGLAND

As the name suggests, Kent has a rich heritage in local food and drink. In Canterbury city center, check out the vast array of local produce at the Goods Shed, or sample local ales, gins and spirits produced in Canterbury at the Foundry Brew Pub. In Dover, take a short trip to the Breakwater Brewery located on the River Dour on the outskirts of town, or take in the sea views at The Dover Patrol.

KENT HERITAGE COAST – LONELY PLANET'S BEST IN TRAVEL

Kent's Heritage Coast running along the Dover coastline was named fourth best global destination in Lonely Planet's Best in Travel 2022 ranking. This is in recognition of its unique history, heritage and iconic natural landscapes and its sustainable tourism. The Via Francigena runs through the town to the coast, terminating on the Dover seafront; with the iconic White Cliffs and Heritage Coast climbing either side of the esplanade, it's worth taking time to explore this internationally award-winning landscape.

STAGE 1

Canterbury to Shepherdswell

Start	Canterbury Cathedral, main entrance
Finish	Shepherdswell, St Andrew's Church
Distance	17.2km
Total ascent	260m
Total descent	150m
Difficulty	Easy
Duration	4½hr
Percentage paved	35%
Lodging	Shepherdswell 17.2km

It's quite possible to walk from Canterbury to Dover in one go, but this would be a very long (33km, 8hr) first day unless you are already trail hardened. Splitting the English section over two days also allows more time in Canterbury, and taking the Dover–Calais ferry in the afternoon sets you up for your first French evening to be in Calais.

The first day's walking is on the North Downs Way (NDW) National Trail through wide valleys and gently rolling chalk downs. Much of the day is spent on paths through or around fields or on tracks and small roads. If dry, the ground will be hard; if wet, it could be heavy going. There are no facilities before Shepherdswell, where there is a pub (open 2–10pm, closed Mon) and a grocery store (open 6am–10pm).

Waymarking of the NDW is good. Look for small blue or yellow square medallions with the acorn symbol for the NDW next to the VF pilgrim. Cyclists may choose the North Downs Way Riders' Route, christened in Sept 2022, which closely follows the walking path.

Regular trains between Canterbury and Dover stop at Shepherdswell, allowing accommodation at either end of the UK stages to be used.

0.0KM CANTERBURY (ELEV 30M, POP 55,240) 🅗 🚻 ⛺ 🛏 🏧 🍴 🏪 ⊕ ⊕ Ⓗ 🛈
(2226.6KM)
Bathed in history, with a stunning cathedral and quaint old city, Canterbury is justifiably one of England's most popular tourist destinations. Its ancient religious lineage has led pilgrims here for centuries, and Sigeric's ascendancy as

Archbishop of Canterbury in AD990 and subsequent documented journey to and from Rome makes it the official starting point of the Via Francigena.

While archaeology points to human habitation here from Paleolithic times, Canterbury entered recorded history as home of the Celtic tribe of Cantiaci. The Romans overcame local peoples in the first century AD and called the town *Durovernum Cantiacorum*. Their army occupied the town, laid out the street grid according to Roman custom, and built defensive walls against barbarian invaders. After their withdrawal in the third century, Canterbury stood empty for a century. Anglo-Saxon and Danish settlers ultimately filled the town, and by the late sixth century it became capital of the Kingdom of Kent. King Ethelbert of Kent married a Christian woman, Bertha, and Queen Bertha's chapel is Canterbury's **St Martin's Church**, oldest in the English-speaking world. With assurance he would receive a royal welcome, Pope Gregory I sent the Italian abbot, Augustine, on a missionary expedition to convert the kingdom. Augustine's mission was successful, and the abbey he established in Canterbury – **St Augustine's Abbey** – would become a center for Christianity until it was dismantled in the English Reformation.

Canterbury spawned many notables, including saints Ethelbert, Alphege, Augustine, Anselm (born in Aosta, a city on the Via Francigena), Mellitus, Theodore, Thomas à Becket, Dunstan, and Adrian. The list of saints includes two martyrs – Alphege, who was killed by Vikings in 1012, and Thomas à Becket, who was murdered in 1170 by soldiers of King Henry II of England, who had famously uttered the ill-fated words, 'Will no one rid me of this troublesome priest?' Admirers built a now-disappeared golden shrine over Becket's tomb, and pilgrims from throughout the world flocked to Canterbury to honor the martyr-priest. Geoffrey Chaucer's 14th-century classic, *The Canterbury Tales*, features 24 stories of pilgrims on their way from London to visit Becket's tomb here.

Canterbury Cathedral is the highlight of any visit to the city. Successive building programs are evident in its mix of Romanesque and Gothic elements, which you might think of as a Gothic tube laid end-to-end with a Romanesque tube separated by a gate in between. Some of the cathedral's windows are older than its current Gothic building. Look for the 'Adam Delving (digging)' window as one of its oldest examples. The site of Becket's murder is a must-see, as is the Cloister and Chapter House. In 1950, builders discovered 12th-century murals in the Crypt. Look for St Augustine's Chair and also the tomb of the Black Prince, one of England's most celebrated military heroes. (Visits are free with pilgrim credential, open daily at 10am, Sundays at 12.30pm, Closes 5pm. Free admission for the renowned 11am Sunday Choral Worship, www.canterbury-cathedral. org.) Ask at the cathedral store entry for a pilgrim's credential stamp and for a member of the cathedral staff to give you a pilgrim blessing for your journey. Timber-framed buildings of the city center make for a charming and relaxed

A remnant of its historic walls, Canterbury's Westgate has served as an entry checkpoint and prison

stroll. Nearby is the **Roman Museum**, which includes a section of Roman pavement discovered after WWII bombing, as well as the famed Canterbury Treasure, a Roman-era silver hoard discovered nearby. Twin-towered **Westgate** is the largest medieval gate in England and sits among gardens on the River Stour on the London side of the old city. Its museum houses relics of its centuries-long use as a jail. Historians consider Canterbury's **city walls**, rebuilt in the 14th century on Roman foundations, some of England's finest remaining medieval battlements.

Modern Canterbury's center is filled with pubs, restaurants, and shops. The older parts of town include Elizabethan-era constructions, but as you walk gradually uphill along High Street you will find modern stores in tasteful, contemporary buildings. With two universities in town, the old city is often filled with young people enjoying life in one of England's most lovely urban settings.

⌂ **YHA Canterbury** O Pr Do R K S 69/87, £17/49/-/-, 54 New Dover Rd, canterbury@yha.org.uk, tel +44 (0)345 371 9010

⌂ **Canterbury Cathedral Lodge** O Pr R Br Cf W S Z 34/60, £-/92/97/-, Cathedral Precincts, www.canterburycathedrallodge.org, tel +44 (0)1227 865350

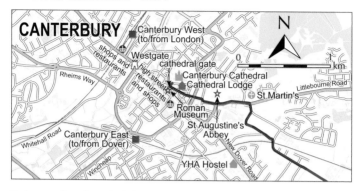

Facing away from the cathedral's main door, head through Christchurch Gate and turn left on Burgate. Continue across the A28 ring road onto Church Street. Facing the **St Augustine's Abbey** entrance, turn half-right (first Via Francigena sign).

In 598 King Ethelbert of Kent granted lands for **St Augustine's Abbey** to Augustine of Canterbury, who had been sent to England by Pope Gregory I to convert the Anglo-Saxons. Ultimately named after its founder, the abbey served as a key religious institution for all of England until its dissolution in 1538 during the English Reformation. The ruins are a UNESCO World Heritage Site and a popular tour (from £7.90, advance booking recommended, www.english-heritage.org.uk/visit/places/st-augustines-abbey).

Pass the abbey visitors' entrance and continue ahead on **Longport**. Pass the entrance to Canterbury Christ Church University and find signs for the North Downs Way (NDW) and take Spring Lane right (**1.0km**). Turn right on Pilgrims Way after 50 meters, and then left in a further 100 meters. Follow the way past houses, cross a railway bridge and past more houses before it meets a track that passes behind a business park and into open country, where the route will stay all day.

Pass **Hode Farm** (**2.9km**) and follow Hode Lane. Join a busy road (take care, no sidewalk) and take the next right at a mini-roundabout. Follow through the village and past the church into **Patrixbourne** (**1.4km**). St Mary's Church is mentioned in the 1086 Doomsday Book and is notable for the 12th-century sculpted south portal and the fine wheel window above the chancel. After some bends in the route, take a NDW path heading left across fields. This climbs and passes a wood. The noise of the busy A2 road intrudes. Continue on a bank above the road and follow the path as it veers gradually away from the road across fields.

Pass **Upper Digges Farm**, keeping left, and cross the Adisham Road B2046 near a cemetery and small reservoir, and continue down into the village of **Womenswold** (**6.7km**) with its 12th–13th-century Church of St Margaret of Antioch.

Take the continuing path across fields, cross a road and cut through a small wood to another road that leads into **Woolage** village. Just before the village sign, turn left down fields (outside the village common). Continue down alongside a road and just before the bottom of the field cross onto the road, which after 50 meters becomes a track.

After a further 20min, join a road, turn left across a railway bridge (**3.2km**) and then immediately right on **Long Lane**. Pass a farm and then turn right past stables. Cross paddocks to another road, turn right across the tracks of the East Kent Railway and then straightaway left. (Going straight here would take you in a few blocks to the train station.) Pass houses, cross fields and emerge at **Shepherdswell Church** (**2.0km**). The Bell Inn pub is alongside the village green. To reach the Co-op grocery store, take the road down for 600 meters. (Description by Jonathan Williams)

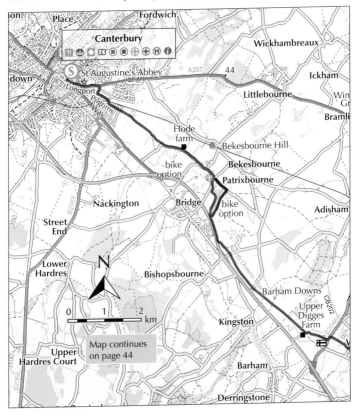

(17.2KM) SHEPHERDSWELL (ELEV 121M, POP 1849) 🍴 ⊕ ⌂ ◉ ◉ ⊕
(2209.4KM)

Originally in the lands of St Augustine's Abbey, the village is included in the Domesday Book as Sibertswold and is spelled Shepherds Well by the National Rail. The 19th-century **St Andrew's Church** sits on the village green at the heart of the community, with the Bell Inn pub opposite. (Train: www.nationalrail.co.uk, ticket machine at the station; or bus: www.stagecoachbus.com)

🏠 **Host Family Pascall** O Pr R Br Dr W S 2/3, £-/25/45/-, Hill Avenue, mikepas53@aol.com, tel +44 (0)776 201 4149, dinner available £10

🏠 **Host Family Rogers** O Pr R K Br Cf W S 3/5, £-/50/50/-, 20 The Glen, susanna2705@hotmail.com, tel +44 (0)785 629 7007

▲ **Coxhill Camping** O R Cf tents ok, £12 pp, Coxhill, CT15 7ND, coxhillcamping@gmail.com, tel +44 (0)786 937 5034, www.coxhillcamping. co.uk

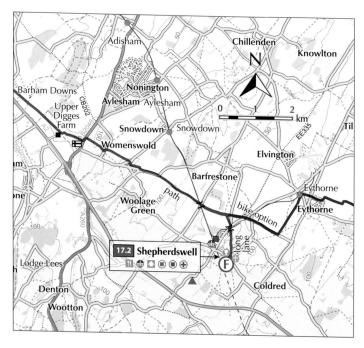

The route to Shepherdswell crosses gently rolling downs covered in grain or hay

STAGE 2

Shepherdswell to Dover to Calais by ferry

Start	Shepherdswell, St Andrew's Church
Finish	Calais, Place d'Arme
Distance	18.6km plus ferry
Total ascent	149m
Total descent	263m
Difficulty	Easy
Duration	4¾hr plus ferry
Percentage paved	46%
Lodging	Dover 14.4km, Calais 18.6km

The route crosses downland on the NDW before descending into Dover. There are shortcuts but not improvements on the route to the ferry terminal. Note that foot passenger tickets are not sold at the ferry terminal, so it's important to reserve your ferry passage online at least a day in advance – see details below.

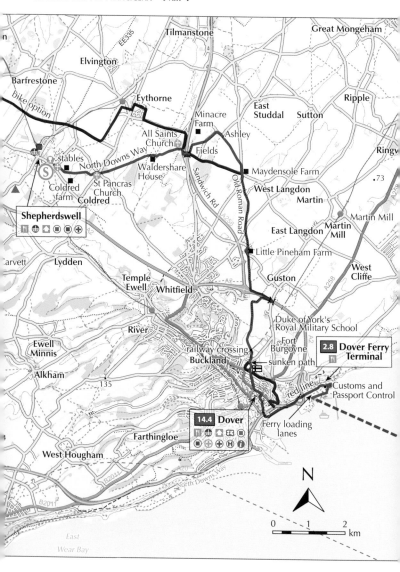

N

0   1   2 km

From the church in Shepherdswell, reverse the final 10 meters of yesterday's stage and find the narrow and signed but eminently missable NDW path to the right that passes alongside the cemetery before dropping down past stables and across a field.

The next field is often ploughed – continue the line you've been following and seek out a marker post on the far side of the crossing. Pass trees and smaller fields to leave **Coldred Court Farm** on your right. Join a road for 10 meters, passing by the tiny **church of St Pancras** (**1.3km**) almost hidden behind earthworks, before taking the NDW directly across the road junction.

Pass through another wood and into a large field, part of the Waldershare Park estate. The path aims just to the left of a wood before dropping past the vast **Waldershare House** (**1.6km**). The 18th-century Queen Anne-style Waldershare House was center of an estate linked to the Monins and Furnese baronets. The NDW takes the driveway for 50 meters then turns left along it past Home Farm before leaving it across fields to the **All Saints church**, no longer in use. The 12th-century church is notable for its memorials to members of the Monins and Furnese families.

Turn right and follow Sandwich Road briefly and then turn left and cross a bridge over the busy A256, then left on a tarmac track towards **Minacre Farm**. Before the farm, turn right across fields, in the second field aiming for the top left corner. Turn left on a small road into the hamlet of **Ashley** (**2.5km**, no services).

Follow the road through Ashley which makes a 90-degree right turn. When the road turns left take a track straight ahead. This crosses fields before joining the line of an old Roman Road that leads to Dover. At a junction by **Maydensole Farm** go ahead and in 100 meters take a poorly signed track left.

The White Cliffs of Dover stand above maritime buildings at the port (photo: Jonathan Williams)

Continue south for 3km, passing a wood and **Little Pineham Farm** before coming to the busy obstacle of the A2 (**4.3km**). The path heads left, over a bridge and follows the south side of the highway. The southern course resumes and becomes a road by a pet-care operation before crossing a railway (**2.7km**). You are now on the descent into Dover.

At a road, the NDW appears to be signed down the road but it's better to continue on a narrow sunken path through a **cemetery**. Continue down Park Avenue. Turn half left on Maison Dieu Road (**1.2km**) and then right on Pencester Road. (It is possible although less interesting to head directly for the terminal, saving 1km, by continuing on Maison Dieu Road and turning left to find the cycle lane and in due course the red line mentioned below.)

By a bus station, cross a small park (Pencester Gardens) with St Mary's church on the right. Follow Church Street to King Street and take an underpass to arrive on the sea front and the end of the NDW (**0.9km**).

(14.4KM) DOVER (ELEV 6M, POP 113,100) 🏨 🍴 🏧 🏦 ⊙ ◎ ⊕ ⊕ ⊕ 🅷 ⓘ
(2195.0KM)

The name 'Dover' derives from the city's location on the River Dour, and its proximity to the European mainland – just 33km – has made it a key transit point since at least the Bronze Age. The Romans called the town *Pontus Dubris* and fortified it against invasion, also building a **lighthouse**, located at Dover Castle, that survives as the tallest Roman-era structure in Britain. **Dover Castle** has stood in one form or another since the Iron Age. It was burned by William the Conqueror in 1066 as he made his way to be crowned at Westminster Abbey. The castle's interior was recreated in the early 21st century and today over 300,000 people visit each year (£27, open daily 10am–5pm, www.english-heritage.org.uk).

Enjoy a stroll on pedestrian-friendly Biggin Street and visit the **Dover Museum** with its Bronze Age boat (free, open daily 9.30am–5pm in season, www.dovermuseum.co.uk). The famed **White Cliffs of Dover** on either side of the city are chalk deposits from the Late Cretaceous epoch that reach a height of 110m above sea level.

🛏 **Maison Dieu Guest House** ⓞ 🄿🅁 🅁 🄶 🅂 6/14, £-/45/52/70, 89 Maison Dieu Rd, info@maisondieu.co.uk, tel +44 (0)1304 204033, brkfst £8, www.maisondieu.co.uk

For the ferry terminal, turn left along the sea front. Pick up a cycle track and follow this as it crosses the main road and heads towards the terminal. Follow the red line for cyclists and pedestrians and carefully read signs to safely cross ferry traffic to arrive at the **passenger terminal** (**2.8km**). (Walking directions by Jonathan Williams)

TO BUY DOVER–CALAIS FERRY TICKETS

For a small fee, ticket aggregators like www.directferries.co.uk allow you to compare schedules and fares before purchasing. Slightly less expensive is to book directly with the ferry companies which include British P&O ferries (www.poferries.com), Danish (www.dfds.com), and Irish (www.irishferries.com). Check in advance to confirm foot passengers are allowed on the ferry of your choice. Cost is generally around £30 for the 90-minute trip, but plan to arrive at the passenger ferry terminal 90 minutes before departure for check-in and passport control. Passports with six months' validity or an EU identification card are required for entry to France. Foot passengers are allowed at the ferry terminal only between 8.25am and 7.15pm daily.

(2.8KM) DOVER FERRY TERMINAL 🚆 (2192.3KM)

From the passenger terminal, a bus will take you to the ferry for security checks and then a scenic ride across the Channel on the ferry's passenger deck. Once in France, a bus will take you to the Calais passenger terminal.

Head to the auto street on the ramp and turn right onto the sidewalk, passing alongside a roundabout onto **Rue Lamy**. Follow this arterial across the low Pont Vetillard bridge and turn right afterward onto Boulevard des Alliés. Curve left with it and as you come to the third block, follow the VF signage left for a pleasant detour into the **Place d'Armes** of modern, central Calais. Continue on Rue Dubout through the passage at the end of the square and turn right to find the **Tour du Guet** in three blocks at Rue de la Mer.

(1.5KM) CALAIS (ELEV 7M, POP 73,911) 🚆 ⊕ 🏠 🅲 ⊚ ⊛ ⊕ ⊕ Ⓗ ❶ (2190.8KM)

Due to its proximity to Britain, Calais has been an important transportation and shipping hub since the Middle Ages. From 1347 to 1558 it was a possession of the English, who saw it as vital for the sale of English tin, lead, lace, and wool on the continent. After winning back Calais from the English, French King François II built the 16th-century Citadel of Calais at the site of a 13th-century medieval fortress. The massive fortifications were completely destroyed, along with much of the city, in WWII. The old city, now mostly composed of post-WWII buildings, centers on the Place d'Armes at the foot of the 13th-century **Tour du Guet** watchtower.

Calais is famed for its lace industry and some 3000 local workers create the machine-made product. In front of the ornate, 20th-century **Hôtel de Ville** is the 1889 Auguste Rodin sculpture **'The Burghers of Calais'** that depicts six volunteers who agreed to surrender to English King Edward III's army in exchange for ending the siege of Calais. The 72m-high belfry of the Hôtel de Ville is accessible by lift (€5–8, open daily in season 10am–5.30pm, closed 12–1.30pm).

🛏 **Centre Européen de Séjour Youth Hostel** ⓞ Pr Do R Cr S Z 84/162, €24/-/-/87, Rue du Maréchal de Lattre de Tassigny, contact@cescalais.com, tel +33 (0)3 21 34 70 20. BYO towel. Posted rate only with VF credential. Self-serve restaurant.

🛏 **Metropol Hotel** ⓞ Pr R Br Cr S Z 40/80, €-/60/91/101, 45 Quai du Rhin, www.metropolhotel.com/en, tel +33 (0)3 21 97 54 00

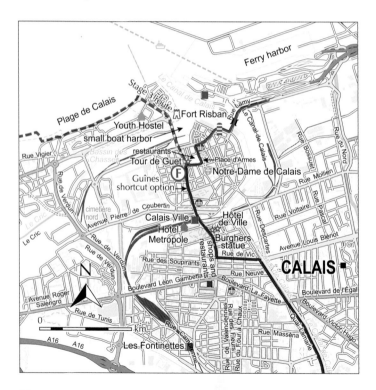

SECTION 2: HAUTS-DE-FRANCE REGION

A two-track trail rises in a forest of young trees after Guînes (Stage 5)

Section 2 overview

The route crosses three departments in this gently hilly agricultural region in the far north of France. Coastal Pas-de-Calais is known for its cool weather and Flemish-Belgian cultural influences. Hills spread out into wide fields in the Somme department near Péronne, with long canals dug for 18th–19th-century shipping. Steep rock hills dot the landscape of the forested Aisne department, most notably at Laon. The entire region has seen many historic battles, with WWI cemeteries keeping solemn watch over countless fallen soldiers.

Because of the relatively flat topography, a single elevation profile for the entire section, rather than for each stage, is included below.

Cap Blanc-Nez looks out over the Channel, with Cap Griz-Nez in the distance (Stage 3)

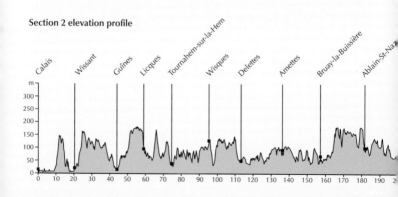

Section 2 elevation profile

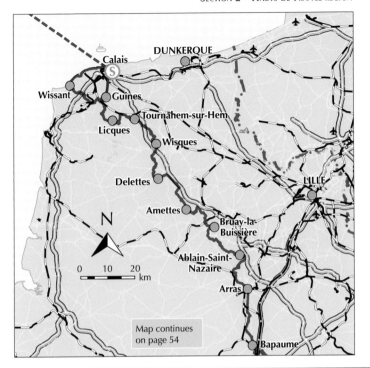

Map continues
on page 54

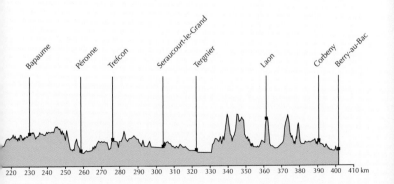

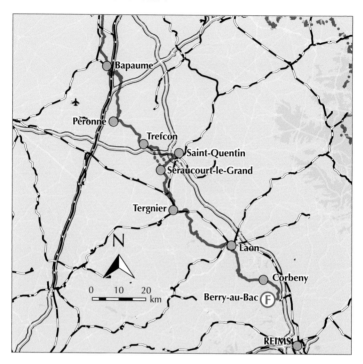

After harvest a farmer prepares his field near Bapaume for the next crop (Stage 13)

STAGE 3
Calais to Wissant

Start	Calais, ferry terminal
Finish	Wissant, town hall
Distance	20.2km
Total ascent	250m
Total descent	240m
Difficulty	Moderate
Duration	5½hr
Percentage paved	31%
Lodging	Sangatte 7.9km, Wissant 20.2km

While there's a shorter way to Guînes, the coastal stage to Sigeric's continental port is the Via Francigena's only true seaside walk. The soft colors of the Côte d'Opale (Opal Coast) make it unforgettable, and the services are plentiful. That said, when you view the Calais town hall tower from Guînes just 8km away after two days' walk you may second-guess your choice. See the map for the shortcut along the #5 Veloroute des Marais, but if time and weather allow, you'll be glad you made space for this lovely stage. Sangatte offers a convenient lunch stop, but its restaurants don't open until noon.

Turn right onto Rue de la Mer, head through the Place d'Armes and cross the Boulevard des Alliés. Continue past the small boat harbor on your right, cross the Pont Hénon, go straight through the traffic circle and just afterward fork left onto Avenue Poincaré. This takes you to the waterfront promenade, where you turn left to follow along the urbanized but still very lovely **Plage de Calais**, with plentiful sun loungers, hotels, cafés and food kiosks in season (WC). On a clear day the White Cliffs of Dover are visible in the far distance.

Past the parking lots, at the round plaza that ends the promenade (**2.2km**), veer right and continue on the wide, sandy beach, which is interrupted at intervals by fence-like rows of wooden pilings, some of which you must squeeze between to proceed. WWII-era German pillboxes, built against an Allied invasion, are visible from the beach. After the fifth row of pilings, turn left onto a path heading up the low bluff.

Before coming to an asphalt road, turn right and follow paths along the bluff until the path finally ends at a gravel road (**4.2km**). Turn right toward a **weather station** and on its left side pick up a concrete sidewalk atop a bulkhead above the beach. Come to a wooden deck on the left with steps leading down to **Sangatte** (**1.5km**, WC, café, snack bar).

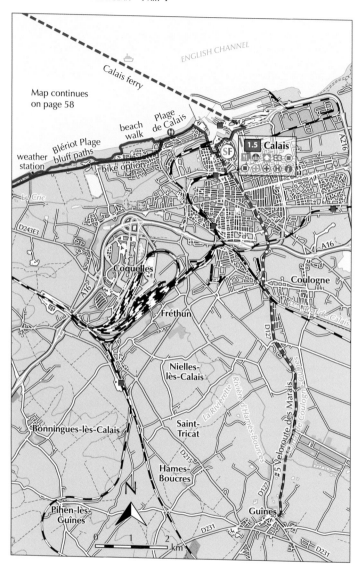

Map continues
on page 58

ENGLISH CHANNEL

Calais ferry

beach walk

Plage de Calais

weather station

Blériot Plage bluff paths

bike option

Le Cric

D243E3

SF

1.5 Calais

A216

Coquelles

A16

Coulogne

Fréthun

D127

Canal de Calais

Nielles-lès-Calais

La Riverette

Rivière d'Hames-Boucres

Bonningues-lès-Calais

Saint-Tricat

D215

Véloroute des Marais

#5

Canal de Coulogne-Guines

Hames-Boucres

D127

Pihen-lès-Guines

N

Guines

D231

0   1   2 km

D231

56

(7.9KM) SANGATTE (ELEV 4M, POP 4789) 🏨 🛏 ⊛ ⊕ **(2182.9KM)**
In the 12th-century, Sangatte was site of a fine seaside fortress of the Counts of
Guînes. Louis Blériot headquartered here in 1909 before becoming the first person to cross the Channel in a heavier-than-air craft. The beach between Sangatte
and Calais is named **Blériot-Plage** in his honor.

⌂ Chez Kerloan 🅿🚻 🆁 5/12, €-/72/-/-, 93 Route Nationale, tel +33 (0)3 21 82 08
50

Return to the sidewalk atop the bulkhead and turn left (or simply follow the D940
road through town), and 100 meters before the sidewalk's end turn left and take a concrete stairway into the west part of the village (**1.1km**, WC, restaurant, hotels, bus), near
the church of Saint-Martin. Turn right onto first a sidewalk then a gravel path along the
D940 and follow it out of town.
After a caravan parking area, fork left onto a dirt road among pastures. The path
now heads uphill on **Noir-Mottes** (Black Clods) hill toward a radio tower and tall,
dark obelisk. As you climb, the road narrows to a pathway. Near the summit, make a
right turn and go through a gate, continuing uphill on the gravel path. Pass the radio
tower, cross the D940 and continue uphill once again on the north side of the bluff to
the WWI monument (**4.4km**) for outstanding views of the sea and shoreline.

The headland at **Cap Blanc-Nez** (Cape White Nose) is a white chalk cliff,
similar to those at Dover. It stands some 32km from Cap Gris-Nez (Cape
Grey Nose), a similar, sandstone headland that is geographically the closest point in France to the British Isles. The monument here remembers the
Dover Patrol from WWI that used the cape as a lookout to prevent German
shipping and submarines from passing. A German pillbox on the hillside
was used in WWII as a defensive outpost against an Allied invasion. The
soft, bluish-green colors of the sea, evident especially here, earn the region
its name, Côte d'Opale.

On the SW side of the monument take the footpath that returns toward the D940,
but before reaching the driveway make a hard right to double back on a path that
heads downhill toward fields along the shore. At the bottom of the hill continue straight
on a grassy path that follows the edge of the bluffs. When the trail ends, take a stairway
to the right (**3.8km**) leading down to the beach. Continue on the beach until turning left
at a stream that flows from the town. Here, in season, you will find beach shacks with
snacks, crêpes, and burgers.
Go straight uphill on the asphalt road and turn right when it ends at the Hôtel
de la Plage Wissant. Two blocks to the right are the Église Saint-Nicolas and *mairie*
(town hall) (**3.1km**).

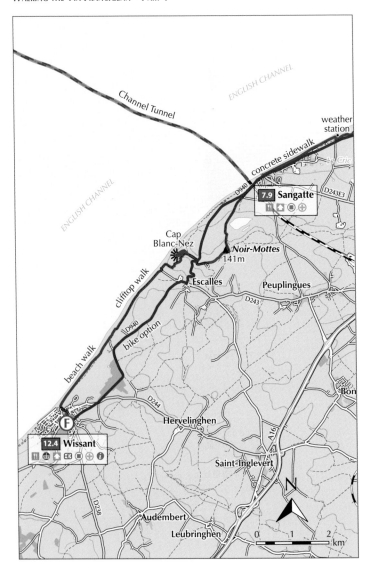

The Via Francigena's final beach walk, with Wissant just a few hundred meters ahead

(12.4KM) WISSANT (ELEV 17M, POP 1078) 🏨 ⊕ 🛏 🅲 ⊙ ⊕ ❶ (2170.6KM)
Stage LXXX of Sigeric and last in the record of his 990 return to Canterbury from Rome, Wissant briefly prospered as a prime cross-Channel launching port until its harbor silted up in the 12th century and it was supplanted by Calais. Thomas á Becket embarked here in 1170 on his way to Canterbury and martyrdom. The name Wissant derives from the Flemish words for 'white sand.' Jacques and Pierre de Wissant are two of the tragic characters depicted in Rodin's 1889 sculpture, 'The Burghers of Calais' at the Calais city hall. (Bus to/from Calais: https://trans-ports.hautsdefrance.fr)

🛏 **Ferme du Breuil** 🅾 🅿ᵣ 🄱ᵣ 🆆 🆂 🆉 3/6, €-/50/60/-, Ferme du Breuil, Route 238 contact@lebreuil.com, tel +33 (0)6 83 52 25 78 (0)3 21 92 88 87, brkfst €1

▲ **Camping Municipal Le Source** 🄲ᵗ 🆆 🆉 391 sites, €-/15/-/-, 3 Rue de la Source, camping@ville-wissant.fr, tel +33 (0)3 21 35 92 46. Restaurant at entrance.

STAGE 4
Wissant to Guînes

Start	Wissant, town hall
Finish	Guînes, Place Foche
Distance	23.4km
Total ascent	332m
Total descent	335m
Difficulty	Moderate
Duration	6¼hr
Percentage paved	43%
Lodging	Landrethun-le-Nord 13.5km, Caffiers 15.8km, Guînes 23.4km

The stage is mostly among fields and forests – beware of mud in wet weather. A highlight is the impressive panorama over altar-like directional tables at Mont du Couple. Since Guînes itself is a roundtrip to and from the trail it feels like a detour. The village is pretty, though, and the Tour de l'Horloge and museum add interest. Otherwise, a continuation to Licques without stopping at Guînes saves 4.5km.

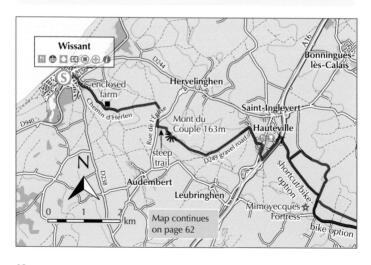

Map continues on page 62

With your back to the WWI monument in front of the town hall, walk straight ahead through town onto Rue Baude. Fork right in two blocks and in a few hundred meters cross the D940. Walk straight across and veer left onto Rue du Fort César, which before long becomes Chemin d'Herlen that takes you out into the wide fields outside town.

Come to a picturesque, **enclosed farmhouse** on your left (**1.8km**) and turn left just afterward onto a gravel road which you'll take uphill until its end. Turn right on **Rue de l'Église** and follow signs left into a nature preserve and then up to the chalky, 161m **Mont du Couple** scenic viewpoint set among WWII battlements (**2.4km**, difficult for cyclists, but worth the exertion).

> As the highest peak for some distance, this **site** has historically been limited to military use, but a 1997 project opened its majestic views to the public. Take time to enjoy the 360-degree panorama and the well-preserved concrete battlements. The distance of 1284km shown to Rome is rather optimistic.

Head slightly downhill on the opposite side to walk along the ridgetop, catching your last glimpses of the sea on the Via Francigena until Lunigiana in Italy. Turn left onto the gravel D249 and before the road takes a sharp left, turn right and head uphill into the town of **Hauteville** (**3.3km**, restaurant, bar).

Once in town, turn right on the main road (D244E1), and at the edge of town a few blocks later turn left. Now you are on a road that doubles around to the back side of town alongside the A16 autoroute. Turn right to cross under the roadway (**1.3km**), and for a 1km shortcut (or in wet weather) continue on this road until it ends rather than turning left on the official route. If you prefer the wooded route, take care on the deeply rutted roadbed, particularly in wet weather. Both routes rejoin on an asphalt road before a left turn on a gravel road.

> If interested, continue on the asphalt road to find the **Mimoyecques Fortress**, built for use by the Germans in WWII for V-3 projectiles targeting London (daily 10am–4pm Apr–Oct, €6.50, http://mimoyecques.fr). The fascinating site includes vast underground tunnels.

Continue to climb, then follow signs left into **Landrethun-le-Nord** (**4.8km**), aiming at the pyramid-topped steeple of its Église Saint-Martin. From this path, on a clear day, you can look back to see the city hall tower at Calais, just 8km away.

(13.5KM) LANDRETHUN-LE-NORD (ELEV 57M, POP 1283) 🏨 🛒 **(2157.1KM)**
Allied bombing raids targeted construction at Mimoyecques Fortress during WWII, which led to destruction of most of this otherwise quiet farming village.

⏶ **Chantebise**, 8 Rue du 8 Mai 1945, chantebise@hotmail.fr, tel +33 (0)3 21 33 64 42

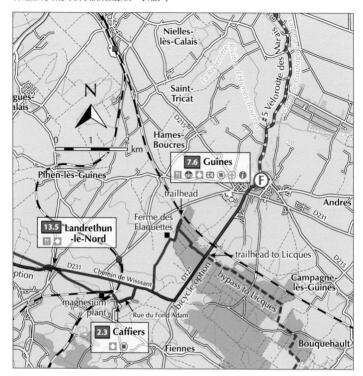

With the church to your right, continue straight in the direction of Caffiers and at the second street fork right onto a two-track grassy path. Cross a two-lane road and continue straight. Cross the wide field toward farm buildings, a town, and tall wind turbines. The road veers left at a grove of trees that hides a rail yard beyond. When it ends, turn right and cross over a series of rail tracks and pass the entrance of the SCORA **magnesium plant** to enter **Caffiers** (**2.3km**).

(2.3KM) CAFFIERS (ELEV 59M, POP 732) 🏠 ◉ (2154.9KM)
This rural village's name is likely derived from the Old Saxon words *catt* and *fyrs* for 'fiery cat' or 'wild cat.'

🏠 **La Ferme des Flaquettes**, Via Romana 170, lesflaquettes@orange.fr, tel +33 (0)6 25 41 27 86

Liberty holds a soldier close in this sculpture in central Guînes.

At the traffic circle in town, turn left onto **Rue du Fond Adam**, which you follow out of town as it sweeps across fields. At its end, turn right on **Chemin de Wissant** and after a further 400 meters turn left onto a gravel road under power lines among fields. Once again you can see Calais in the distance.

The farm road comes to an end at **Ferme Les Flaquettes** (**2.8km**, see info above), and you turn right. In 150 meters, just before a wood, turn left and follow the road to a trailhead where you turn right onto a path into the thick woods. Follow signs to the D127 road (**2.2km**) where you turn left. Soon, signs point you right at a trailhead (**0.2km**) that leads to Licques, the end of the next stage. Take this right if you're bypassing Guînes. Otherwise, continue straight on the road for a quick (although auto-oriented) shortcut to come to Place Foche in **Guînes**, just below the Tour de l'Horloge (**2.5km**).

(7.6KM) GUÎNES (ELEV 6M, POP 5619) 🏨 ⊕ 🛆 🄲 ◉ ⊕ 🛈 (2147.2KM)
The town has Roman roots but slipped out of the historical record until 928 when Sifrid the Dane made it a Viking stronghold. Later that century it was visited by Archbishop Sigeric as his Stage LXXVIII 'Gisne.' Sir Baldwin II, Count of Guînes, built a stone castle at the site of the Viking fortress as well as its first stone walls. The fortifications allowed the French to hold out against the English in 1351 and then the English against the French in 1520. Spanish attacks destroyed the fortress, but the picturesque **Tour de l'Horloge** (clock tower) was built at the site in 1763 (€6, www.tour-horloge-guines.com). France's King Francis I and England's King Henry VIII met at nearby **Balinghem** in the Field of the Cloth of Gold summit of 1520. While the area's once-extensive marshland has largely been drained, the **Guînes canal** still connects the village to the port at Calais.

🛏 **La Forge** 🄾 🄿🅃 🅁 3/12, €-/-/60/-, 32 Rue Guizelin, tel +33 (0)6 61 86 44 50, (0)6 62 99 44 50 www.chambrehotelaforge.com

⛺ **La Bien Assise** 🅁 🄶🅁 🅆 🅂 🅉 €16 tent, Avenue de la Libération, www.camping-la-bien-assise.com/en, tel +33 (0)3 21 35 20 77, restaurant, pool

STAGE 5
Guînes to Licques

Start	Guînes, Place Foch
Finish	Licques, Place du Bas
Distance	16.3km
Total ascent	233m
Total descent	172m
Difficulty	Easy
Duration	4½hr
Percentage paved	32%
Lodging	Licques 16.3km

A stage set mostly on forest trails, with farm roads through fields mixed in. Views on the ridgetop just before Licques add perspective to the rolling countryside. In wet weather the stage can feel like a slog through mud along some of the forest pathways. The D215 offers an easy shortcut for bikes or walkers who don't mind asphalt.

Retrace your steps from yesterday to leave town, forking left off the D127 at the asphalt road just before a small **shrine** of two statues. After a time the road turns to dirt and heads out to the fields. When it ends just before the railroad tracks, turn left and follow signs to the bridge crossing over the Calais mainline rail tracks. Continue into the woods where soon you find a gravel road (**3.7km**) that continues the Licques shortcut trail you skipped yesterday. Turn left and follow the road uphill.

Heading south now, you begin zigzagging on a series of forest roads set in a diagonal, SW/NE grid. Watch for mud here in wet weather. Finally, the last road comes to an end and you turn left and pass through a **red-and-white gate** (**4.2km**) onto a farm road that curves right as it makes its way through grain fields. Soon turn right in the direction of farm buildings, and after passing directly through them, turn left on **Rue du Mât**, which leads to Gîte du Mât (for groups of 20–40, www.gitedegroupe-gitedumat.com), followed soon by a Via Francigena **rest area** (**1.5km**).

Now turn left onto an asphalt road leading across fields with the town of Hermelinghen on your right. Follow signs left to briefly join the D248 highway until turning right onto a gravel road alongside a wood. Jog right at a driveway and head uphill toward the edge of the village of **Le Ventus d'Alembon**, following signs left and back into the fields before the settlement. Follow this wide trail as it gradually leads

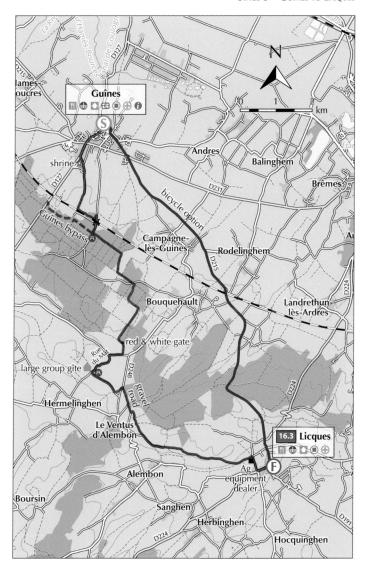

Licques becomes visible as a gravel road leads from the woods into the fields before town

uphill, first through a settlement, and then gently curving left. Now views open to the villages of Alembon and Sanghen.

As the road begins downhill you now see Licques and its large, boxy, Church of the Nativité de Notre-Dame. Pass between buildings of an **agricultural equipment dealership** (**6.1km**) and turn right, going uphill on Rue de l'Abbé Pruvost. Pass the Place du de Gaulle and the town's church, then turn left onto Rue du Bourg, heading downhill to find the heart of town at the end of the street (**0.8km**).

(16.3KM) LICQUES (ELEV 87M, POP 1597) 🏠 ⊕ 🛏 ◉ ⊕ (2130.9KM)
The village is dominated by the imposing but plain 18th-century **Church of the Nativité de Notre-Dame**, former chapel of the 12th–19th-century **Abbey of Notre-Dame de Licques**. This once-rich abbey was successively plundered by French, English and Spanish armies during its long life, and its monks were finally dispersed in the French Revolution. (Bus: www.sitac-calais-opale-bus.fr)

▲ Camping Le Canchy 🟥 🟥 🟥 1/4, €17/-/-/-, tents €11 830 Rue de Canchy, campinglecanchylicques@orange.fr, tel +33 (0)6 88 70 66 79, (0)3 21 82 63 41, www.camping-lecanchy.com/en, brkfst avail

▲ Camping Pommiers des Trois Pays 🟥 🟥 🟥 🟥 🟥 24 tent pitches, 273 Rue du Breuil, contact@pommiers-3pays.com, +33 (0)3 21 35 02 02, www.pommiers-3pays.com, bar on site

STAGE 6
Licques to Tournehem-sur-la-Hem

Start	Licques, Place du Bas
Finish	Tournehem-sur-la-Hem, town hall
Distance	15.0km
Total ascent	233m
Total descent	282m
Difficulty	Easy
Duration	4hr
Percentage paved	67%
Lodging	Audenfort 3.0km, Tournehem 15.0km

A turn uphill after Audenfort may seem an ordeal – especially considering the D217 on the valley floor – but it actually makes for easier access to the jewel of the stage: the 15th-century Chapel of Saint-Louis, a scenic ruin set on a ridge overlooking the Hem Valley and beyond.

Turn right at the end of the main street and head out of town on Rue Antoine de Lumbres. Continue through the neighborhoods of town until you turn left after a **soccer pitch** (**0.7km**) onto Rue de la Commune. At the first fork, go right, heading out into the fields. The road becomes a farm road and then ends at the asphalt **Rue de Cahem**, where you turn right. Soon turn right again at a large dairy barn and continue right on a two-track dirt and grass road. Turn right at the next asphalt road and enter the farming hamlet of **Audenfort** (**2.3km**).

(3.0KM) AUDENFORT (ELEV 51M, POP<50) 🏠 (2127.9KM)
A quiet, riverside village of homes and barns.

🏠 **Gîte Sainte-Thérèse** 🅾 ⓟ Ⓓ ⓡ ⓚ ⓦ Ⓢ 3/6, €-/60/75/90, 54 Rue d'Audenfort, gitesaintetherese62@gmail.com, tel +33 (0)7 49 19 03 59, (0)7 52 07 40 72

Turn left on Rue d'Audenfort and at the next fork go left and uphill. As the road curves right, try to go straight onto a usually-overgrown path in a bramble between two fields that leads uphill in 200 meters to the D217 **Route de Licques**. If the path is overgrown, simply follow the road uphill and turn left on the D217 to find to the path's end. Cross the road onto the **Route du Val** and follow this uphill toward the village of Yeuse.

Turn right after the self-serve **strawberry kiosk** (**4.8km**) on Rue de la Chapelle, which you follow as it curves 90 degrees to the right. Fork left at the **Church of Saint-Martin à Yeuse** and continue out of town, following the road as it makes a sharp left. Turn onto gravel soon afterward and head across fields toward a forested hill, which you will walk around on its north side with good views to Calais in good weather. Passing the woods, a left turn takes you to the starkly beautiful ruins of the **Chapelle de Saint-Louis** (**4.0km**).

Many legends surround the ruins of the 15th-century **Chapelle de Saint-Louis**, including hints of pagan worship, third-century Roman army encampments, and forgotten underground tunnels. The building was reassembled to its current form in 1930, and left intentionally unfinished.

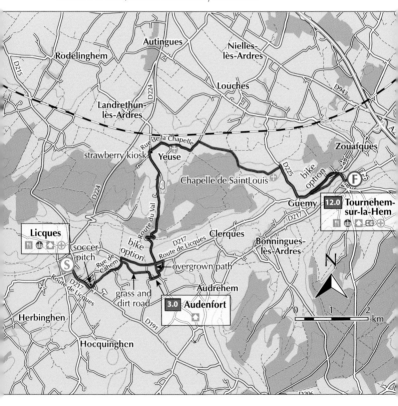

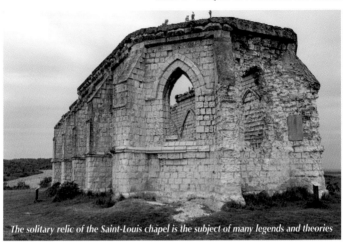

The solitary relic of the Saint-Louis chapel is the subject of many legends and theories

After exploring the chapel ruins, head downhill on the path next to the chalky drive and turn right onto the **D225** asphalt road, taking it downhill while avoiding speeding cars. Arrive at the farming hamlet of **Guemy** (**1.5km**), where you turn left just before a gorgeous ruin of a farming estate. After a second farm, fork right onto a grassy path alongside a narrow line of trees among fields, or in wet weather simply continue on the asphalt road. Turn right onto the D217, and when it ends turn left and find the town hall of **Tournehem-sur-la-Hem** one block on the right (**1.8km**, café).

(12.0KM) TOURNEHEM-SUR-LA-HEM (ELEV 39M, POP 1354) 🍴 ⊕ ⌂ 🄲 ⊕
(2115.9KM)
Roman troops rested here in 57BC, and in the Middle Ages the town hosted one of the network of castles protecting the counts at Guînes. Between 1346 and 1595 it was held variously by British, French and Spanish forces, and only a 16th-century **gate and tower** survived the destruction of the town's Spanish battlements by the French in 1595.

🛏 **Chez Lysensoone**, 2/4, €-/-/45/-, 30 Rue Valenciennes, henri.lysensoone@orange.fr, tel +33 (0)3 21 35 60 56

STAGE 7
Tournehem-sur-la-Hem to Wisques

Start	Tournehem, town hall
Finish	Wisques, Abbaye Notre-Dame
Distance	19.8km
Total ascent	375m
Total descent	293m
Difficulty	Moderate
Duration	5½hr
Percentage paved	50%
Lodging	Leulinghem 17.2km, Wisques 19.8km

A stage of expansive views of vast fields of grain on undulating countryside leading over hill and dale. At stage end is Wisques with its two landmark abbeys plus a fine hotel and restaurant.

Facing the town hall, go left, uphill and take the first right turn after the pharmacy onto Rue de Broukerque. Continue two blocks until the road ends and turn left, heading toward the church. Cross the D217 and fork left in the direction of Laronville on Rue Blanche, walking uphill.

Fork left at the first opportunity onto **Rue de Saint-Omer** and find yourself out amongst fields and farms – although this area appears to be slated for additional suburban-style homes. The official route takes a left for a loop through the fields, but continuing straight on this road shaves about 400 meters off the day.

Soon follow signs to a right turn onto a **grassy path** that doubles as a farm trail where views of vast fields of crops on rolling hills open to your left. Pass what looks like a tall barn, which once was actually a windmill, now plucked of its blades. Afterward, go straight ahead, cross an asphalt road onto a two-track gravel road, followed by another asphalt road (the **D221**) which you cross and just afterward turn right when the gravel road ends. This road too ends, and here you turn left onto the **D222** (**5.3km**) with views ahead to the village of Mentque.

Climb up the ridge and cross over the A26/E15 Autoroute des Anglais, which if you were a car would carry you between Calais and Reims in under 3hr. To get there in 19 days on foot, continue straight.

Turn right at the next road, where you pass alongside an extensive **chalk quarry**. Continue straight, keep away from the highway, and pass a second, older quarry. The

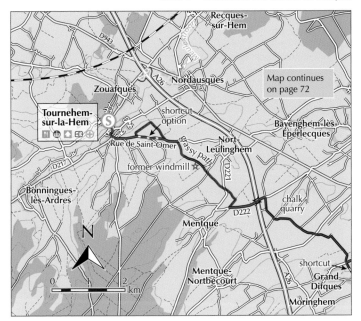

road makes a jog left before continuing straight to the outskirts of **Grand Difques**, where you come to the D207 asphalt road, named here Rue Principale (**4.5km**).

Turn left and continue toward the fields, turning right onto the 'Voie Antique, **La Leulane**,' for a few hundred meters on this ancient thoroughfare between Thérouanne and the Channel. The road ends and you turn right toward a **poultry farm** and then left when the road ends. Follow this road for a sharp left turn and then a sweeping curve through a small wood, heading once again to fields on the other side.

The road surface turns to asphalt before you cross the D214 and it comes to an end in the village of **Cormette** (**3.6km**). Passing a few homes, fork right, heading downhill. Just after starting back up, turn right onto a grassy and pleasant path between fields that leads to the asphalt D206 with its row of evenly spaced trees, where you turn right.

At the next road, turn left in the direction of Leulinghem to enter the village of **Leuline**. Turn right on Chemin des Marronniers (Chestnut Path) and continue until it ends at the heart of the hamlet (**2.3km**, bakery open mornings and afternoons, closed every Wednesday and Sunday morning). Turn right and a block later turn left onto an asphalt road leading out to the fields again. When this road ends, turn right, still in the fields.

Cross the asphalt D208 to enter the village of **Leulinghem** (**1.5km** ⌂ La Ferme du Pré Vert 5/15, 8 Rue de la Mairie, valise2010@hotmail.fr, tel +33 (0)7 82 89 84 97, www.lafermeduprevert.fr) with its 12th-century Church of Saint-Maurice that honors the fourth-century martyr we will come to know later at Saint-Maurice, Switzerland. On July 18, 1389, Richard II of England and Charles VI of France met here to sign the Truce of Leulinghem that led to 13 years of peace during the Hundred Years' War.

Now on the D212, continue through the village back to the fields. Straight ahead you can now see the towers of Saint-Oyen to the left in the distance. The road ends, you turn right, and then cross under the **D942** highway into the outskirts of Wisques. On your left you pass **Abbaye Saint-Paul à Wisques** and on your right you soon pass along the walls of the Abbaye Notre-Dame de Wisques. At the end of the wall, turn right to head up to the **Notre-Dame abbey**, the stage end (**2.7km**).

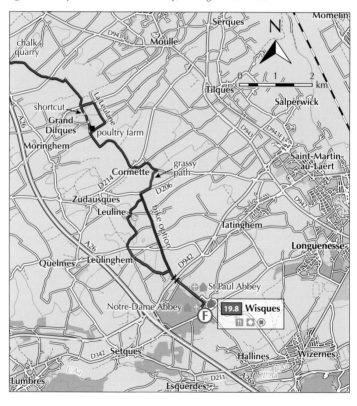

The Abbey of Notre-Dame of Wisques

(19.8KM) WISQUES (ELEV 112M, POP 256) 🏨 ⛺ ◉ **(2096.1KM)**
The tiny village hosts not one but two Benedictine abbeys – the **Abbaye Saint-Paul** for men that occupies a 15th-century castle, and the **Abbaye de Notre-Dame** for women, set in a 19th-century neo-Gothic edifice.

🛏 **L'Abbaye Notre-Dame** 🄾 ᴾʳ 🅁 🄺 ᴮʳ ᴰʳ 5/10, €20/-/-/-, 24 Rue de la Fontaine, ndwisques@wanadoo.fr, tel +33 (0)3 21 95 12 26. Demi-pension €30.

🛏 **L'Abbaye Saint-Paul**, €15/-/-/-, 31 Rue de l'École, stpaulwisques@gmail.com, tel +33 (0)3 21 12 28 55

🛏 **La Sapinière** 🄾 ᴾʳ 🅁 🄺 ᴮʳ 🄲ʳ 22/55, €-/98/140/-, 12 Route de Setques, lasapiniere2@wanadoo.fr, tel +33 (0)3 21 38 94 00, www.sapiniere.net, restaurant, rates include demi-pension, kitchen closed Sun noon–Mon noon

STAGE 8
Wisques to Delettes

Start	Wisques, Abbaye Notre-Dame
Finish	Delettes, Rue du Centre
Distance	18.0km
Total ascent	201m
Total descent	278m
Difficulty	Easy
Duration	4½hr
Percentage paved	35%
Lodging	Delettes 18.0km

This stage is at first among shaded forest trails and then beneath wide-open skies in vast grain fields. Indolent cows will find your presence the highlight of their day. Continuing on to Thérouanne offers an inexpensive overnight option at Gîte Eden.

From the Abbaye Notre-Dame, head downhill and turn right at the first street, the Route de Setques **D208/E1**. Turn left into the woods and follow this road across the A26-E15 Route des Anglais, heading into the town of **Esquerdes**, where the road ends (**2.3km**).

Veer left (bar) and turn right immediately onto Rue Léon Blum. Cross the Aa River, certain to be atop any alphabetical river list, and go right at Rue de la Poste. Head toward the monumental 12th–17th-century Saint-Martin Church, with its elegantly tall, hexagonal steeple atop a square central tower. Turn left here, cross the rail tracks, turn left just afterward, and then right after the town's **cemetery** to begin a climb among crops and pastures. Remain on this road through fields, a forest, and then out of the forest climbing to more fields, this time host to a farm of tall wind turbines.

A row of trees is dwarfed by the wind turbines beyond

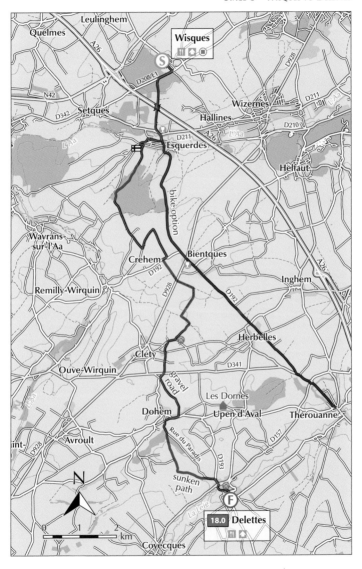

Pass between a pair of these whooshing generators and turn left before a third. From this high point you can count more than 30 wind turbines near and far. A right turn at a clump of trees leads you uphill and over the ridge to the D192 in the hamlet of **Crehem** (**5.9km**, no services), suburb of the farming village of Bientques (bar) a short distance west. Turn right on the D192 and then left before the hamlet's last building to head back out to the fields.

The path becomes a grassy farm track between fields, finding asphalt before crossing the **D928** Route Nationale. Although you see ahead of you the town of Herbelles, turn right at the bottom of a draw to zigzag instead toward the town of Cléty. Come to a **picnic area** in town (**3.1km**), and although the signs point you left to avoid pavement, a right turn on Rue d'Herbelles and a left on Basse-Rue saves steps.

Cross the tree-lined **D341** highway and then turn left onto a gravel road that skirts the town of Dohem on fields to its east. The road ends at the asphalt D190, finally, in **Dohem** (**3.0km**), where you turn right (a left turn on the D190 leads to Delettes' sole lodging, Les Dornes, and then an option to continue on tarmac onward to Thérouanne on the following stage). Continue straight, forking off the D190 in two blocks at a small chapel and heading downhill.

Take the first left, the **Rue du Paradis**, and fork right on your way out of town onto a gravel road that leads through fields and then woods, continuing as it meanders into woods at the bottom of a valley and finally ends. Turn left and begin a climb on the rutted and **sunken path**. Make your way to the top and find you are near the village of Delettes. Come to a small grassy picnic area and turn right onto the **D193** and in a block come to the **D157** (**3.2km**).

Cross the road and turn right in 50 meters onto a sidewalk that brings you alongside a shallow riverbed. Veer left to follow the channeled stream as it curves toward the heart of town. Cross two narrow channels of the **Leie River** and come to an automobile road. Turn left on asphalt, passing **picnic tables** of this riverside park, and passing a basketball court. Curve right and come to the D193 Rue du Centre of **Delettes** (**0.5km**).

(18.0KM) DELETTES (ELEV 43M, POP 1183) 🍴 ⬆ (2078.2KM)
This small farming village on the Leie River is an amalgamation of four prior villages, giving it three parish churches. Most notable is the stout 17th-century **St Maxime**.

⬆ **Les Dornes**, 4/8, €-/65/80/95, 520 Rue des Deux Upen, D'Upen d'Aval, lesdornes@lesdornes.com, tel +33 (0)6 88 82 55 96, www.lesdornes.com

STAGE 9
Delettes to Amettes

Start	Delettes, Rue du Centre
Finish	Amettes, Church of Saint-Sulpice
Distance	22.8km
Total ascent	263m
Total descent	221m
Difficulty	Moderate
Duration	6hr
Percentage paved	48%
Lodging	Thérouanne 4.2km, Liettres 12.2km, Auchy-au-Bois 19.3km, Amettes 22.8km

A stage of familiar farm roads through familiar fields and woods. A ruined château in Liettres is a highlight, as is stage end Amettes, with its charming church and historic birthplace of Saint Benoit, both worthy of a brief exploration.

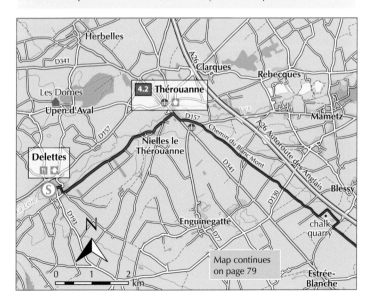

Map continues on page 79

Turn left at the D193 Rue du Centre and then left at the next street, **Rue Haute**, which you follow for another long block before turning left on Rue de Nielles. This asphalt road carries you out among fields to **Nielles le Thérouanne**, the next town (**3.2km**, rest area, WC after church). Continue on the same road through town and into **Thérouanne**, where the road ends at the D341 Grand Rue (**1.0km**).

Lamps recovered in archeological digs at Thérouanne show the lost city's ancient heritage

(4.2KM) THÉROUANNE (ELEV 37M, POP 1135) ⊕ 🏠 **(2073.9KM)**

Thanks to Charles V, Holy Roman Emperor, little remains of the glory of Thérouanne. Founded by the Gauls as Tarwanna, capital of the Morini tribe, it was known in Roman times as Civitas Morinorum. In the Middle Ages it was a prosperous city and important religious site, boasting the largest cathedral in all of France. After his defeat by the French in 1552 at Metz, Charles V besieged Thérouanne and determined to wipe it from the map. He ordered all the buildings dismantled, the streets plowed, and the fields salted. The original site of the city is now an open field to the north of town. It would have been there in 990 that Archbishop Sigeric visited as Stage LXXVII 'Teranburh.'

The well-done **Maison de l'Archéologie** holds many finds from the ancient and medieval urban area (6, Place de la Morinie, www.patrimoines-saint-omer. fr, closed Mon–Tues). Modern Thérouanne is stretched out along the Grand Rue with its bustle of cars and trucks, and the all-important supermarket is at the SE edge of town.

🏠 **Gîte Eden** **Pr** **Do** **R** **K** **W** **S** **Z** 3/8, €22/-/-/-, 30 Grande Rue, lamaisonpresdumoulin@laposte.net, tel +33 (0)6 80 10 79 07, (0)3 21 93 23 13, Linens €8. Alain Millamon host, open Apr 15–Oct 15

Turn right on the Grand Rue and then fork left in 300 meters on the **D157** (go straight to find the town's grocery store in 500 meters). Fork right off the D157 in 500 meters, this time onto the **Chemin du Blanc Mont**, which puts you once again out into the fields, climbing at first on asphalt and then gravel. A kilometer to the left is the noisy Autoroute des Anglais.

Cross a row of trees and just afterward the asphalt **D130** and continue on over the low summit. Circle left around a chalk quarry (which prior to its flattening in the

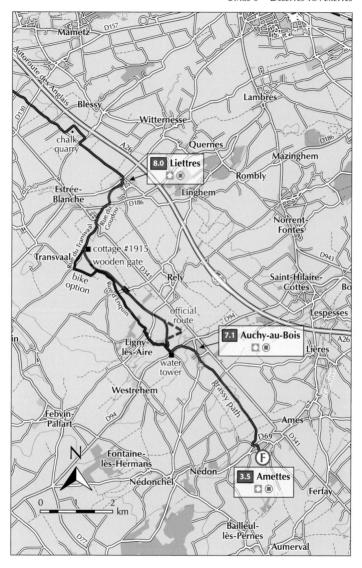

mining operation perhaps was a chalk mound that earned the road its name), and continue to the asphalt road just before the town of Liettres, where you turn right. Turn left in one block onto the Rue du Mairie to come to the center of town (**8.0km**).

(8.0KM) LIETTRES (ELEV 52M, POP 247) ⬛ ◉ (2066.0KM)

The privately owned **Château de Liettres** or 'Hamel Domain' dates from at least the 15th century, while the current building dates from 1720. The walls of its cylindrical towers are 5m thick in some places. (Bus: www.tadao.fr)

⌂ **Les Chambres du Relais** 🄾 🄿🅁 🅁 🄱🅁 🅆 🅂 2/4, €-/42/55/-, 4 Rue du Moulin, chambresdurelais@gmail.com, tel +33 (0)6 84 49 49 03, https:// leschambresdurelais.webnode.fr. Ask for pilgrim price, incl demi-pension with credential, res req.

⌂ **Les Chambres de la Lacquette**, 4 Rue de l'Église, leschambresdelalacquette@ hotmail.com, tel +33 (0)6 77 69 26 38

Take the first right turn to find yourself on a tree-shaded lane heading through a park with benches. Through the trees you can catch glimpses of the château just across the Laquette River. The lane becomes lost in the grass and you veer slightly left, following signs, to cross the small river on a bridge. Arriving at the asphalt **D186** Rue de Lambres roadway, turn right. Turn left at the first street, the **Rue du Goudou**, and pass through trees and small fields to the **D341**, where you jog left onto the **Rue du Transvaal**, bringing you to the hamlet of **Transvaal**, which is in the shadow of a tall, dome-shaped, wooded mound with a half-dozen wind turbines spread behind it.

Turn left at an intricately detailed brick **cottage numbered '1915'** (**2.3km**). The route becomes a wide, dirt path after passing through a wooden gate on a route that leads over the wooded ridge ahead. Fork left onto a grassy path before the **Rue**

Cloudy skies before Amettes

d'Enquin and enter a quiet forest. Cross a pedestrian bridge over the road between Ligny-lès-Aire on your right and Rely on your left and continue straight, through woods and then fields.

Cross an asphalt road and either take the longer, official route that makes a hard left turn ahead, or simply curve right on a grassy farm road between crops, also leading directly to the tall, concrete water tower. Either way, turn left at the asphalt road leading to the **water tower**, and once there, turn left on the **D94** in the direction of Auchy-au-Bois. Fork right at the first asphalt road, and then turn right at the Rue de Pernes (**4.8km**) to arrive at the heart of the village.

(7.1KM) AUCHY-AU-BOIS (ELEV 98M, POP 397) 🏠 ◉ (2058.8KM)

Towers of the **Château de Fromental** in this agricultural village are currently used as farm buildings. The **Church of St Gilles** dates from the 17th century. (Bus: www.tadao.fr)

🏠 **Ferme de la Vallée**, 4/8, €-/50/60/70, 13 Rue Neuve, brigitte.de-saint-laurent@wanadoo.fr, tel +33 (0)3 21 25 80 09, demi-pension €23, http://lafermedelavallee.com

Turn right and head straight downhill, forking left just before the **Church of Saint-Gilles**. This takes you downhill to cross a creek and then uphill on the other side, the tallest climb of the day. Continue straight, out into the fields, with the tree-lined D341 across the fields on your left.

The road becomes a grassy path as it crosses another road and you continue toward a low ridge covered in crops. Soon see the elegantly tapered steeple of the Saint-Sulpice church ahead. The road ends at the bottom of the hill in town, and you turn left on the **D69** Rue d'en Bas, taking a right in two blocks onto Rue du Crinquet to find the church at the heart of the village (**3.5km**).

(3.5KM) AMETTES (ELEV 85M, POP 487) 🏠 ◉ (2055.4KM)

This farming village's most famous son is St Benedict Joseph Labre (1748–1783 – Saint Benoît), who at 16 took up the life of a mendicant pilgrim and visited shrines across Europe. In his last years in Rome he lived as a homeless man in the Colosseum, where his devotion was noted by locals who declared him a saint at his death. He is buried at the Santa Maria ai Monti church in Rome where he died, and his birth home here is located just below the church. He was canonized in 1881 and is patron saint of homeless people. (Bus: www.tadao.fr)

🏠 **La Ferme des 2 Tilleuls** 🅞 🄿🅻 🄳🅾 🅁 🄺 🄱🅁 🅆 🅂 4/12, €15/48/60/70, 2 Rue de l'Église, fermedes2tilleuls@wanadoo.fr, tel +33 (0) 38 81 34 15, (0)3 21 27 15 02, brkfst €6, hosts Colette and Jean-Baptiste Gevas. Baggage transport avail

STAGE 10
Amettes to Bruay-la-Buissière

Start	Amettes, Church of Saint-Sulpice
Finish	Bruay-la-Buissière, Rue René Cassin
Distance	21.1km
Total ascent	270m
Total descent	292m
Difficulty	Moderate
Duration	5¾hr
Percentage paved	62%
Lodging	Burbure 8.5km, Bruay-la-Buissière 21.1km

The stage is a serpentine walk along old railroad grades among *terrils* (slag heaps), heading uphill to the outskirts of Bruay-la-Buissière. Since industrial Bruay is shaped like a spread-eagle octopus, you'll want to allow an extra few kilometers to see the sights or find your overnight lodging.

Keeping the church on your right, curve right with the road and continue straight, passing the Catholic school on your left and then the **Foulon Chapel**. This tiny neoclassical oratory was built in 1855 to honor the Virgin Mary. Fork left after the **cemetery** and after 200 meters in the woods fork right to put yourself on the **Chemin des Morts**.

Now the road begins a gradual climb through the fields, passing a slender radio tower and making a 90-degree left turn before ending at highway **D341**. Turn right here and continue to the town of **Ferfay** (**3.5km**). Turn left at an alley called 'Sentier de Burbure' and follow it past the **cemetery**, after which you turn right on an asphalt road.

Come to another asphalt road, the **Rue du 19 Mars 1962** (commemorating the ceasefire in the French Algerian War), where it is best to turn left since in another few hundred meters the official route is blocked. Follow this road across the **Rue Salvatore Allende**. The road heads out to the fields, turns to gravel, and the official route rejoins.

Soon the level road comes under the shade of trees and then comes to a small concrete bridge. Just afterward turn right on a **narrow trail**, which you follow downhill into a gully, shaded under dense foliage. You are now in the Corridor Biologique de la Scyrendale, part of an old rail line that has been turned into a nature corridor to connect the Woods of St Pierre and the Nave Valley. Fork right at a low, stone memorial, find the wooden steps and continue alongside a field to cross the **D916** roadway. This leads you past the **cemetery** and to the Rue Noémie Delobellein and the heart of **Burbure** (**5.0km**).

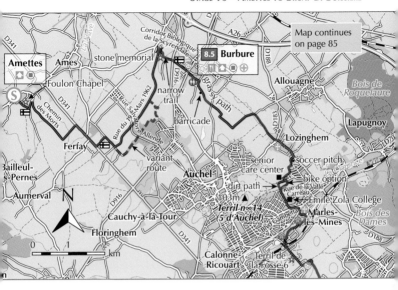

(8.5KM) BURBURE (ELEV 58M, POP 2925) 🏠 🏕 ◉ ⊕ **(2046.9KM)**
A **memorial** stands at the heart of the town, commemorating the lives of the 104
local men who died in WWI. (Bus: www.tadao.fr)

🏠 Gîte d'Étape du Presbytère ◎ ᴅᴏ ᴿ ᴷ ᴡ ˢ ᴢ 3/8, €17/-/-/-, Place de l'Église,
  mairie.burbure@wanadoo.fr, tel +33 (0)3 21 61 02 00, https://burbureviagite.
  wordpress.com

Cross the road (bakery) and continue on Rue du 11 Novembre, which you follow
until it ends. Turn right here and immediately fork left onto a grassy path that curves
left, crossing a **barricade**, and continuing uphill among pastures. Now you begin a
zigzag pattern, leading you in a SE direction toward the tall, slender steeple of the
Saint-Riquier church in **Lozinghem** (3.9km). At the stop sign in town, fork left and cross
the D183. Continue through town, passing the church and *mairie* before turning right
on the narrow Rue des Champs Dorée.

Here you catch first clear sight of a **terril**. Dark, often 150m high, these piles
of debris are left from 300 years of underground coal mining in this area.
Once considered unsightly, they are increasingly seen with affection as a sign
of ancestral labors and their will to survive.

83

This terril, or slag heap, is a living testimony to the miners who populated the area

This becomes a two-track gravel road, heading up a low ridge before signs lead you left at a gate to walk across a grassy park near a **soccer pitch**. Come to a road and go right, turning right again onto a path in just 50 meters. Turn left to walk around a **senior care center**, then turn left at a break in the road barricade just before a green cell tower to go downhill on a **dirt path** through a wood.

The path squeezes out to a street which soon crosses the Rue de la Valle Carreau, to enter Marles-les-Mines. Note the uniform homes on the right, characteristic of local mining towns. Continue past the Emile Zola College until the road ends at Boulevard Gambetta in **Marles-les-Mines** (**2.6km**, restaurant). Turn left and then right at the flamboyant, brick town-hall building. Pick up Rue de l'Egalité to the left of the town hall and follow it as it curves downhill, turning right to head into a park before the brick Saint-Vaast church.

Follow a wide gravel path through the park, then cross the **Clarence River** after the parking area and pick up another gravel path on the river's opposite bank. Before coming to the large pond, turn left at the Chemin de Quenehem (**1.7km**), now in the town of **Calonne-Ricouart** ⌂ L'Auberge des Gourmets, Rue du Mont Saint-Eloi, +33 (0)3 21 62 26 58, http://lesgourmetscalonnix.free.fr.

Now you begin an uphill dodge between *terrils* on the outskirts of Bruay-le-Buissière. Go uphill, passing **Terril de la Fosse 6**. A German bombing run in 1940 created a dust explosion at this mine that killed 34 miners. Turn left at the end of the road and follow the **Rue de Bruay** (bakery) as it curves right. Continue as the road curves right and then turn left on Rue du Soleil. Make a left on Rue LeClerc and right at Rue Gaston Blot, the next through street, leading downhill through a park where you cross the **D302** arterial.

Catch an asphalt path across the road, and cross the **Lawe River** on a wooden pedestrian bridge. Follow the path clockwise around the pond (cyclists go right), heading through a lawn to the **D941** road, which you cross. Jog left to head uphill on the

Rue Chopin among identical mining houses. Test your musical acumen as you pass streets named for Auber, Massenet, and Gounod. Turn left on Bizet and pass Ravel, before turning right onto Rossini. Take a path to the right at the road's end to end at **Rue René Cassin** at the edge of town (**4.4km**, groceries).

(12.7KM) BRUAY-LA-BUISSIÈRE (ELEV 62M, POP 24,474) 🔲 🌐 🏠 🄲 ◉ ⊕ ⊕ ⊕ (2034.2KM)

In 1987 the communities of Bruay-en-Artois and La Buissière were combined into a single town. Although the coal-mining industry was shuttered in the 1960s it was replaced with today's prosperous chemical manufacturing. Most famous of the town's buildings is the 47m tall **Hôtel de Ville**, dedicated in 1927 and adorned with notable stained-glass windows. Archbishop Sigeric's return from Rome included Stage LXXVI 'Bruwaei.'

⌂ **Béthanie**, 215 Rue Paul Eluard, annie.bureau@numericable.fr, tel +33 (0)6 75 97 99 19, (0)6 75 33 31 41, demi-pension possible

⌂ **Le Cottage** 🄾 🄿🅃 🅁 🄱🅁 🄳🅁 🄲🅃 🅆 🅂 🅉 20/40, €-/62/62/-, 292 Avenue De La Libération, lecottagehotel@wanadoo.fr, tel +33 (0)3 21 53 14 14, restaurant, €18 demi-pension w/o drinks, €7 brkfst, 2.4km from trail

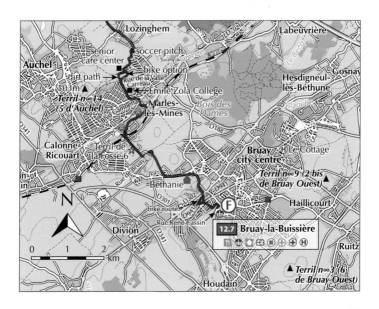

STAGE 11
Bruay-la-Buissière to Ablain-Saint-Nazaire

Start	Bruay-la-Buissière, Rue René Cassin
Finish	Ablain-Saint-Nazaire, Ruine de l'Ancienne Eglise
Distance	24.7km
Total ascent	406m
Total descent	378m
Difficulty	Moderately hard
Duration	7hr
Percentage paved	37%
Lodging	Houdain 2.6km, Ablain-Saint-Nazaire 24.7km

The forests of Parc d'Olhain and Bois de Mont offer shade and beauty, which contrasts with the stark and somber introduction to this region of WWI battlefields. Near the stage end is the largest French military cemetery, Notre-Dame de Lorette, filled with memories of tragedy and courage.

Turn right before the supermarket and follow the gravel trail as it becomes a narrow dirt track curving left on its way out of town. Continue on this pleasant, shaded path under the **D301** highway bridge, over La Lawe stream, and coming to the D341 at the edge of **Houdain** (**2.6km**).

(2.6KM) HOUDAIN (ELEV 57M, POP 7622) 🍴 ⊕ ⌂ 🅒 ⊙ ⊕ ⊕ (2031.6KM)

The **Church of St-Jean-Baptiste** dates from the 13th century, although the town itself is much older, with archaeological evidence from Celtic and Roman times. Wars in this strategic region of France have reduced the town to rubble many times, most recently in WWI. (Bus: www.tadao.fr)

⌂ **Gîte des Collines d'Artois**, 3/7, €-/-/82/-, 99 Place de la Gare, bernardhoudain@wanadoo.fr, tel +33 (0)3 21 54 14 21, (0)6 23 16 58 05 (two-night minimum)

The path continues briefly as an alleyway between two homes and then comes to a road next to a brick utility building where you turn left, leaving the calm path and turning onto a suburban street. Follow this down to cross **La Lawe** once more, and then climb up through fields. Watch for signs at the fourth left that lead you into the village of **Rebreuve-Ranchicourt** (**3.0km**).

In the village, with its channeled but burbling stream, turn left on Rue du Château and climb first past the 18th-century **castle** and then to the D341 just beyond. Turn left on the D341 and follow it to **Rue d'Olhain**, where you turn right at a veterinary clinic to continue first among suburban homes and then onto gravel into the fields. Soon turn left at a gravel road in the direction of the wooded ridge on your left.

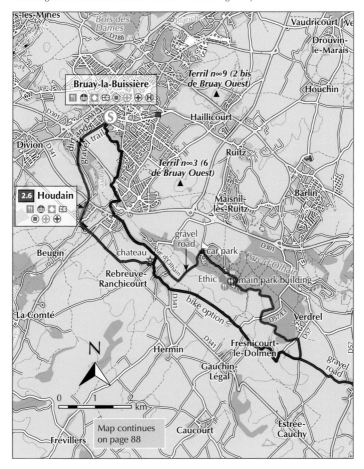

Map continues
on page 88

Once at the woods, begin a significant climb on a mountain path of chalk, turning right after a parking area and then continuing to climb into **Parc d'Olhain**. Parc d'Olhain is a private, outdoor, forested amusement park with a suspended net course, four-season luge, outdoor pool, miniature golf, restaurants, and RV campsites, see www.parcdolhain.fr. ⌂ **Ethic Étapes Parc d'Olhain** 29/153, €20/-/-/-, Rue de Rebreuve, reservation@parcdolhain.fr, tel +33 (0)3 21 27 91 79.

One of the many entertaining features of the Parc d'Olhain is its tilting tower (photo: European Association of the Via Francigena ways)

Follow signs past the swimming pool and *parcours* areas to the main building (**3.5km**, restaurant, WC) which you pass on your right. Continue to the large lawn, finding the route clearly marked to the path at the left side. Once in the woods again, take the path to the right, staying just inside the woods as you pass pastures and a golf course and come to the **D57/E3 road** (**2.7km**) which you cross to continue along the edge of the forest. Finally, signs lead you through the heart of the forest and you come out into the open at the **D57** (**1.5km**).

Turn left briefly toward the village of Verdrel, but then cross the road and continue south, away from Verdrel, in the direction of Servins instead, on a narrow farm

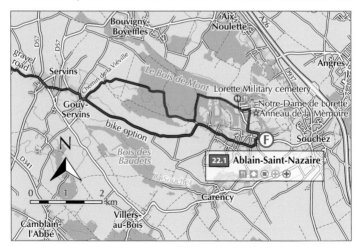

road. At the first intersecting farm road, turn left and begin uphill on an unmarked, two-track, gravel road. Continue into town, turning right at the stop sign onto the D57 in **Servins** (**2.3km**).

Pass the park and WWI monument and fork left on Chemin Croisé. Turn right at the D57/E1, and right again in town at Le Chemin de Bouvigny. Curve left with the road to come to the town hall, then turn left, off the D57 and onto the **Chemin de la Viéville**.

Head back out across fields, and fork left then right to head through woods. This puts you on **Le Bois de Mont**. Follow signs that lead you right, then downhill to the edge of the woods, then once again uphill into the forest. A final right turn in the woods puts you on the path, with fields on the left, that leads to the vast cemetery at **Notre-Dame de Lorette** (**8.1km**).

Originally the site of an 18th-century chapel honoring a pilgrimage to Loreto, Italy (hence 'Lorette'), this ridge was the scene of several WWI battles and now houses the largest French **military cemetery** in the world, hosting remains of over 40,000 soldiers. The neo-Byzantine basilica and ossuary tower were completed in 1932. The beautiful and heartbreaking Anneau de la Mémoire (Ring of Memory) sculptural display, 345 meters in diameter, is engraved with the names of the 580,000 soldiers killed in the region between 1914 and 1918 without regard to nationality, gender or religion.

Either head straight through the cemetery to the domed necropolis (entrance on the opposite side) or follow along on the right side, looking for an easy-to-miss path opposite the necropolis leading downhill into town. Curve left with the road, which

Over 40,000 French WWI soldiers are buried at the cemetery and ossuary of Notre-Dame de Lorette

becomes Rue de la Blanche Voie as it enters town. Curve right with it to come to the Ruine de l'Ancienne Eglise, the stage end (**1.0km**).

(22.1KM) ABLAIN-SAINT-NAZAIRE (ELEV 87M, POP 1891) ⊞ ⬈ ◉ ⊕ ⊕
(2009.6KM)
The entire village, including its 16th-century flamboyant Gothic Church of Saint Nazarius, was destroyed in May 1915 by shellings from French forces during the Second Battle of Artois. The church's ruins were left standing as a poignant reminder of the shocking death toll – 105,000 lives lost in two weeks' fighting. (Bus: www.tadao.fr)

🏠 **Les Chemins de Lorette** ◨ Pᴛ ◻ ◻ Bʀ Dʀ ◻ ◻ 1/2, €-/35/70/-, 8a Rue de Lens, gite-lescheminsdelorette@orange.fr, tel +33 (0)6 82 38 00 06. Fri, Sat, Sun only. Brkfst incl, €25 demi-pension, check-in after 5.30pm, res req, email or WhatsApp

STAGE 12

Ablain-Saint-Nazaire to Arras

Start	Ablain-Saint-Nazaire, Ruine de l'Ancienne Eglise
Finish	Arras, Hôtel de Ville
Distance	22.5km
Total ascent	258m
Total descent	275m
Difficulty	Moderate
Duration	6hr
Percentage paved	62%
Lodging	Souchez 2.8km, Mont-St-Éloi 10km, Maroeuil 14.3km, Arras 22.5km

An extra hour spent in Souchez allows a visit to one of France's top WWI museums. Afterward, farm roads take you to the stark and beautiful ruins of the abbey at Mont-St-Éloi. You'll continue on asphalt roads and bike lanes through a park and across the threshold of lovely, Flemish-themed Arras, one of the most beautiful and vibrant cities of the Via Francigena.

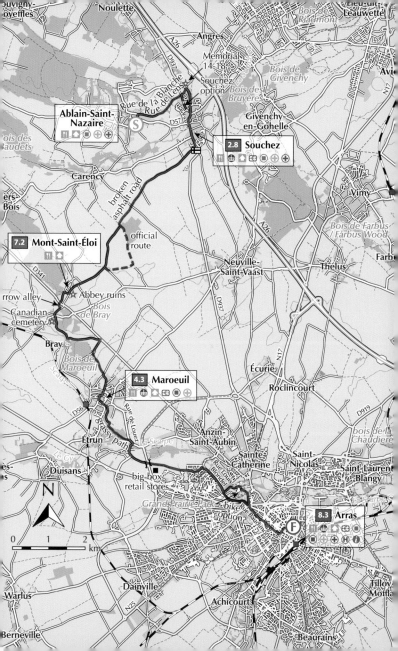

Noulette

Bois de Riaumont

Cléuigny-Leauwette

A26

Angres

Mémorial 14-18

Bois de Givenchy

Avi

Rue de la Blanche

Souchez option

Bois des Bruyères

N17

Ablain-Saint-Nazaire **S**

Rue de l'Ense

D57

Givenchy-en-Gohelle

2.8 Souchez

A26

Carency

Vimy

Bois de Farbus / Farbus Wood

Farbu

s des audets

rs Bois

broken asphalt road

official route

7.2 Mont-Saint-Éloi

D341

Neuville-Saint-Vaast

D937

Thélus

row alley

Abbey ruins

Canadian cemetery

Bois de Bray

N17

A26

Bray

Bois de Maroeuil

La Scarpe

Écurie

Roclincourt

4.3 Maroeuil

D56

Rue de Louez

Brassy Path

Étrun

La Scarpe

Anzin-Saint-Aubin

Sainte-Catherine

Saint-Nicolas

Saint-Laurent Blangy

D919

bois de la Chaudière

Duisans

big-box retail stores

Grands Prairie Park bike option

F

8.3 Arras

N25

Dainville

Achicourt

Tilloy Moffla

Warlus

Berneville

Beaurains

N

0   1   2 km

Return to Rue de la Blanche Voie and turn right. The road's name changes here to **Rue de Lens**, and you follow this as it turns to gravel. Turn at the signs to head to central Souchez and skip the museum, or go straight to the D937 for an hour of introspection to learn more about the WWI battle at this site.

> This road was front line of the **Second Battle of Artois** in May 1915, with German forces on the left and French and Allied forces on the right. One block to the left is the Memorial 14–18 History Center, a striking, black and blocky museum that houses photos, maps, and period films documenting the fighting at this location (www.memorial1418.com, closed Mon–Tues).

Turn right to come to the center of town at D57 Rue Pèri Brossolette (**2.8km**).

(2.8KM) SOUCHEZ (ELEV 74M, POP 2509) ⬛ ⊕ ◪ ⓒ ◉ ⊕ ⊕ (2006.8KM)
As with many towns in this region, sporadic warfare over centuries destroyed the town and forced its rebuilding. This includes battles in 1213, 1303, and, most notably, 1915. After WWI the town's rebuilding was sponsored in part by the Kensington neighborhood of London. The central square of Souchez is named Place Kensington and a nearby street is named after Rice Oxley, former Kensington mayor. (Bus: www.tadao.fr)

♠ **Le Domaine des Loups**, 4/8, €-/-/119/-, 31 Rue du Docteur Wagon, contact@ ledomainedesloups.com, tel +33 (0)6 32 62 27 21, http://ledomainedesloups. com, luxury tourist accommodation

Turn right just before the **cemetery**. The road soon ends and you fork right on broken asphalt, leading out into the fields. Cross several farm roads as you see Mont-Saint-Éloi ahead, a hilltop village with the tower of a ruined church. Finally the road ends (**3.8km**) and you turn left. Here either make an immediate right turn for a shortcut to save 700 meters or follow signs to take the following right. The two rejoin before heading up the hill and arriving at the abbey ruins in the village of **Mont-Saint-Éloi** (**3.3km**, restaurant).

(7.2KM) MONT-SAINT-ÉLOI (ELEV 135M, POP 1014) ⬛ ◪ (1999.6KM)
Saint Vindicianus established the once-powerful Abbey of Saint Eligius (Éloi) in the sixth century. Its 16th-century buildings were dismantled in the late 18th century during the French Revolution, and in WWI they were further reduced in height by shelling. What's left was intentionally preserved as a stark reminder of the tragic cost of war.

🏠 Chez Fifine Ⓞ Pr R K Cf W S 3/7, €-/50/70/80, 21 Rue de Douai, contact@ chez-fifine.fr, tel +33 (0)6 89 72 04 65, available to drive to nearest store for groceries

🏠 Accueil Pèlerin Degouge Pr K Br Dr W S 1/2, €-/10/20/-, 9ter Rue du Général Barbot, jpcdegouge@gmail.com, tel +33 (0)6 76 92 56 51, €10 brkfst

Turn right at the ruins, heading downhill, and then turn left at the next street, continuing downhill. Cross the **D341** and continue on an alleyway between two buildings. The alley becomes a narrow path that turns left to follow alongside a pasture. Turn right at the next road, and at the bottom of the hill turn left and then make an immediate right to pass the WWI **Canadian cemetery** on your right. Soon arrive in the village of **Bray** (**1.7km**, bakery).

The route now aims at the town of Maroeuil with the Woods of Maroeuil park in the way. Turn left on Chemin des Douze and then turn right onto a tree-lined promenade just before the D341. Once at the woods, turn left onto a forest path, heading downhill onto a farm road among the fields. The road ends at an asphalt road where you turn right. This road curves left and becomes Rue du Fresnoy, which leads to Place Hagimont at the heart of **Maroeuil** (**2.6km**, bakery, restaurants a block SE).

(4.3KM) MAROEUIL (ELEV 78M, POP 2611) 🔟 ⊕ 🏠 Ⓒ Ⓜ ⊕ (1995.3KM)
Documents attest to the existence of this town on the Scarpe River as early as 680. In the seventh century, at the death of her husband, Lady Bertille, noble lady of Maroeuil, sold her possessions and returned to her birthplace here to pray, build a church and serve the poor. She was canonized in 1081 as Saint Bertille of Maroeuil and the **church** at Rue de l'Église is dedicated in her honor.

🏠 Domaine de la Tilliére, €45/person, 113 Chemin de Bray, contact@ domainedelatilliere.com, tel +33 (0)3 21 58 79 30, (0)6 71 27 97 74. Hunters' lodge.

Follow the D56 until you turn left on Rue du Four. After two blocks, fork right on Rue de la Source where you walk alongside La Scarpe stream, first on a road and then on a **grassy path**. Pass through a gate and turn right on **Rue de Louez**, making an immediate right onto Rue de la Scarpe at a historic watermill (**2.2km**).

The road curves left and crosses under the N25 highway and becomes a gravel path on the back side of big-box retail outlets. After the path curves left, away from tall apartment blocks, turn right onto **Rue Louis Blondel**. Turn left into the **Grand Prairie Park** on Chemin des Maçons and come once again to La Scarpe stream, which you follow alongside before forking away from the stream, across a large field, and over

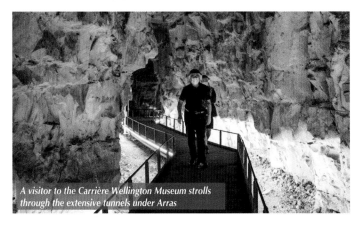

A visitor to the Carrière Wellington Museum strolls through the extensive tunnels under Arras

two pedestrian bridges in this lovely park. A stairway after the second bridge leads to a narrow alleyway heading uphill, which you follow until coming out into a busy six-way intersection at the edge of downtown Arras.

Go left to cross three streets until turning left onto **Rue Baudimont** (**4.7km**), which leads downhill through the picturesque city. At Rue Désiré Delansorne turn left, and in three blocks come to the Place des Héros and the Hôtel de Ville of **Arras** (**1.4km**).

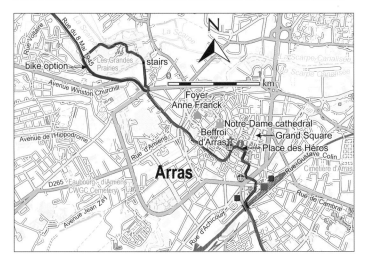

(8.3KM) ARRAS (ELEV 70M, POP 47,052) ⏸ ⊕ ⬜ ⓒ ⊙ ◎ ⊕ ⊕ ⓗ ⓘ **(1987.0KM)**
Strangely unknown to people outside France, this capital of the Artois region is
one of the historic and atmospheric gems of the Via Francigena. Situated at the
confluence of the Scarpe and Crinchon rivers, Arras has been the area's primary
urban center since the Iron Age and was Stage LXXV 'Atherats' of Archbishop
Sigeric in 990. In the Middle Ages the Abbey of Saint Vaast became a center
of medieval art, and the town was famous for its troubadour poets. By the 14th
century Arras was known throughout Western Europe for its cloth industry and
tapestry making.

When King Louis XI of France took control of Arras in 1477 he razed the
walls, expelled the residents, and renamed the town 'Franchise.' A few short
years later the town was ceded to Austria, which kept it until giving it to Spain
as part of the Spanish Netherlands. During this period the city's central squares
were built, and the flamboyant town hall and belfry were dedicated. The elaborate Gothic **Cathedral of Notre-Dame-et-Saint-Vaast of Arras** was destroyed in
the French Revolution and the Abbey of St Vaast church was rebuilt along neoclassical lines to replace it.

During WWI Arras was just 10km from the front lines, which led to the
destruction of three-quarters of its buildings, including the beloved belfry and
cathedral. After the war these key buildings were painstakingly rebuilt along their
original lines, with the town hall gaining art deco influences to blend with its
Gothic structure. The urban center of Arras today evokes its Flemish roots, with
gabled buildings closely clustered on narrow streets and large, open squares.

The highlight of a visit to Arras is an elevator ride and a 40-step climb past
the carillon bells to the top of the city hall's clock tower, the 75m-tall **Belfry of
Arras** (€3.50). The **Musée des Beaux-Arts** fills the former Abbey of Saint Vaast and
has a notable collection of Flemish and Dutch paintings (www.arras.fr/culture/
musee-des-beaux-arts.html).

Starting in the Middle Ages, stone was quarried from under the city, resulting
in a network of tunnels some 22m underground. These were expanded by New
Zealand miners in WWI, resulting in over 20km of underground passageways
that can now be visited in the **Carrière Wellington Museum** that commemorates
the miners, 41 of whom died while tunneling (www.carrierewellington.com, reservations recommended, wear warm clothing).

🛏 **Maison Saint-Vaast** ⊙ Pr Do Br Dr G S Z 31/70, €25/30/43/48, 103 Rue
d'Amiens, maison.diocesaine@arras.catholique.fr, tel +33 (0)3 21 21 40 38,
http://arras.catholique.fr/accueil-hotellerie, credential required, brkfst €6, dinner €12

🛏 **Foyer Anne Franck** ⊙ Pr R Br 21/48, €contact, 21 Rue du Bloc, tel +33 (0)3
21 71 24 83. Residence for young workers, pilgrims accepted.

STAGE 13
Arras to Bapaume

Start	Arras, Hôtel de Ville
Finish	Bapaume, Place Faidherbe
Distance	26.4km
Total ascent	242m
Total descent	191m
Difficulty	Moderate
Duration	6¾hr
Percentage paved	66%
Lodging	Boisleux-St-Marc 9.4km, Bapaume 26.4km

After the long, urbanized-but-service-rich exit from urban Arras, the topography changes from bumpy to flat. Fields now come in three sizes: vast, vaster and vastest. Someone in a hurry could walk or cycle the spacious shoulder of the D917, which is sprinkled with eateries, but the walking route itself is also direct, if lacking in food and water. Bapaume is a comfortable crossroads town with some of its charm restored after its destruction in WWI.

Return to Rue Baudimont (now Rue Gambetta) or simply follow signs left to the **train station**, Gare d'Arras. Turn right at the station and pick up Rue Brazzart. After one long block, turn left at the D917, aptly named the **Rue de Bapaume** (grocery, bakery) since you follow it all the way out of town in the direction of Bapaume. After Jules Verne Park, turn right onto Rue Robespierre (**4.0km**) in the suburb of **Beaurains**.

Pass under a **water tower** and then under the **D60** roadway and continue on this paved road out into the fields. Before the next town, take a right fork that leads to a neighborhood of brick homes and then the D34 in the village of **Mercatel** (**2.0km**, no services). Cross the D34 and continue straight through fields, heading under the railroad tracks and passing the **Sunken Road WWI cemetery**. Over 200 fallen soldiers from the Somme offensive of 1916 are buried here.

Continue ahead toward a gap between the towns of Boisleux-au-Mont (train) on the right and Boisleux-Saint-Marc on the left. After a small, domed wayside chapel the road turns right and ends at the **D35** (**3.3km**).

(9.4KM) BOISLEUX-SAINT-MARC (ELEV 75M, POP 212) 🛏 ◉ (1977.6KM)
'Boisleux' likely derives from the Celtic word 'bail,' meaning fort or castle. The town appears in records as 'Bailius' beginning in 1119. (Bus: www.bus-artis.fr)

🏠 **Chez Malassingne**, 2 Rue de Mercatel, tel +33 (0)9 72 49 86 86

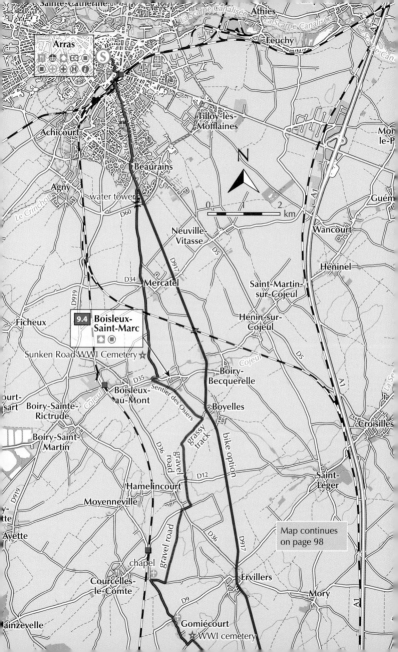

Arras

S

Sainte-Catherine
Athies
Feuchy
La Scarpe Canalisée
La Scarpe Canalisée
Mor-
le-P

Achicourt
Tilloy-les-
Mofflaines

N

Agny
Beaurains
water tower
D60

Guém

0   2
km

Neuville-
Vitasse
A1

Wancourt

D34
Mercatel
D917
D5

Héninel

D919
Saint-Martin-
sur-Cojeul

Ficheux
9.4 Boisleux-
Saint-Marc
Hénin-sur-
Cojeul
D5

Sunken Road WWI Cemetery ☆
Cojeul
D35

Boiry-
Becquerelle
A1

urt-
sart
Boiry-Sainte-
Rictrude
Cojeul
Boisleux-
au-Mont
Sentier des Osiers
Boyelles

Boiry-Saint-
Martin
D36
grassy track
gravel road
bike option

D919
Hamelincourt
D12

Moyenneville
gravel road
D36
D917

Ayette

Map continues
on page 98

chapel
Ervillers
Mory

Courcelles-
le-Comte
D9

A1

ainzevelle
Gomiécourt
☆ WWI cemetery

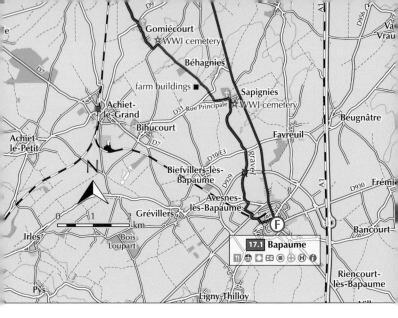

Look across and to the right for a gravel road, where you climb up steps, veer left, and begin on a shaded path named **Sentier des Osiers** (Wicker Trail). Cross two roads and continue on this wooded path among fields toward Boyelles, where the path ends before town. Turn right onto an asphalt road, passing a farmhouse and heading again into the fields, this time toward the village of Hamelinecourt. The road becomes a **grassy farm track**, and partway before town turn left on a gravel road and continue, crossing the **D12** and continuing until the road ends at a T-junction.

Turn right here, cross the **D36**, and then fork left. When this road ends at a T-junction, turn right toward a line of trees and the hamlet of Courcelles-le-Comte (restaurant, train) beyond. Turn left before a small **chapel** and follow this road until it ends at the D9 in the village of **Gomiécourt** (8.7km).

Turn right and then make an immediate left to pass the Church of Saint-Pierre, continuing through this town of homes and barns out into the fields. Very soon the road ends at an asphalt road and you turn left, then take the first right, across from the small Gomiécourt South **WWI graveyard**. The cemetery contains 206 British Commonwealth and 27 German burials from a battle fought at this site in August 1918.

Pass the large barns of a dairy farm and cross the **D31** afterward. Although straight ahead you can now see the steeples of Bapaume, continue on gravel to the next road, the D31/E1 **Rue Principale**, where you turn left instead to enter the village of **Sapignies** (3.8km). Turn right from the Saint-Pierre Church next to the town hall and pass a German **military cemetery**. The Sapignies military cemetery holds 1550 German burials from 1914–18.

'Beat palms' is the source of the town of Bapaume's name, as is remembered on this monument in front of the town hall

The road continues downhill and out into the fields. Cross the **D10/E3** and continue on gravel. Cross a bridge over the **D929** highway (**2.3km**) and when the road ends at the Rue d'Achiet, turn left onto a pink gravel sidewalk. Turn right before a neo-Gothic chapel and then left at the next street, now in the village of **Avesnes**. Turn right on the Rue d'Albert and left before the home improvement store. A left at the Rue de la Croix Saint-Jacques takes you in four blocks to Place Faidherbe at the center of **Bapaume** (**2.3km**).

(17.1KM) BAUPAUME (ELEV 122M, POP 4157) 🏨 ⊕ 🏠 🄲 ⊙ ⊕ 🄷 ❶
(1960.5KM)

The area is sometimes called the 'Seuil de Bapaume' ('Bapaume threshold') because of its position between the Artois and Somme regions. The name derives from the Flemish Batpalmen, meaning to 'beat your palms' after suffering or hardship, and the town's crest includes three hands with open palms. Rome called the town Helena during the centuries before it was overwhelmed in the Gallic invasions.

Nearly 2300 soldiers lost their lives in the 1871 Battle of Bapaume during the Franco-Prussian War, and, as with many towns in the area, Bapaume was devastated in shelling during WWI due to its key position in the Battles of the Somme, when it changed hands four times between 1914 and 1918. In WWII Bapaume saw intense fighting during the German invasion and its mayor, Abel Guidet, was imprisoned at the Gross-Rosen Camp, where he died in 1944. Abel-Guidet Square is named in his honor. (Bus: https://transports.hautsdefrance.fr)

🛏 **Institute St Eloi**, 36 Rue Marcellin Gaudefroy, bapaume@cneap.fr, tel +33 (0)3 21 07 14 20, Mon–Thurs only

🛏 **Le Refuge**, 17 Rue de la République, odile.samain@orange.fr, tel +33 (0)3 21 22 11 92, (0)6 18 99 75 73, tent ok

🛏 **Le Gourmet** 🄾 🄿 🅁 🄱 🄳 🄲 8/16, €-/54/56/-, 10 Rue de la Gare, contact@le-gourmet.fr, tel +33 (0)3 21 07 20 00, www.le-gourmet.fr, brkfst, demi-pension avail, closed Sun nights and 3 weeks in Aug

🛏 **Hotel de la Paix**, 11 Avenue Abel Guidet, contact@hoteldelapaix-bapaume.fr, tel +33 (0)3 21 22 28 28, (0)6 01 68 51 84, www.hotel-de-la-paix-bapaume.com, closed Sun nights

STAGE 14
Bapaume to Péronne

Start	Bapaume, Place Faidherbe
Finish	Péronne, WWI museum, Place Audinot
Distance	28.7km
Total ascent	238m
Total descent	307m
Difficulty	Moderately hard
Duration	7¾hr
Percentage paved	75%
Lodging	Péronne 28.7km

This flat stage enters the Somme department and then the Somme Valley, notorious as scene of some of the most intense and tragic battles of WWI. Today the region is crisscrossed by major highways and TGV train lines, with dozens of tall wind turbines in silhouette against the skyline. Péronne's Museum of the Great War is well worth a visit, and the town itself features a friendly historic center of shops and restaurants with a Saturday farmers' market.

From the main square, head south on Rue de Péronne, which becomes D917/Avenue Abel Guidet. Pass the **WWI memorial** and then a supermarket and make a right turn on Rue de Lesboeufs. Soon you are on an asphalt road out among fields and wind turbines. Fork left onto gravel at a tall **crucifix** with the TGV tracks and the A1/E15 on your left and come to a **cemetery**.

> Used after nearby battles in late 1918, the **Beaulencourt British Cemetery** contains 700 Commonwealth graves, of which over 300 are unidentified. The adjoining Thilloy Road Cemetery contains another 241 war dead.

Turn left and pass the **Thilloy Road Cemetery** before continuing over the tracks and motorway and curving right toward the north edge of **Beaulencourt (4.8km)**. To find a quieter route south than the D917, the route now turns left, and after crossing the **D917** heads north on gravel out into the fields, toward the tower of Saint-Pierre church in **Riencourt-lès-Bapaume**.

When the road ends at the asphalt **D11/E3**, turn right to head south toward the tall steeple of Saint-Pierre church in Villers-au-Flos, passing the **Manchester British Cemetery**. Riencourt changed hands twice in WWI and 72 East Lancashire soldiers from 1917–1918 actions are buried here. After the Riencourt cemetery, the official route turns left to circle north of Villers-au-Flos; however, the recommended route goes through Villers-au-Flos, saving 2.2km.

Stay on the asphalt road to enter **Villers-au-Flos** (**2.8km**) and go straight at its traffic circle. Turn right before a small grassy park, then right again, forking left before the cemetery onto Rue de Barastre. Under high-tension powerlines, fork right onto gravel,

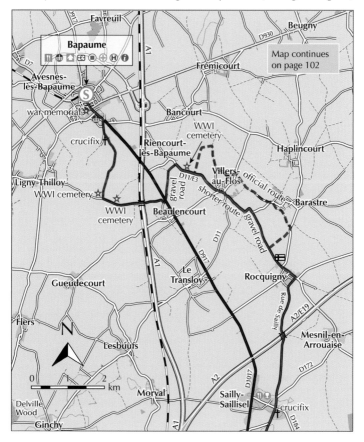

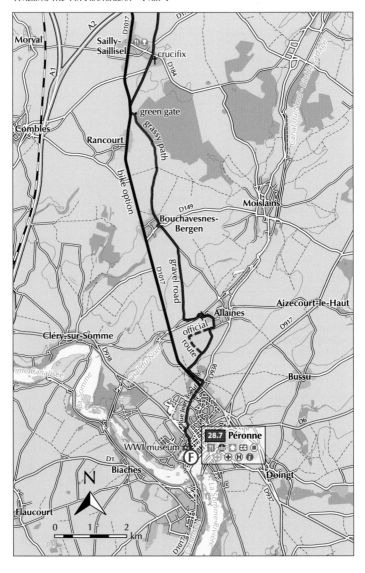

with Barastre now visible on the left. The official route rejoins, you pass another **cemetery**, and arrive in **Rocquigny** (3.2km, no services, benches behind church).

Pass the launchpad-style church tower and turn right one block afterward on **Rue de Sailly**. Fork left at the end of town, once more in the fields. Cross over the **A2/E19** highway, pass a tall cell/microwave tower and join the **D172** road which meets the D184 in **Sailly-Saillisel** (4.0km, benches left, bar and restaurant four blocks right).

Continue through town, and when the D172 curves right at an outdoor **crucifix**, instead go straight. This road ends and you briefly merge with the **D1017** highway until 200 meters later you turn left onto a gravel road, heading toward woods. Just before a **green gate**, turn right to walk alongside the woods on a **grassy path**, heading gradually downhill.

Continue briefly in the woods and, on reemerging, across fields you can see the steeple of the church of Rancourt on the right. Continue straight to arrive at the D149 in the town of **Bouchavesnes-Bergen** (5.2km, no services). Turn left and then make an immediate right, heading uphill for the first climb of the day. On the downhill, turn right on a **gravel road** and continue a long, slow descent, now among low, rolling hills.

The gravel road ends at an asphalt road before the Canal du Nord, which requires a left turn to catch the **canal bridge** (3.4km) just after a grain elevator. After the bridge, curve through the village of **Allaines** and take the first street right. Cross a low bridge and take the first right (Rue Verte) and either follow signs straight onto a gravel road or continue on this road to save 600 meters as it curves south to meet up with the other route before a cemetery.

After the cemetery and before the highway, turn left to climb among homes and barns. At a stop sign before the D43, turn right and follow **Rue Jean Toeuf** down into town, turning right on Rue Jean Mermoz after Rue Toeuf curves left, and turning left again on Avenue de la République to arrive at the WWI museum and Place André Audinot in the center of town (5.2km).

(28.7KM) PÉRONNE (ELEV 52M, POP 9011) 🏨 ⊕ 🛏 🏧 🅒 ⊗ ⊕ ⊕ 🅗 🅘 (1931.8KM)
The 12th-century **Château de Péronne** is centerpiece of the town and houses the excellent **Historial de la Grande Guerre**, the largest WWI museum in Europe (€10, open daily in season, www.historial.fr/en). While the town is notable for its role in the WWI Battles of the Somme, its historical pedigree is far more extensive and has earned it two Croix de Guerre awards and one Légion d'Honneur. French Kings Charles the Simple and Charles the Bold were imprisoned in the castle dungeons (929 and 1468, respectively), and one of France's heroines, Catherine of Poix (also known as Marie Foure), led the defense of the town in 1536 against Charles V of Austria. Bombardments in WWI and WWII left little of the medieval city, but modern Péronne's rebuilt brick and stone buildings are a pleasant hint at its medieval past, and its riverside location gives it a gracious feel. (Bus: https://transports.hautsdefrance.fr)

The museum contained in the Château de Péronne houses extensive exhibits of WWI memorabilia

🛏 **Auberge de Jeunesse des Remparts** ⬛Ⓞ ⬛Pr ⬛Do ⬛R ⬛Br ⬛Cr ⬛S 25/137, €-/37/59/79, 17 Rue Beaubois, resa@aubergedesremparts.net, tel +33 (0)3 22 88 41 10, demi-pension except Sun

⛪ **Saint-Jean-Baptiste Parish**, €Donation, 15 Rue Saint-Jean, paroisse. de.peronne@wanadoo.fr, tel +33 (0)3 22 84 16 90, Tues–Sat

STAGE 15

Péronne to Trefcon

Start	Péronne, Place Audinot
Finish	Trefcon, Rue Principale
Distance	17.7km
Total ascent	135m
Total descent	92m
Difficulty	Easy
Duration	4½hr
Percentage paved	38%
Lodging	Vraignes 11.8km, Trefcon 17.7km

Cool weather brings mosquitoes to the forest trails after Péronne, and weekends bring noisy ATV riders. In between the forested bookends of the stage are farm roads, often paved in asphalt, as well as villages of post-WWI brick homes where few opportunities for water present themselves. Be certain to stock up on supplies and mosquito repellent before leaving Péronne.

From Place Audinot, head uphill on Rue Louis XI and turn left onto the D1017 Rue Saint-Fursy. Now make an immediate right on Rue Saint-Jean. Follow this two blocks until it ends at Boulevard des Anglais, where you turn left to follow alongside the gardens of La Cologne River. When this road ends at the D199, turn right (café) onto a pink gravel sidewalk. Before the road turns right, go straight onto a gravel road where you pass through a **white gate** and continue under trees and alongside marshes.

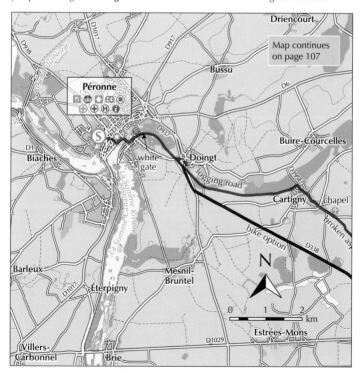

Map continues on page 107

Come to an option to turn left into **Doingt** (**2.5km**, no services). The village of Doingt was Archbishop Sigeric's LXXIV 'Duin' overnight; however, it was completely leveled in WWI and few visible sights of its medieval origins remain. Either take the option left (turning right after the D937 overpass) or continue straight, generally following the south banks of La Cologne. After you cross an asphalt road the path becomes a logging road. Watch for mosquitoes in wet weather in this shaded, marshy terrain. Finally, turn right at the D194E asphalt road (**3.9km**) to enter **Cartigny** (no services).

Head uphill in this village of brick homes in the direction of Hancourt. At the top of the hill find yourself on a country road among fields stretching into the distance, dotted with clumps of trees. After a yellow, stone **chapel** at the end of a promenade of trees fork right, off the D194, onto a **road of broken asphalt** that leads to the village of **Bouvincourt-en-Vermandois** (**3.4km**, no services) where the road ends.

Zigzag through town to the pleasant, asphalt Rue de Vraignes, which you follow to the D15 in the next village, **Vraignes-en-Vermandois** (**1.9km**).

(11.8KM) VRAIGNES-EN-VERMANDOIS (93M, POP 148) 🏕 (1916.9KM)
Local artist and poet Hector Crinon (1807–70) became famous for his political satires based on life in Picardie.

▲ Camping Hortensias, €14 campsite, 22 Rue Basse, campingdeshortensias@gmail.com, tel +33 (0)3 22 85 64 68, www.campinghortensias.com, mobile home rental, meals available

With its owners' house gone, a family tomb is slowly overcome by the forest before Trefcon

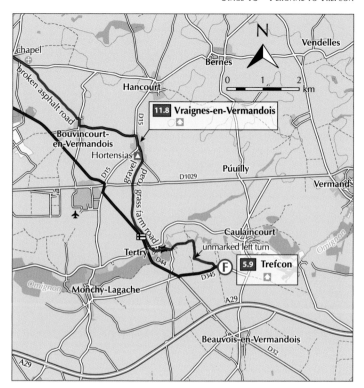

Turn right on the D15 and continue through this village of modest turn-of-the-century homes, forking left on Rue Basse after the Church of Saint-Pierre and passing the Hortensias **campground**. Before the last, quaint barn in town, fork right on a gravel road leading out into the fields. Cross the **D1029** highway and fork left afterward onto a grassy farm road, heading into a narrow wood between two fields. Here you may see skydivers landing at the airfield to the right.

Pass a community **cemetery**, and cross the D45 to enter the town of **Tetry** (3.3km, no services) on its Grand Rue. Curve past the parish church and town hall (benches) and cross **L'Omignon**, a quiet stream, on a pedestrian bridge. Fork left onto gravel and take another fork left on a road leading into woods on the edge of a large field. As the road begins to climb in the woods clockwise around the field, watch carefully for an **unmarked turn** onto a dirt path that climbs to the left. Pass the village cemetery and soon arrive at the D345 Rue Principale in the hamlet of **Trefcon** (2.6km).

(5.9KM) TREFCON (ELEV 97M, POP 94) ⌂ (1914.1KM)

This tiny farming settlement is part village, part crossroad. Its name originally was Saint-Martin-des-Prés after its former parish church. In WWI it became part of the Hindenburg Line and its buildings and trees were leveled. Today its population numbers less than half its pre-WWI total.

⌂ Le Val Domignon Ⓞ Ⓟⓡ Ⓓⓞ Ⓡ Ⓚ Ⓑⓕ Ⓓⓡ Ⓢ 2/4, €25/-/62/-, 3 Rue Principale, le.val.domignon@wanadoo.fr, tel +33(0)3 23 66 58 64, (0)6 99 19 95 47, horses, canoes, demi-pension available

STAGE 16
Trefcon to Seraucourt-le-Grand

Start	Trefcon, Rue Principale
Finish	Seraucourt, town hall
Distance	28.2km (shortcut options can deduct up to 15.7km)
Total ascent	174m
Total descent	200m
Difficulty	Moderately hard (duration via Saint-Quentin)
Duration	7¼hr
Percentage paved	72%
Lodging	Attily 5.8km, Saint-Quentin 16.8km, Seraucourt 28.2km

Although it's possible Sigeric diverted to enjoy the charming city of Saint-Quentin, the official VF/GR145 route's left turn here feels like a detour. If you're looking to save time and don't mind skipping an interesting city, take the bike option shortcut through Étreillers and save 15.7km or the walker shortcut through Savy to save 11.2km. On the other hand, if you like pretty cities you'll enjoy the center of lovely Saint-Quentin, the largest town between Arras and Reims.

Turn left on Rue Principale, heading east and pass the village's water tower. Cross the quiet **D34** and continue on gravel. The road ends and you turn left toward a row of trees.

Bike option to Seraucourt-le-Grand

A right turn just afterward leads to the **D733**, where you turn right and continue to **Étreillers** (3.6km, bar, bakery, grocery, pharmacy). Cross the D68 and turn left on the

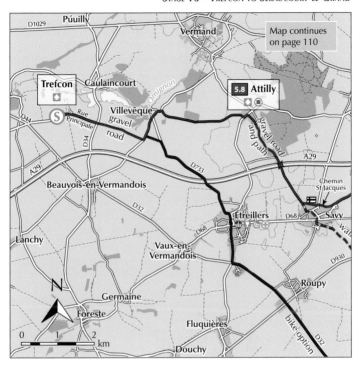

D32, which you follow into **Seraucourt-le-Grand** (**6.5km**, construction on the Somme bridge closed the route to cars in 2022, but pedestrians and bikes can cross).

Main route
On the main route, come to the idyllic village of **Villevêque** (**3.3km**, no services) with its immaculately tended gardens, turn right and off the D73 to head again into the fields. This road ends at the Grand Rue in **Atilly** (**2.5km**).

(5.8KM) ATILLY (ELEV 117M, POP 402) 🏠 ⊚ (1908.3KM)
The settlement likely dates to Roman times. After the devastation of WWI, the wall of just one building was still standing. (Bus: www.cap80.com)

🏠 **Ferme de Vivien Legrand**, 27 Grand Rue, contact@lafermedevivien.fr, tel +33 (0)6 29 43 40 34

Once in town, turn left on the Grand Rue and immediately right on Rue du Prozet, heading uphill. When the road curves left, instead go straight on a gravel driveway leading to a dirt path that continues through woods on the west side of the road. Continue through fields and woods, cross a gravel road, and take a bridge over the **A29** motorway to the first road in **Savy** (**3.1km**).

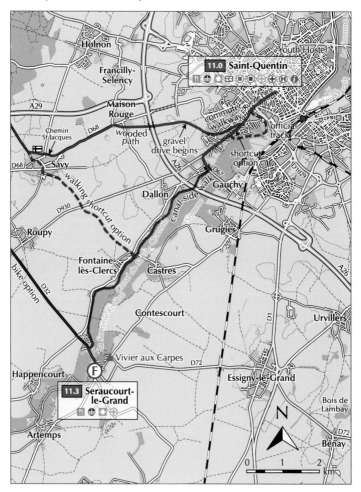

Walker shortcut option to Seraucourt-le-Grand
At the edge of Savy, signs point to another option to miss Saint-Quentin. Go straight on Rue du Château d'Eau toward the D68 at the town's church. Cross onto Rue des Écoles and turn left onto Rue de Fontaine. Cross the **D930** and continue to the road's end on Rue de Saint-Quentin in **Fontaine-lès-Clercs**. Continue on the next street to the right to cross the **Canal de Saint-Quentin** (4.5km) and continue left toward **Seraucourt-le-Grand**.

Sunset leaves a warm glow on the Basilica of Saint-Quentin

Main route
In Savy, a left on the official Francigena route through Saint-Quentin is marked '**Chemin Saint-Jacques**,' a grassy road between a field and a pasture. Pass the village cemetery and merge onto a path alongside the **D68** in the direction of Maison Rouge. The path ends just before the village and you fork right before a bus stop onto a narrow, **wooded path** across a small parking area.

Cross an asphalt road and then cross under the **A26** Autoroute des Anglais as the path becomes more pleasant. Join a gravel drive, cross another gravel road, and pick up a narrow path, once again under trees. The path becomes a **commuter walkway** for office workers and students. Turn left on the busy Rue de Paris arterial to continue up to the main square and Hôtel de Ville (7.9km).

(11.0KM) SAINT-QUENTIN (ELEV 99M, POP 55,407)
🏨 ⊕ 🛏 🅒 ⓜ ⓞ ⊕ ⊕ Ⓗ ⓘ (1897.3KM)
Originally a Gallic town and then Roman *Augusta Veromanduorum*, Saint-Quentin was renamed after Quentin of Amiens, who was martyred here in AD287. Pilgrimage to venerate his tomb led to the establishment of a major monastery, now the **Basilica of Saint-Quentin**. Located at a ford of the Somme River, Saint-Quentin's position between the Champagne and Flanders regions made it a trade capital in the late Middle Ages. Beginning with the Hundred Years' War (1337–1453), the city suffered many setbacks including plague and its destruction in 1557 by the Spanish Army, which left it deserted for two years. The town was overrun by the Germans in 1916 and the war left 80% of the city's buildings

severely damaged. The Basilica of Saint-Quentin, though heavily damaged in WWI, has been restored to much of its former glory, and the **Hôtel de Ville** was restored in 1926 with art deco embellishments. Despite its ravishments, central Saint-Quentin has the atmosphere of an ancient city and makes a pleasant overnight stop. (Bus: https://buspastel.fr)

🏠 ▲ **Camping & Auberge de Jeunesse**, 10/60, €10/-/-/-, camping €4, 87 Blvd Jean Bouin, www.saint-quentin.fr/51-camping.htm, tel +33 (0)3 23 06 94 05, open mid May to mid Sept

Retrace your steps on Rue de Paris, coming to the Square Romain Tricoteaux, where just afterward you turn left onto Rue de Vieux Pont on the official route that follows alongside the canal. Recommended alternative: It is wiser simply to continue on Rue du Paris instead, since the official path along the canal is overgrown and isolated.

Back on the Rue de Paris, at the D67 turn left to pass a roundabout and cross the **Canal de Saint-Quentin** (**4.2km**). Turn left to enjoy a quiet walk along this canal, passing opposite the towns of **Dallon** and **Fontaine-lès-Clercs**.

The **Canal de Saint-Quentin** was conceived in the 16th century but remained incomplete until Napoleon ordered its completion beginning in 1801, and it was dedicated in his presence in 1810. The canal was part of the Hindenburg Line of German defenses during WWI, and was recaptured during the Hundred Days Offensive of 1918.

In a little over 3km, just before Seraucourt, fork left with the canal and follow this road until it ends at the D32 (bar). Turn left and in 400 meters find the Saint-Martin church and town hall in **Seraucourt** (**7.1km**).

(11.3KM) SERAUCOURT-LE-GRAND (ELEV 71M, POP 774) 🍴 ⊕ ⌂ ⊕
(1886.0KM)
Before WWI, the town hall and Church of St Martin stood adjacent to each other on a large town square. By the war's end, only small portions of the church remained standing as the town was totally destroyed. On Sigeric's journey it was listed as LXXIII 'Martinwaeth.'

🏠 **Municipal Hostel**, Via Romana 170, mairie.seraucourt@orange.fr, tel +33 (0)6 82 12 20 61

🏠 ▲ **Camping Vivier aux Carpes**, tent €10/person, caravan €-/25/35/-/-, 10 Rue Charles Voyeux, contact@camping-picardie.com, tel +33 (0)3 23 60 50 10

STAGE 17
Seraucourt-le-Grand to Tergnier

Start	Seraucourt-le-Grand, town hall
Finish	Tergnier, canal road and Ave Jean Jaurès
Distance	18.8km
Total ascent	97m
Total descent	112m
Difficulty	Easy
Duration	4¾hr
Percentage paved	77%
Lodging	Tergnier 18.8km

Familiar farm roads carry you to Jussy, and afterward canal-side paths lead quickly and easily to Tergnier – unless poor trail maintenance at the canal blocks your way beginning in Jussy. An asphalt alternative can be used if vegetation along the path is overgrown, and after Mennessis the path, now paved in asphalt, is clear. Consider continuing to La Fère or even Bertaucourt to shorten the next day's long stage.

From the town hall, continue onto the D72 Rue du Jeu d'Arc. When this road curves left, go straight instead onto a gravel and cobblestone road heading into the fields. The road ends at the D341, where you go straight in the direction of the lattice-like steeple of the Saint-Sulpice church in the village of **Clastres** (**5.0km**, no services).

Turn right at the D34 after the church, pass the *mairie* and school, then take the first left – an alley called Rue de Becquemin – which curves around to Rue de la Longue Ruelle, where you turn left and follow until it ends. Now turn left on the **Chemin du Burguet**, again heading into the fields. This long road takes you to the D8 at the village of **Jussy** (**3.5km**).

Go straight one block (picnic tables on right) to the bridge over the Canal Saint-Quentin and inspect the condition of the north canal-side path, which may be overgrown with vegetation. If it looks passable, take the path left (north side of canal), following it all the way to the D1090 outside **Mennessis** (**5.2km**). If the path looks overgrown, as is often the case, head south through town, forking left onto **Rue Edmond Osset** to follow the bike option (see map).

The two options rejoin on the canal-side path where it meets the **D1090** (**0.6km**). Continue alongside the canal until the second auto bridge, where you leave the path to enter **Tergnier** (**4.6km**). The town hall and services are across the canal and beyond the railroad tracks.

Contescourt

Urvillers

Seraucourt-
le-Grand

S

Essigny-le-Grand

bike option

Artemps

Benay

Cerizy

Bois de
Lambay

ncourt

Somme

Clastres

Montescourt-
Lizerolles

Hinacourt

Gibercourt

Ly-
Fontaine

Chemin de Burguet

Canal de Saint-Quentin

Jussy

official track - if accessible

Remigny

Rue Edmond Ossel

Flavy-le-Martel

bike option

Liez

Mennessis

Canal de Saint-Quentin

first auto bridge

Frières-Faillouël

N

0   1   2
km

Villequier-
Aumont

18.8 Tergnier

second auto bridge

F

Canal de la Sambre à l'...

Saint-Quentin

Tergnier's Art Nouveau city hall stands in the town's central square

(18.8KM) TERGNIER (ELEV 56M, POP 15,475) 🍴 ⊕ 🏠 Ⓒ ⊛ ⊕ ⊕ (1867.2KM)
Among French towns, Tergnier is quite young, its first appearance in records coming in the 17th century and its formal establishment in 1793. The town's development was enhanced in 1843 by the completion of the **Picardy Canal** and in 1853 with completion of the rail line to Reims and Amiens. Tergnier changed hands several times in WWI, and in WWII over 16,000 bombs were dropped on the city's transportation and industrial infrastructure by Allied forces.

🏠 **Parish Notre-Dame de Thérigny**, 43 Rue Racine, tel +33 (0)6 86 35 53 15, (03) 23 57 01 06

▲ 🏠 **Camping La Frette**, six mobile homes avail with 2–8 places each from €70/night; two tent lodges 4–6 places each from €45/night, Rue de la Prairie, camping.lafrette@ville-tergnier.fr, tel +33 (0)3 23 40 21 21

STAGE 18
Tergnier to Laon

Start	Tergnier, canal road and Ave Jaurès
Finish	Laon, town hall
Distance	39.5km (options can deduct 2.7km)
Total ascent	478m
Total descent	348m
Difficulty	Hard (duration)
Duration	10¼hr
Percentage paved	53%
Lodging	La Fère 6.2km, Bertaucourt 11.5km, Cessières-Suzy 28.1km, Laon 39.5km

The official stage is long due to the relative lack of services in this stretch, so it makes sense to extend the previous stage to either La Fère or Bertaucourt in order to make this stage more manageable. Though the D1044 offers a direct route to Laon (perfect for cyclists at 24.2km from La Fère), the VF instead aims for a walk through the Forêt de Saint-Gobain as a respite from farm roads and fields. The result is a green and quiet stage, at least until the D750 before Laon. Resist any temptation to skip the uphill climb at stage end into medieval Laon, because it's one of the most authentic medieval towns in France and one of the highlights of the Francigena. At its summit is the must-see Notre-Dame de Laon, a surviving wonder of the Middle Ages.

Continue on the canal-side road, pass under a railroad bridge, and follow the road through a 90-degree bend at its confluence with the **Canal de la Sambre à l'Oise**. At the next auto bridge, cross to the other side (picnic tables) and continue in the same direction, now on the canal's south side.

Continue through **Beautor** (restaurant), which straddles the canal, go under the railroad bridge again, and then at the next bridge leave the canal and turn right onto the **D338** (groceries). In 800 meters turn right at the roundabout and then turn right again on Rue de la République to come to the town hall in downtown **La Fère** (**6.2km**).

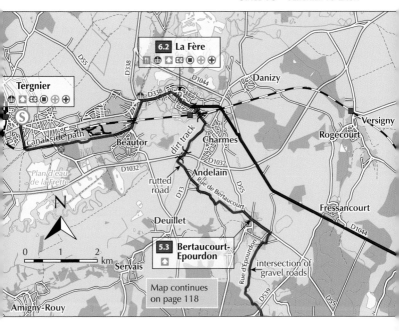

(6.2KM) LA FÈRE (ELEV 50M, POP 2869) 🍴⊕🛏🅲◉⊕⊕ **(1861.0KM)**
The town entered the pages of history when Eudes I, King of the Franks, died
here in 898. While under Spanish control, King Henry IV of France besieged the
city for two years beginning in 1595. By blocking the Oise River he flooded the
town, which then surrendered. Alexander Dumas's fictional character Athos in
The Three Musketeers was revealed to be Count of La Fère, and would also be
featured in two later novels. In WWI the town was part of the Hindenburg Line
of German defenses. (See online resources for tourist accommodation options.)

Continue along the street with its many restaurants, cross the Oise River and after
the park turn right on Square Foch. Head through the tunnel under the railroad tracks
and, now in **Charmes**, turn right onto Rue du Petit Charmes (**1.0km**, bakery). Pass
among homes as the road becomes a dirt track through fields and small woods.

Cross the **D1032** road in a culvert-like tunnel and 250 meters later turn left on
a deeply rutted road heading uphill among pastures. Come to the first barns and
then the D13/Rue Principale in **Andelain** (**1.9km**, no services). Cross the road and

117

continue on **Rue de Bertaucourt**, which winds through town, past the village church of Saint Denis, and back into the fields. Head uphill, and soon after meeting a gravel road turn left to find the D55 roadway, where a right takes you north of the village of **Bertaucourt-Epourdon** (2.4km).

> **(5.3KM) BERTAUCOURT-EPOURDON** (ELEV 102M, POP 593) 🏛 (1855.7KM)
> The rural villages of Bertaucourt and Epourdon were merged together in the 1790s.
>
> 🛏 **Gite des 3 Geais**, 3/6, €-/-/60/-, 9 Rue Georges Domissy, http:// gitedes3geais.e-monsite.com/reservation/gite, tel +33 (0)6 12 32 81 90, house and cottage

Watch for a right turn onto either Rue du Carolus or Chemin de Mont Calleux, both of which take you southbound into the fields on **Rue d'Epourdon**, passing the tumbledown relics of a once-grand farm manor. Continue straight through a hilltop **intersection** of gravel roads where now you can see Les Bruyères on your left and ahead a series of low, wooded ridges.

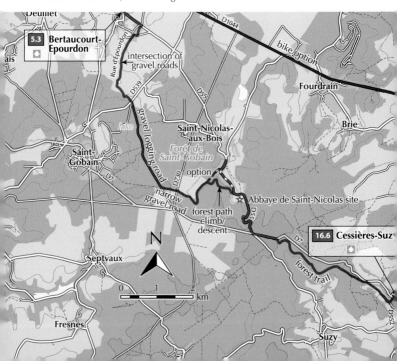

At the bottom of the hill the road turns to sand and heads left toward the asphalt **D539** (**3.3km**). Cross the road and pick up a gravel road, marked as a logging road, which will make a straight trajectory through the **Forêt de Saint-Gobain**.

Once a forest owned by the Abbey of Saint-Nicolas-aux-Bois, the **Forêt de Saint-Gobain** became a royal forest under Henri IV. In WWI it held a position on the Hindenburg Line and the network of trenches built in this tranquil wood suffered continual bombardment.

Pass a small lake and continue on the gravel road, which is paved in asphalt on steeper climbs. At a junction atop a hill, turn left onto a narrower gravel road. Cross the **D730** asphalt road and continue on gravel, heading downhill. Come to an option to go left toward the missable village of **Saint-Nicolas** (**5.3km**, no services), or turn right to climb the hill for a 0.9km shortcut.

The options rejoin on the D55 after town. Pass the original site of the **Abbaye de Saint-Nicolas-aux-Bois**, where only a few remnants of 15th-century buildings can be seen. Continue to the top of the hill, where the road meets the **D7** highway. Turn left here and walk along this quiet highway for the next 700 meters before turning right onto a gravel road.

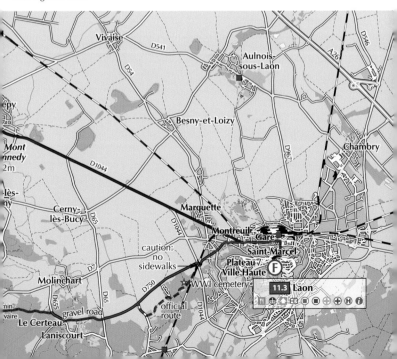

The road soon becomes a dirt path, ultimately becoming a delightful and fairly flat **forest trail** following the general trajectory of the D7 roadway. Keep straight at the next intersections and again meet the D7 road before the next town, but before touching asphalt turn right to continue on gravel. Turn left on Rue Buet to come to the D7 in **Cessières-Suzy** (**8.0km**) where you turn right to enter the town.

(16.6KM) CESSIÈRES-SUZY (ELEV 105M, POP 764) ⬆ (1839.1KM)

Cessières is mentioned in documents from 631, when Saint Cagnoald of Laon built a chapel to St Nicholas here. The village was completely destroyed in WWI. It was merged with its neighboring community of Suzy in 2019.

⬟ La Forestière, 7 Ruelle Bluet, email@domain.com, tel +33 (0)3 23 24 19 07

Turn right on the **D552** then left on the **Chemin du Calvaire**, which soon turns to gravel as it crosses the D26 and heads out of town. After a time you'll be able to see ahead the distant ridge with the towers of the grand churches of Laon. The road becomes a forest path, crossing through the woods and coming to the D655, where you turn right, in the direction of Laniscourt, to arrive at the edge of the hamlet of **Le Certeau**.

Stone walls and a defensive tower show this farm below Laon is many centuries old

Watch carefully for signs pointing to a narrow **gravel road** where you turn left off asphalt just after a small orchard before town. Continue to the asphalt **D65**, which you cross to walk on the **D750** going straight ahead. Come to signs pointing the official route to the right, which loops out to find more pleasant terrain and to pass a German military cemetery, costing an extra 700 meters. Both routes rejoin just before the side-walk-free **D1044 bridge** where you turn right to cross the tracks and left just afterward to continue into the lower city of Laon, joining with the D181 to follow signs towards the *gare* (train station).

Once at Rue Place de l'Homme (**10.5km**), where a left turn takes you in a block to the trains, turn right instead and walk uphill on Avenue Camot. Follow signs to the city center, which lead to the town hall near the top of the hill in the medieval city at Rue du Bourg (**0.8km**). Turn left on Rue Châtelaine to arrive at Notre-Dame de Laon in three blocks.

(11.3KM) LAON (ELEV 178M, POP 28,688) 🏨 ⊕ 🛏 🅲 ⊚ ⊚ ⊕ ⊕ 🅗 ❶
(1827.8KM)

Bertrada of Laon was wife of Pepin the Short and mother of eight children, including, in 747, Charlemagne, greatest of the Frankish kings and Holy Roman Emperor. Laon's position on a 100m mountain ridge amidst the flat plain of Picardy is key to its strategic importance over centuries. Named by the Gauls Bibrax, it was called *Alaudanum* or *Lugdunum Clavatum* by the Romans who used it as an important imperial redoubt against uprisings by the Franks and successive invasions by Burgundians, Vandals, Alans, and Huns. In the Middle Ages Laon was a key city of the Franks, who endowed its cathedral with vast lands. In 990 Archbishop Sigeric visited here and recorded it as his Stage LXXII 'Mondlothuin.' The theological school of Anselm of Laon (died 1117) was influential in medieval scholasticism.

A revolt against Bishop Gaudry of Laon in Eastertide 1112 led to the burning of the episcopal palace, a fire that ultimately consumed the Romanesque cathedral, which led to the building of its spectacular Gothic replacement. The Abbey of St Martin was established in 1124, and its 12th-century chapel survives as the parish **Church of St Martin**. The city was scene of the 1814 Battle of Laon, a defeat for Napoleon's armies. One hundred years later the German army captured Laon and held it until an Allied offensive in 1918. Since Laon's buildings survived many of the devastating wars of the 20th century, the old city offers tourists and Francigena pilgrims the flavor of a medieval French town. Its **Bouvelle Court gate**, its narrow **Rue Châtelaine**, and its cathedral complex all evoke a long-ago time.

Cathedral of Notre-Dame de Laon

After the conflagration of 1112, Laon's new cathedral was built using the then-new Gothic style that had originated at Saint-Denis just 50 years earlier. The result is one of the premier architectural treasures of France. The building was completed in essentially its current form in the 12th-14th centuries, though some minor 19th-century modifications strengthened the structure and allowed installation of the large pipe organ. Above the façade, look for the life-sized oxen sculptures that honor the beasts of burden who delivered stone to the site. In the French Revolution Laon lost its bishopric, which demoted the cathedral to parish church status. Without diocesan activities and at the center of the quiet, hilltop old city of Laon, the building is a tranquil and beautiful setting for contemplation. (Bus: www.tul-laon.fr)

The interior of the 12th–14th-century Cathedral of Laon is famous for its brilliant light, made possible through its airy Gothic structure

🛏 **Le Refuge des Cordeliers** 🅞 🄿🅣 🅁 🄺 🅦 🅂 3/8, €-/50/50/50, 12 Rue des Cordeliers, lerefugedescordeliers@gmail.com, tel +33(0)6 76 28 11 19, Guillaume Dussart

🛏 **Accueil Pèlerin**, €Donation, 22 Rue du Cloître, email@domain.com, tel +33 (0)6 81 19 53 56, Mme Tordeux

🛏 **Hotel les Chevaliers**, 3 Rue Sérurier, hotelchevaliers@aol.com, tel +33 (0)3 23 27 17 50

STAGE 19
Laon to Corbeny

Start	Laon, town hall
Finish	Corbeny, village church
Distance	29.6km (options can deduct 2.1km)
Total ascent	298m
Total descent	381m
Difficulty	Moderately hard (duration)
Duration	7¾hr
Percentage paved	44%
Lodging	Corbeny 29.6km

After leaving medieval Laon's hilltop center and its less picturesque modern, lowland suburbs, this is a delightfully calm and pastoral stage set on mostly well-groomed pathways with gentle ups and downs among fields and forests. Lac de l'Ailette and the ruins of the Abbey of Vauclare are scenic highlights. Prepare for mud and mosquitoes in damp weather, with intermediate services only at Bruyères.

With your back to the town hall, turn slightly right to find a passageway across the street between a shop and a restaurant. Take the steps downhill through the historic Chenizelles gate and turn right on a cobblestone street of the same name. Follow this uphill to a wide and easy stairway, and at the top veer onto cobblestoned Rue Thibesard in the direction of the tall church ahead, the 12th-century **Eglise Saint-Martin**.

Turn left at the church and go downhill to **Porte de Soisson**, a scenic remnant of Laon's 13th–16th-century walls. Cross the street and continue downhill on the wide asphalt road that becomes a cobblestone then dirt path. At the stop sign in the lower city, turn left on **Rue Romanette** (groceries, restaurants, tourist hotels), which becomes Rue Pompidou after the first roundabout. At a stoplight, turn right on the **D967**, cross under the N2 roadway bridge, and continue straight on the D967 through the village of **Ardon** (**4.6km**, restaurant).

Continue out of town, cross L'Ardon River, and turn left onto Rue Sainte-Salaberge, named after the local saint and seventh-century abbess. Shortcut option: Turn left just afterward onto Chemin de l'Hippodrome to save a few hundred meters. From the official route, cross the Chemin de l'Hippodrome and continue on a **gravel path**, first among the fields and afterward through the woods. After joining with the **Rue du Bois Brûle** (Burnt Forest Street), come to Rue Porte de Laon in the town of **Bruyères-et-Montbérault** (**4.2km**, groceries, restaurant).

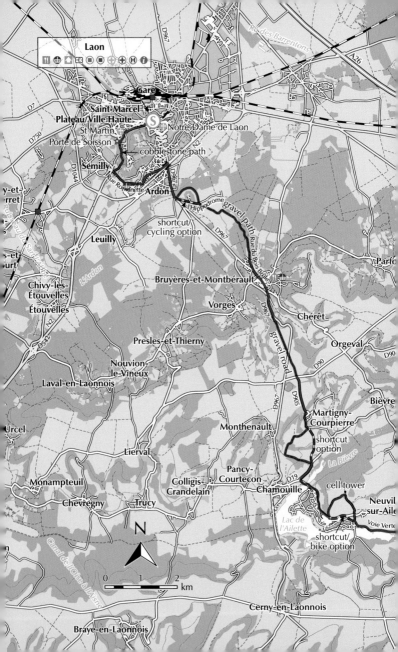

Fork left toward the square steeple of the town's church and continue outside town to join the **D967** at a roundabout, heading uphill on the asphalt sidewalk. After the last houses of town, fork right onto a gravel road, continuing the climb. Cross the **D967** and then the **D90** to reach a summit. Now on the **D905**, head downhill toward the needle-like spire of the Church of Saint-Martin in **Martigny-Courpierre** (**4.5km**).

Martigny-Courpierre was completely destroyed in WWI bombardments. Its current buildings are all post-war, including the lovely art-nouveau church.

At an intersection before the bottom of the hill, turn right onto a gravel farm road. Shortcut option: Continuing straight on the D905 saves 0.9km. The road ends at the D19, where you turn left to take a pedestrian bridge that snakes across **La Bièvre River** under the auto bridge. Pick up a nature path after the parking lot that follows to the left of the quiet auto road, heading uphill. At a parking area veer left onto a grassy farm road that continues the climb. Now views of Lake Ailette – an artificial lake created along the Ailette River in the 1980s – open ahead.

Come to a summit and turn left. Shortcut option: Continuing straight instead to the D19 roadway and taking the second left saves a climb plus a distance of 0.9km. Climb through woods and turn right at the **cell tower** at the summit. Cross the D19 in the town of **Neuville-sur-Ailette** (**5.7km**, no services) and continue to the **Voie Verte de l'Ailette** bikeway of light brown crushed rock, where the shortcut rejoins and you turn left. The Vélo Route Voie Verte de l'Ailette is a 17km route linking Monampteuil to Vauclair. The bike trail heads alongside the lake until it ends at an asphalt road where you turn right before picking up the gravel **Chemin du Roi** on the left. Head through the woods and just before the **Étang des Moines pond**, turn right to cross the D886 at the entrance to the ruins of **Vauclair Abbey** (**4.4km**, WC).

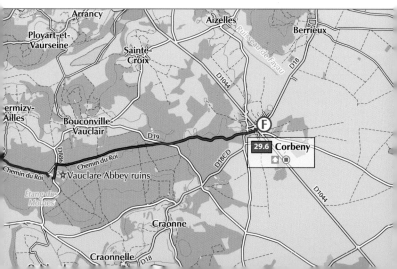

The haunting ruins of the Abbey of Vauclair

The haunting ruins of this one-time Cistercian **abbey**, founded by St Bernard of Clairvaux in 1134 and active until the French Revolution, were reduced to their current state by heavy bombardment during WWI.

After a visit through the ruins, continue north on the D886 and return to the graded, gravel **Chemin du Roi** on your right, once again in the quiet woods. Cross the asphalt **D19** and continue straight as the road joins the D18CD before arriving at the village church at the heart of **Corbeny** (**6.3km**).

(29.6KM) CORBENY (ELEV 92M, POP 767) 🔼 ◉ (1798.2KM)

The Abbey of Corbeny was home to the relics of sixth-century Saint-Marcouf, believed to have power to heal scrofula, also known as 'king's evil.' Whether for this reason or because of its central location in the Frankish kingdom, it was often visited by royalty during its long history. Even so, the town never grew beyond about 3000 inhabitants in size. In 990 Archbishop Sigeric stopped here as his Stage LXXI 'Corbunei' and in 1429 King Charles VII passed through, with Joan of Arc in his retinue. Napoleon Bonaparte was housed here during the Battle of Craonne, and the Prussian army headquartered in the town in 1870. WWI saw the total destruction of Corbeny, which by 1929 was rebuilt into its contemporary form as a pleasant and quiet crossroads village. (Bus: https://transports. hautsdefrance.fr)

🏠 **Chemin des Dames** Pr R Br Dr Gr W S Z 21/49, €-/55/65/90, 4 Rue Pierre Curtil, hotelchemindesdames02@gmail.com, tel +33 (0)6 22 57 32 24, (0)3 23 23 95 70, (0)6 22 57 32 24, restaurant with demi-pension €17 pilgrim price, €86 for 2 pilgrims in 1 room with demi-pension, closed Aug

STAGE 20
Corbeny to Berry-au-Bac

Start	Corbeny, village church
Finish	Berry-au-Bac, town hall
Distance	11.1km
Total ascent	42m
Total descent	78m
Difficulty	Easy
Duration	2¾hr
Percentage paved	66%
Lodging	Berry-au-Bac 11.1km

Farm tracks among vast fields of grain with wide views over broad valleys characterize this short and easy stage. The intermediate town of Juvincourt offers no facilities, while Berry-au-Bac has just the one lodging. To continue to Hermonville would allow more time the following day to enjoy the delights of remarkable Reims.

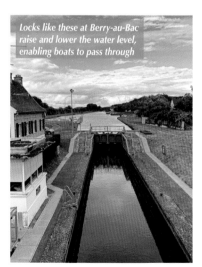

Locks like these at Berry-au-Bac raise and lower the water level, enabling boats to pass through

Turn right at the church onto the D1044, and then make the first left onto the **D62** in the direction of Juvincourt. The asphalt sidewalk ends and you continue on this quiet, country road through grainfields and occasional woods between fields. The road ends at the D89 in **Juvincourt-et-Damary** (**5.2km**, no services).

Cross the D89 and jog right onto Rue de l'Abrevoir and continue through town. Pass a farm-implement dealer and in 100 meters fork left to follow a gravel road between farmland and woods which shelter a quiet stream, La Miette. The road becomes a path and turns away from the woods to cross the **D925** where it once again becomes a road as it enters town. Turn right on Rue des

Écoles and find the town hall in three blocks when the road ends at the D1044 in **Berry-au-Bac** (5.9km).

(11.1KM) BERRY-AU-BAC (ELEV 56M, POP 655) 🍴 🛏 ◉ (1787.1KM)
Settlements from the Neolithic period have been found by archeologists here, and the town is located near the site of Julius Caesar's defeat of the Belgians at the Battle of the Aisne in 57BC. Berry-au-Bac reappears in history when its bridge was the site of an 1814 skirmish during the Napoleonic Wars. France used armored vehicles here for the first time in 1917 when it launched a tank offensive against German forces. The WWI **National Necropolis of Berry-au-Bac** holds the remains of 3972 French, British, Russian and Belgian soldiers. (Bus: https://transports.hautsdefrance.fr)

🏠 **Emmaüs Centre**, www.facebook.com/emmausReims.Berryofficiel, Av du Gl de Gaulle, tel +33 (0)3 23 79 95 88

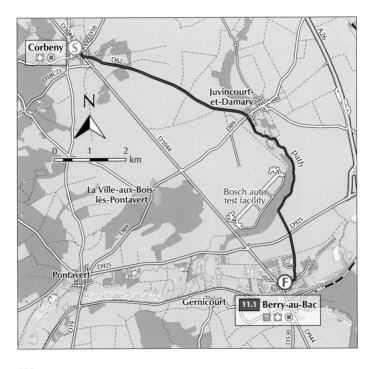

128

SECTION 3:
GRAND-EST REGION

Châteauvillain's streets are quiet on an early weekend morning (Stage 36)

Section 3 overview

The Via Francigena crosses the departments of Marne, Aube, and Haute-Marne in this northeast region of France, where wine is king. Look for vast hillside vineyards where the soils and climate have made the region's premier sparkling wine – Champagne – the international beverage of celebrations. Forests begin to predominate as the route gently climbs up the Marne Valley.

A windmill near Verzenay formerly used to grind grain now serves as a Champagne museum (Stage 22)

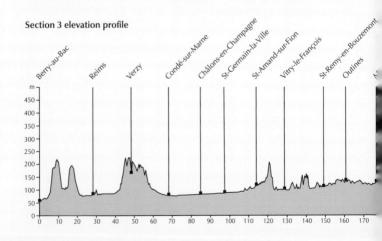

Section 3 elevation profile

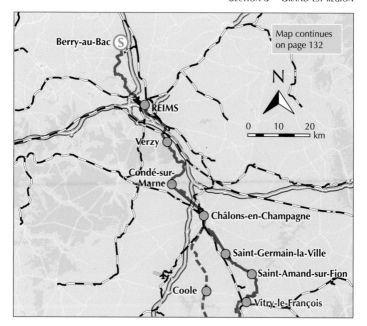

Berry-au-Bac Ⓢ

Map continues on page 132

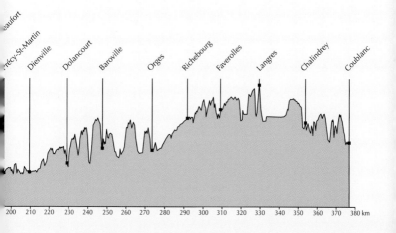

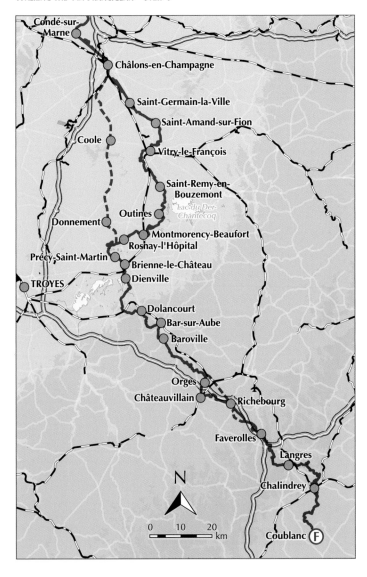

STAGE 21
Berry-au-Bac to Reims

Start	Berry-au-Bac, town hall
Finish	Reims, cathedral
Distance	28.5km
Total ascent	286m
Total descent	256m
Difficulty	Moderately hard
Duration	7½hr
Percentage paved	47%
Lodging	Hermonville 12.2km, Reims 28.5km

After Cormicy the route climbs and descends on easy paths among Champagne vineyards, resulting in a healthy thirst for the local vintage. At Hermonville wheat fields once again abound, but a long forest trek – sometimes busy with motorcycles on the weekend – offers a change of scenery. Enter Reims – technically the largest city on the VF until Rome – on a series of nature and bike trails, with a relaxing walk on the Coulée Verte pedestrian/bike path along the Marne. After a dozen urban blocks, find yourself at one of Europe's finest medieval cathedrals set in a very walkable and charming city center.

Turn left onto the D1044, cross the **Aisne River** on the auto bridge and continue, crossing two channels of the Canal Latèral à L'Aisne. Fork right on the **D530** and after the last houses turn right to head into the fields. Shortcut option: Continue on the D530 (see map 'bike option') to save 1.4km. On the left you can see the next town, Cormicy.

At the last utility pole, turn left onto another farm road. Cross the D530 and a block later turn right to come to the D32 in **Cormicy (5.2km**, bar, restaurant, pharmacy). Turn right and uphill to continue on the D32, passing the church and *mairie*. Turn left on Rue du Bois de Pré, continuing uphill. Turn left just after house #1 toward vineyards of champagne grapes. Zigzag through vineyards in a SW direction, aiming at a grassy path heading toward the woods.

Once at the woods, turn left between the woods and vineyards and then leave the vineyards behind as you pick up a quiet, **forest path**. Once on the woods' opposite side, continue through fields to a summit where you turn left on a **gravel road** that brings you to the **D30** highway. Turn left here and follow the road into town, where it meets the D530 at the town hall of **Hermonville (7.0km)**

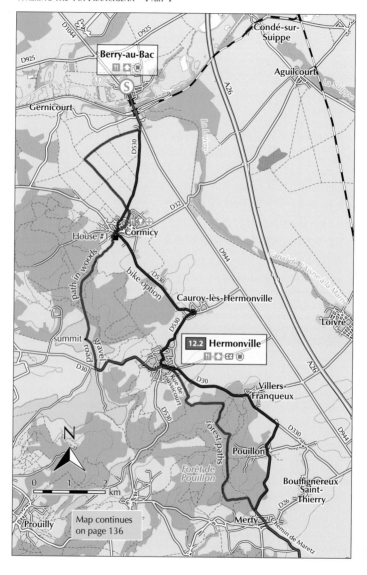

Map continues
on page 136

(12.2KM) HERMONVILLE (ELEV 104M, POP 1447) 🍴 ⛺ Ⓒ ⊛ **(1774.9KM)**

'Villa Herimundi' is mentioned in records as old as the sixth century. The town and its surroundings were variously properties of the Abbey of Saint-Thierry and the Abbey of Saint-Remy in Reims. During the Hundred Years' War in 1317 the town was plundered by forces of the Duke of Lancaster. Six centuries later it served as a rear base for the French army during the Second Battle of the Aisne, which lasted over six months in 1917 and cost approximately 350,000 lives. (Bus: https://transports.hautsdefrance.fr)

⛺ **La Grange en Champagne**, 6 Rue de l'Église, lagrange.hermonville@gmail. com, tel +33 (0)3 51 42 08 20

⛺ **Bienvenue Chez Florine**, 12 Rue Saint Martin, email@domain.com, tel +33 (0)3 26 08 90 57

Pass the Place de la Mairie and one long block later veer right onto **Rue de Toussicourt** which you follow out of town and into the fields. Cross a narrow wood to walk alongside a field on your left, followed by another wood leading to a field you pass on your right. Turn left and into the **Pouillon Forest** on a wide, dirt track.

At a summit, turn right and now head straight south through the woods. After a grainfield on your right, fork right. Signs of motocross dirt bikes are everywhere, and on weekends these woods are full of their sounds. The path passes another field and curves eastward. At a third field, turn right and come to an asphalt road where you turn right and after a time, with views of Reims in the far distance, you come to the D26 in **Merfy (7.1km)**.

Vineyards stretch out on the hillside between Hermonville and Reims

Cross the D26 and continue to descend as the road becomes **Chemin de Maretz** and heads through grainfields. At the bottom of the hill, turn left before a field under a promenade of **maple trees** and continue on this narrow but quiet paved road through fields as it crosses the A26/E17 motorway.

Turn right on an asphalt road under **power lines**. Go around a red metal gate to find a narrow path on the right. Pass the sewage treatment plant and at the end pick up a **bike trail** on crushed brown gravel. Now in an industrial zone, continue to your first view of the now-channelized River Marne.

Continue along the bike trail as you enter the city, comfortably away from urban traffic. After the convention center across the canal, take the stairway (or elevator) up to the bridge deck and cross the river. You now see brass Via Francigena markers embedded in the sidewalk which you follow up the Rue de Vesle among shops and businesses until turning right either after the Opéra de Reims or the Palais de Justice to find one of the world's truly great Gothic cathedrals at the heart of the Via Francigena's largest city until Rome: **Reims** (**9.2km**).

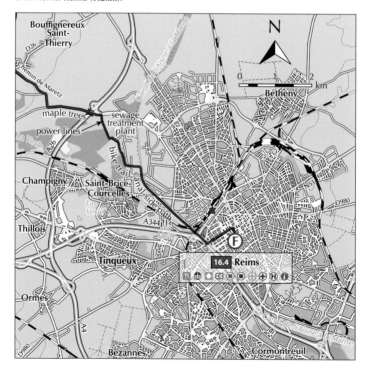

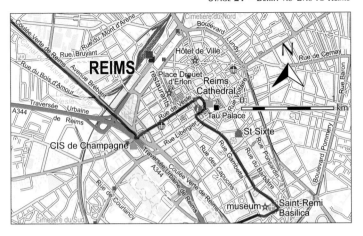

(16.4KM) REIMS (ELEV 86M, POP 196,565) 🔢 ⊕ 🏠 🄲 ◉ ◉ ⊕ ⊕ ⊕ 🄗 *i*
(1758.5KM)

Ancient capital of the Remi tribe of Gauls, the early influence of Reims grew due to its alliance with insurgent Roman legions under Julius Caesar. During the Pax Romana it came to be called Durocortorum and is believed to have had a population as high as 100,000 people. The decline of Rome's military power brought successive invasions and the city was sacked first by the Vandals in 406 and then by Attila the Hun in 451. The resulting power vacuum led to the rise of the Frankish king, Clovis, and his 496 baptism at Reims by St Remigius (St Rémi in French) would permanently connect Reims with the divine right of France's Catholic monarchy.

Popes found the city important enough to journey here to meet with Kings Pepin the Short and Charlemagne, and beginning in 1179 until the end of the French monarchy in 1825, nearly every French king was consecrated at the Cathedral of Reims. According to legend, St Remigius's tomb was found to include a small vial of fragrant oil which he purportedly used when he baptized King Clovis. That vial and its contents, the 'Holy Ampulla,' became a sacred treasure of the Abbey of Saint-Rémi and with great fanfare was transported to the Cathedral for royal consecrations where a few drops were used in the anointing of a king. Prior to their consecration, kings and their courts sojourned at the nearby royal Palace of Tau. The three sites – the Cathedral, the Abbey of Saint-Rémi, and the Palace of Tau – are together a UNESCO World Heritage site.

Archbishop Sigeric stayed here in his stage LXX 'Rems.' During the Hundred Years' War, Joan of Arc stood next to King Charles VII in the cathedral as he was consecrated King of France, and her statue adorns the cathedral main plaza. (Bus: https://transports.hautsdefrance.fr)

Cathedral of Nôtre-Dame de Reims

If you're already tired of Gothic cathedrals, plan to skip any other church but this. The Reims Cathedral is widely recognized as one of the finest in the world, which was undoubtedly the vision of its creators who laid its first stone in the year 1211. On the north portal, look for the famous Ange au Sourire (Smiling Angel) de Reims. Once inside the main doors, turn around to see the statues of the kings' gallery beneath the brilliant rose window. In fact, over 2300 statues

Stone tracery allows expanses of glass in the two rose windows above the main entry of the Reims Cathedral

adorn the building. A large portion of the church's 13th-century windows survive, and nearly as dear are the 1974 windows by Marc Chagall. The cathedral was subjected to a devastating artillery barrage in WWI, when it was hit by a total of 288 shells. The 15th-century roof, supported by oak beams, was a total loss, and a complete rebuilding took place after the war when wooden roof supports were replaced by a non-flammable structure.On May 7, 1942 General Dwight Eisenhower of the Allies accepted the surrender of German forces at his headquarters here – a surrender which took effect the following day in what would become known as 'VE Day,' which ended WWII in Europe. On July 8, 1962 Charles de Gaulle of France and Konrad Adenauer of Germany celebrated a 'mass of reconciliation' in the cathedral – a ceremony that was repeated here 50 years later by François Hollande and Angela Merkel. The combined effect of its momentous history in war and peace, its stunning architecture, and its humbling scale make this one of the highlights of the Via Francigena.

Other sites in Reims

All major sites are easily accessible on foot or by bike from the Via Francigena, and most Reims museums can be enjoyed for a fee of €5 each, see https://musees-reims.fr. The **Palace of Tau** holds prized antiques from the cathedral as well as garments worn by French kings. Remnants of the Holy Ampulla are housed here, as well. The 11th-century **Basilica of Saint-Rémi**, located along the Francigena's exit from Reims, is the largest Romanesque-era church in Northern France and its museum holds prized 16th-century tapestries and marble capitals from the fourth century. Notable for its 17th-century splendor is the **Hôtel de Ville**, adjacent to the cathedral. The standing collection of the **Musée des Beaux Arts** includes works by Renoir, Matisse, Monet, and Gauguin. The **Musée de la Reddition** (Museum of the Surrender) chronicles the surrender at Reims of German forces in WWII.

Many shops can be found in the center city, particularly along Rue de Vesle. Restaurants are clustered around the Place Drouet d'Erlon, between the cathedral and train station. Reims is one of the capitals of the production of Champagne, and several cellars in the center city make it possible to spend a day simply enjoying an urban bubbly tour.

⌂ **CIS de Champagne** Pr R K Br Dr Cr W S Z 79/198, €-/30/-/-, 21 Chaussée Bocquaine, info@cis-reims.com, tel +33 (0)3 26 40 52 60, €6 brkfst, www.cis-reims.com, closed some weekends if not hosting groups

⌂ **Van den Borre**, 1/3, €-/60/70/85, 51 Rue Eugène Desteuque, mj.vandenborre@orange.fr, tel +33 (0)6 19 89 74 76, (0)3 26 09 40 16

⌂ **Maison Diocésain St Sixte**, 23/38, €contact, 16 Rue du Barbatre, secretariat@maisonsaintsixte.fr, tel +33 (0)3 26 82 72 50

STAGE 22
Reims to Verzy

Start	Reims, cathedral
Finish	Verzy, town hall
Distance	20.1km
Total ascent	197m
Total descent	73m
Difficulty	Moderate
Duration	5¼hr
Percentage paved	65%
Lodging	Verzenay 17.7km, Verzy 20.1km

Reims, Verzenay and Verzy are all on the Champagne map, so if you don't imbibe here you're not a true champagnophile. After a couple dozen urban blocks, the route follows canals and then heads south at Sillery. A narrow and sidewalk-free highway takes you across the valley to the Champagne vineyards, followed by a pleasant, wooded road above Verzenay. The wooded road continues to Verzy, a charming French town aiming to spread bubbly cheer throughout the world.

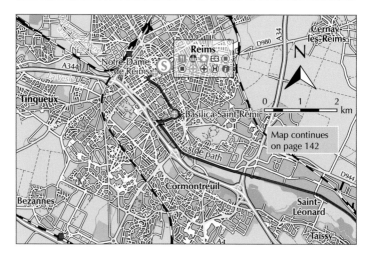

Map continues on page 142

A cyclist rides through Champagne vineyards near Verzenay (photo: European Association of the Via Francigena ways)

With the glorious cathedral behind you, go straight ahead. Turn left at the stoplight in one block on **Rue Chanzy** and continue among commercial storefronts on this arterial. Pass an enormous church on your right and just afterward turn right onto Rue Saint-Julian to come to the entry (south side) door of **Basilica Saint-Rémi** (**1.7km**). After touring this historic church, continue downhill either through the pedestrian arcade or the street on either side.

Cross the canal and turn left at the next street to pick up the **canal-side path**, beautifully set under majestic maple trees. The canal turns gracefully left and right, then makes a more pronounced right turn before the next town, where you pass under the Rue du Petit Sillery and then turn right at the marina to come to the D8 in **Sillery** (**10.1km**, bar, café, pharmacy).

Turn left and then make a right onto the **D308** in the direction of Verzenay. Now among grainfields, cross over the A4/E17 motorway and then the TGV tracks. Take the first **asphalt road** left to head up into the Montagne de Reims, rolling hills of champagne grapes and your tallest climb so far on the Francigena. Follow signs on your right to the **Moulin de Verzenay windmill**.

> The landmark **Moulin de Verzenay windmill** was built in the 19th century to grind crops of wheat, barley and rye. It ground its last meal in 1903 and since 1972 has housed the Mumm Champagne winery.

(17.7KM) VERZENAY (ELEV 190M, POP 1102) 🍽 ⊕ 🏕 ⊕ (1740.8KM)
Surrounding the village are **vineyards** of the Montagne de Reims subregion of Champagne, classified as 100% Grand Cru, the highest level of quality. The **Phare de Verzenay** is a lighthouse built to publicize a winery which today houses a Champagne museum that offers a sweeping view over the region (€9, open daily 10am–6.30pm in season, www.phare-verzenay.com).

🔺 **Gîte l'Haumière**, 35 Rue de Mailly, michelehb@orange.fr, tel +33 (0)6 83 97 21 45

Now either return to the mountainside road for a quiet, shaded, and car-free walk to the next town, or simply continue on the winding D26 to come to Verzy. From the mountainside route, at the road's end at the D34, turn left and then pick up Avenue de la Gare, turning right at the D26 and finding the town hall of **Verzy** in two blocks (**2.4km**).

(2.4KM) VERZY (ELEV 168M, POP 1069) ⅲ ⊕ △ ⓒ ⊕ ⊕ (1738.4KM)

The village is mentioned in records as early as 530 as belonging to Suavegothe, daughter of Sigismond, King of Burgundy. Today it is one of the charming hill villages closely linked with production of Champagne, particularly for its use of Pinot Noir grapes on north-facing vineyards.

🛖 🛖 Champagne Alain Lallement **Pr R K Br Gr W S** 2/8, €-/30/60/88, 7 Rue Carnot, champagne.alain.lallement@club-internet.fr, tel +33 (0)3 26 97 92 32, (0)6 74 94 66 09, closed Aug

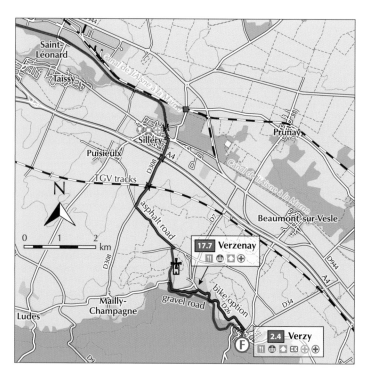

STAGE 23
Verzy to Condé-sur-Marne

Start	Verzy, town hall
Finish	Condé-sur-Marne, Place Siot
Distance	19.9km
Total ascent	100m
Total descent	226m
Difficulty	Easy
Duration	5hr
Percentage paved	48%
Lodging	Condé-sur-Marne 19.9km

A well-graded road leads from above Verzy out into the vineyards and then toward fields of grain at the Marne's wide valley floor. After grain fields it is pleasant if somewhat repetitive canal-side paths all the way to Condé.

Make your way back up to the gravel road at the top of town. One of many ways is to continue through Verzy on the D26, turning right at Rue de la Fontaine, and then left onto Rue de Bourgeat. Once on the Côte Gaucher gravel road above town, follow it along the left side of the valley through the **Forêt Domaniale de Verzy**, one of France's 1300 national forests.

After the French Revolution, 690,000 hectares of **forests** belonging to the French crown and 340,000 belonging to monasteries were nationalized. The forest is home to the world's primary stock of twisted dwarf beech trees, believed in previous times to be home to demons and witches.

The forest road is well graded and comfortable, with no signs of anything nefarious. When it ends, find yourself among vineyards again, looking down toward the village of Villers-Marmery (bars, restaurants), which the track passes as close as 0.5km. Continue, alternating between woods, vineyards, and fields of row crops, and come to the familiar **D26** (**5.7km**).

Turn left and then right to pick up a farm road that takes you between fields to the hamlet of **Billy-le-Grand** (**3.4km**, wineries). Head through the hamlet on the ironically named Grande Rue and turn right at the **D319** at the village's far end. Two blocks later a left turn puts you on **Rue de la Voûte**, which you follow to the end of the Canal de l'Aisnes à la Marne, turning right after the white service building onto the grassy road that follows along and above the canal's far side.

Beaumont-sur-Vesle

Verzenay

Mailly-
-ampagne

Verzy

(S)

Vesle

Sept-Saulx

D308

A4

D34

D944

Les Petites-
Loges

Villers-
Marmery

gravel road

Forêt Domaniale de Verzy

gravel road

D26

D944

A4

farm road

Billy-le-Grand

canal tunnel

Canal de l'Aisne à la Marne

D994

Trépail

Rue de la Voûte

D319

D19

Louvois

xières-
utry

Vaudemange

east side canal path

D19

La Live

D34

Bouzy

Ambonnay

west side canal path

D37

Isse

canal
option

Tours-sur-
Marne

D1

D19

19.9 **Condé-sur-Marne**

(F) canal lock

Place Lt-Jean Siot

La Marne

Canal latéral à la Marne

Aigny

D1

Vraux

Cherville

N

0   1   2
km

A canal emerges from a tunnel to continue through forested flatlands near Billy-le-Grand

Cross the **D19** and continue on a grassy road above the canal. Cross to the west side of the canal and either continue on the canal road or go through the town of **Isse** (7.3km, no services), returning afterward to the canal. Just after a lock, come to the **D1** roadway. The signs mysteriously point you straight ahead, but it's much easier to turn right here on the D1 and find, after two blocks, the pavilion-covered central square, Place Lt. Jean Siot in **Condé-sur-Marne** (3.5km).

(19.9KM) CONDÉ-SUR-MARNE (ELEV 80M, POP 666) ⛺ 🏠 ◉ **(1718.5KM)**
The first time *Condetum supra Matronam* enters the historical record is in the year 850. The village was destroyed in 1380 in the Hundred Years' War, again in 1652 by Charles IV of Lorraine, and again in 1940, when fighting between the French and German armies leveled 80% of the village's buildings. The most significant economic event was the 1837 construction and 1869 completion of the **Marne and Aisne à la Marne canals**, respectively, which eased export of the region's crops. (Bus: www.sitac.net) Conde is a town of few services, but its location among fields and at the confluence of two canals makes it a pleasant stopover.

⛺ **La Clé des Champs**, 3/10, 2 Rue Albert Barré, denis.wolter@orange.fr, tel +33 (0)3 26 68 94 75, (0)6 85 66 53 64

STAGE 24
Condé-sur-Marne to Châlons-en-Champagne

Start	Condé-sur-Marne, Place Siot
Finish	Châlons-en-Champagne, Rue Jean Jaurès bridge
Distance	17.0km
Total ascent	34m
Total descent	31m
Difficulty	Easy
Duration	4¼hr
Percentage paved	84%
Lodging	Châlons-en-Champagne 17.0km

The entire stage can be walked along the right side of the canals, but the official track takes a left turn toward Vraux to give some variation. Châlons-en-Champagne is a charming town – Reims on a smaller scale – and its central square gives it a quiet and almost cosmopolitan charm.

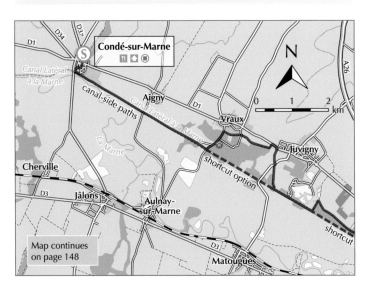

Map continues on page 148

From the covered square, take the street next to the bakery, Rue de la Libération, toward the church tower. Curve around the church and take the first left, which leads you across the **canal**. Turn left onto the canal-side road on the far side. Stay on the right side of the canal until you come to a bridge on the left (**4.8km**), pointing you left across the bridge on the official route that goes through the village of **Vraux** (no services), followed by the edge of **Juvigny** (no services) before returning to the canal's north side. Shortcut option: Instead of crossing the bridge to Vraux, continue along the canal's south side to save 1.4km.

A WWI memorial stands outside the cathedral at Châlons-en-Champagne

The official route veers away from the canal once more after Juvigny, while the southside route continues without detour to the locks before the city of Châlons-en-Champagne after the official route rejoins. As industrial buildings become more dense, watch for a bridge that carries you to the church spires in town. Cross under the bridge and come up on the far side to climb to the bridge deck, where you come to **Rue Jean Jaurès** (**12.2km**).

(To continue to the center city, turn right, cross the canal, and continue as the road name changes to Rue de la Marne and in a half-dozen blocks you come to its end at Place du Maréchal Foch.)

(17.0KM) CHÂLONS-EN-CHAMPAGNE (ELEV 83M, POP 51,257)
🍴 🏨 🏪 🈁 ⊙ ⊙ ⊕ Ⓗ ❶ (1701.5KM)

Then called *Catalaunum*, Châlons was founded at the intersection of the Roman Via Agrippa and the River Marne. Here in 274 Roman Emperor Aurelian defeated Tetricus I of Gaul in the Battle of Châlons that claimed over 50,000 lives. In the Middle Ages, Sigeric stayed here as his Stage LXIX 'Chateluns' and Châlons became famous for its cloth-making. The prosperous economy aided in creation of landmark churches including the 13th-century **Cathedral of Châlons** and the 12th–13th-century **Collegiate Church of Notre-Dame-en-Vaux**.

An 18th-century renewal project led to the realignment and widening of roads that put the **town hall** on an axis of elegant view lines from the river, adding to the regional capital vibe – a status Châlons scores over its larger and wealthier neighbor, Reims. In October 1921, at the request of the US military, remains of four American WWI soldiers were disinterred and brought to the city hall (the city was then called Châlons-sur-Marne). After confirming that injuries suffered in battle had resulted in their deaths, one of the bodies was transported to Arlington National Cemetery where it was interred in the Tomb of the Unknown Soldier on November 11, 1921. (Bus: www.flixbus.com)

🏠 **Paroisse St-Etienne**, 1/2+, €Donation, 1 Place Notre-Dame, paroisse@ paroisse-cc.fr, tel +33 (0)7 68 72 40 51, (0)3 26 64 18 30

🏠 **Auberge de Jeunesse** 🅳🅾 🆁 🅺 🆂 🆉 6/25, €20/-/-/-, 2 Avenue du Général Patton, ajchalons@orange.fr, tel +33 (0)3 26 26 46 28, closed Christmas to New Year

🏠 **Les Catalaunes** 🅾 🅿🆁 🆁 🅺 🅱🆁 🆆 🆂 2/3, €-/45/75/90, 48 Rue Vieilles Postes, lescatalaunes@gmail.com, tel +33 (0)6 83 03 23 45, kitchen by adv req, brkfst incl

🏠 **La Canopée** 🅾 🅿🆁 🆁 🅺 🆆 🆂 4/8, from €-/20/40/60, 11 Rue des Martyrs de la Résistance, contact@gite-canopee.com, tel +33 (0)6 47 82 73 42, www.gite-canopee.com, 3 gîtes & 1 priv room

🔺 **Aquadis Loisirs** 🅿🆁 🆁 🅺 🅱🆁 🅳🆁 🅶🆁 🆆 🆂 🆉 4/6, campsites and bungalows, €call, Rue de Plaisance, camping.chalons@aquadis-loisirs.com, tel +33 (0) 03 26 68 38 00, snack bar in season

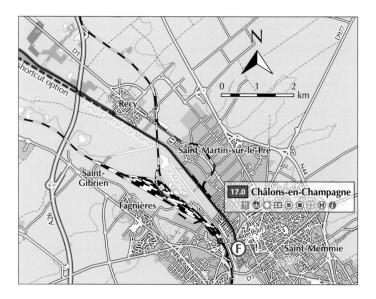

STAGE 25
Châlons-en-Champagne to Saint-Germain-la-Ville

Start	Châlons-en-Champagne, Rue Jean Jaurès bridge
Finish	Saint-Germain-la-Ville, D28 canal bridge
Distance	12.4km
Total ascent	22m
Total descent	18m
Difficulty	Easy
Duration	3hr
Percentage paved	81%
Lodging	Saint-Germain-la-Ville 12.4km

To provide a more interesting itinerary with adequate services, the Via Francigena/ GR 145 departs from Sigeric's historic route through the Coole Valley and follows the Marne Valley instead, with its slightly more plentiful services and interesting sights. The Coole route (see map and description below) tempts with 37km less distance and 1–2 fewer days, but the lack of basic infrastructure makes it a challenging walk, though it is excellent for cyclists who can cover it in just one day. The official stage to Saint-Germain includes a flat and direct option along the canal, making it a quick and easy outing, with the option of combining it and the next stage into a single day.

The route to Sainte-Germain-la-Ville follows the canal among tall forests

On Rue Jean Jaurès, head west toward the Marne River and turn left just before it onto Chemin du Barrage. Pass the **Jard Anglais park**, cross a pedestrian bridge, and continue as the road becomes a gravel path under trees. Go under the **D3** highway and continue in the shaded trails along the river.

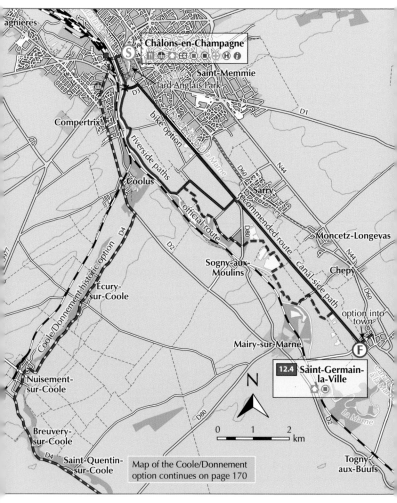

After a time, the signs direct you up a steep bank, but instead you can turn left to take a more gradual grade up the path. Soon afterward come to wide fields on the left, and see the town of **Coolus** across the river. Signs now lead you left and away from the river. At the two-track gravel road (**4.9km**) just afterward you come to a choice of routes. The official route turns right to take a serpentine expedition among fields and woods between the Marne and the Moivre Canal to the east, making a complicated, potentially muddy, and 1.2km longer route.

Recommended route
Instead, go to the end of the gravel road and turn right, which leads after just one left to the comfortable path along the Moivre Canal. Once at the Moivre Canal (**2.2km**), cross the D80 and pick up the **canal-side path** on the right, which you follow all the way to the D28 bridge (**5.3km**), where a left turn takes you into **Saint-German-la-Ville** in two long blocks.

(12.4KM) SAINT-GERMAIN-LA-VILLE (ELEV 86M, POP 548) 🔲 ◉
(1689.1KM)
This small village bears the name 'La Ville' because of the discovery of a Roman villa nearby. The town's **church** dates from the 12th–13th century and much of its interior construction is original. In 1944 a WWII RAF bomber crashed nearby and its crew is buried in the church cemetery. For the first time in this region on the Via Francigena we see half-timbered construction techniques. (Bus: www.stdm-transport.fr)

🔺 **Les Perrières** 🅾 P̲r̲ R̲ K̲ B̲r̲ D̲r̲ C̲r̲ W̲ S̲ 5/14, €-/45/65/75, 7 Rue de Châlons, denis.lesaint@wanadoo.fr, tel +33 (0)6 70 35 40 32, (0)6 86 67 29 94, brkfst €6, demi-pension €25

Coole/Donnement historic route option (37.3km)
Because of the distance, the uniform scenery, and the relative lack of services among the tiny villages, this route works better for cyclists, who will find many local pedalers along the way enjoying the open spaces and lack of auto traffic. Walkers will find it lonely and should not undertake it without making advance plans for accommodation, food, and water. On the bright side, the route is historic – Sigeric went this way – and it even includes a dusty stretch of once-Roman-now-gravel road, although it otherwise retains few traces of its ancient past.
    Directions: Cross the canal and Marne from central Châlons and turn left on Rue Loyer which becomes the D2. After Coolus (**4.0km**) fork right onto the D4 and follow it through Nuisement-sur-Coole (**2.9km**), Écury (**3.8km**), Nuisement (**2.9km**, restaurant), Fontaine (**11.4km**, 🔺 **Host Family Pelouard**, 21 Rue Montsuzon, +33 (0)3 26 70 60 29), Vésigneul (**1.9km**), Coole (**6.6km**, 🔺 **Host Family Songy**, 13 Rue de Châlons,

+33 (0)7 71 85 70 27, ♠ Host Family Dulieu, 1 Chemin du Puit, +33 (0)6 61 85 71 45), and Sompuis (**6.6km**, grocery).

At Sompuis pick up the D12 and continue through Humbauville (**4.3km**), and Le-Meix (**2.3km**, ♠ CAT Center, Rue Four, +33 (0)3 26 72 41 20), where you fork left onto gravel on the one-time Roman road through farmland to Corbeil (**6.9km**, ♠ Refuge Romain, +33 (0)3 26 72 31 04) and Donnement (**7.6km**, ♠ Council Hostel, Salle des Fêtes, +33 (0)9 67 78 06 28, ♠ Host Family Berton, 15 Rue de Dampierre +33 (0)3 25 37 53 93, ♠ Host Family Martin, 1 Voie Creuse, +33 (0)6 24 38 81 38). From Donnement continue on the D24 to Braux-le-Petit (**4.8km**) and Rosnay l'Hôpital (**3.8km**, bar, accommodation).

STAGE 26
Saint-Germain-la-Ville to Saint-Amand-sur-Fion

Start	Saint-Germain, D28 bridge
Finish	Saint-Amand-sur-Fion, Church of Saint-Amand
Distance	17.1km
Total ascent	75m
Total descent	54m
Difficulty	Easy
Duration	4¼hr
Percentage paved	24%
Lodging	La-Chaussée-sur-Marne 9.0km, Saint-Amand-sur-Fion 17.1km

The route now branches off the Marne and onto the Fion River before returning at Vitry-le-François. A medieval vibe prevails, thanks to the half-timber construction on homes and barns, which is plentiful here and for the next few stages. The surprisingly lavish (for the town's size) Gothic church at Saint-Amand is well worth a visit and is usually open.

If you've entered Saint-Germain, return to the canal-side path and then continue along the canal. The path becomes somewhat overgrown, but continue on to the D54 bridge that crosses left over the canal at **Pogny** (**4.0km**, bar, grocery). For services, turn left to follow the D54 to the opposite side of town. Otherwise, turn right on the D54 and continue for a few hundred meters before turning left on a **gravel road** at an outdoor sports center.

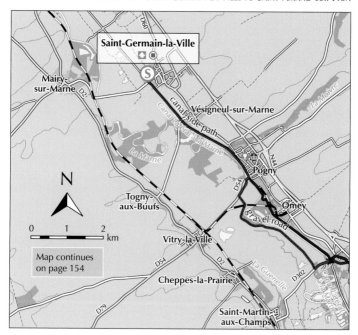

Cross the disused railroad tracks and continue through fields alongside the woods with the Marne on your left until this road ends at the **D302**, where you turn left to cross the Marne and the canal into **La Chaussée-sur-Marne**. Fork right after the canal and continue to the center of town at Rue du Colonel Caillot (**5.0km**).

(9.0KM) LA CHAUSSÉE-SUR-MARNE (ELEV 96M, POP 796) 🏠 🅒 ◉ **(1680.1KM)**
Early 20th-century excavations discovered a Gallic settlement at this site. (Bus: www.stdm-transport.fr)

🛏 Ferme de la Chaussée-sur-Marne, 2/6, 85 Rue de Cournier, monique-chavary@orange.fr, tel +33 (0)3 26 72 94 87, (0)6 28 74 39 46

Turn right on Rue Caillot and pass the D60 sign that offers a 7km journey on the auto road to the next town. Instead, turn right onto Avenue du Jolly south of town into countryside. At a curve, fork left onto a two-track **gravel road** marked for motorcycles.

The nave of the church at Saint-Amand-sur-Fion is dwarfed in size by its transept and apse

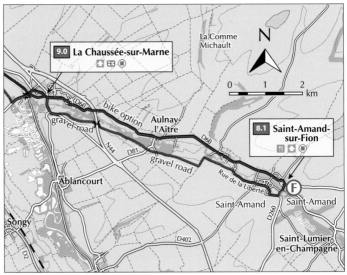

Now cut through woods and fields, cross a gravel road, cross under the **N44** highway, and continue on through fields.

Cross the **D81** highway and when the road ends, turn left. In a few hundred meters turn right before the woods. The road suddenly ends at **Rue de la Liberté**, where you turn right. Pass a gîte that rents by the week or weekend, and continue, coming to Rue du Pont Mathieu. To visit the center of town it is best to turn left to the D60 where you would turn right to find the village's sparse offerings. Or you can continue straight, winding through town to the D260, where you find the village's centerpiece, the historic **Church of Saint-Amand** (8.1km).

(8.1KM) SAINT-AMAND-SUR-FION (ELEV 108M, POP 1025) 🍴 🏠 ◉
(1672.0KM)

This quiet town of half-timbered homes and barns is listed among the most beautiful villages of France. The Hospitallers of the Order of St John of Jerusalem established an outpost here in 1189 to protect pilgrims. The surviving, large, and oddly shaped **church** includes a large transept and apse of 13th-century construction, while the much smaller nave suggests a 12th-century date. Still, the result is an interior of great beauty and surprising symmetry. The size and quality of the church's porch hints at either a onetime cloister or a shelter for pilgrims under its wide roof. (Bus: www.stdm-transport.fr)

🏠 **La Cour en Bas** 🅞 🅿f 🆁 🅚 🅑r 🆆 2/6, €-/49/64/76, 5 Petite Rue de l'Église, sylvain.lanfroy@wanadoo.fr, tel +33 (0)3 26 74 60 50, www.les2cours.com, brkfst incl, reserv req, épicerie and bakery avail in village

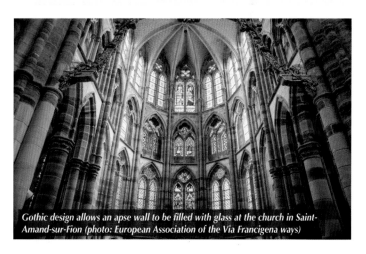

Gothic design allows an apse wall to be filled with glass at the church in Saint-Amand-sur-Fion (photo: European Association of the Via Francigena ways)

STAGE 27
Saint-Amand-sur-Fion to Vitry-le-François

Start	Saint-Amand, Church of St-Amand
Finish	Vitry-le-François, Place d'Armes
Distance	14.9km
Total ascent	146m
Total descent	160m
Difficulty	Easy
Duration	4hr
Percentage paved	35%
Lodging	Vitry-le-François 14.9km

The lonely lookout atop Mont de la Forche is one of the Francigena's more memorable viewpoints. Before this high point are wide open grainfields, and afterward is a snug and shaded walk through a wood that, while seemingly a zigzaggy detour, is actually the optimal pedestrian or cyclist entry to Vitry. The small city is the largest settlement until Langres, about 250km distant.

With the church behind you, turn left and head up the **D260** roadway, forking left at the first opportunity onto a well-graded **gravel road** leading into the woods. Emerge in the fields on the other side. The road ends at a **children's play field** where you turn right on an asphalt road going uphill. This road soon ends and you turn right on a two-lane road, forking left on gravel, behind a **hay barn** and heading uphill. Now out of sight from civilization, this stretch through vast fields can either evoke a joyful solitude or a sense of isolation.

Finally, the road appears to end, but continue straight and then take the next right, climbing to **Mont de la Forche (7.0km)**. This lonely lookout with a bench under a tall tree affords spectacular views over the surrounding countryside, with Vitry-le-François tucked in the valley below. Continue along the road and curve with it left and steeply downhill. Go straight at the bottom of the hill and, when the road curves to the right, instead turn left and head downhill through trees. A tiny, abandoned, 19th-century chapel, well worth exploring, stands at the end of an arcade of trees before the woods.

The path descends quickly, leading to the end of **Rue Sainte-Geneviève**, which you follow for two blocks. Fork right on an asphalt driveway and in 30 meters catch a two-track **alleyway** leading behind homes. Fork right at the bottom of the hill and begin a forest walk on a wide path leading uphill to the **N44** highway **(4.7km)**.

Carefully cross the N44 and turn right afterward to find an asphalt road curving downhill. Follow signs left at a **pasture** and come to a canal, which you cross to continue left (south) on the **canal-side path**. Follow signs down a bank to a street that heads west from the canal, **Chemin du Mont Bergeon**. Take it two blocks to a roundabout and turn left.

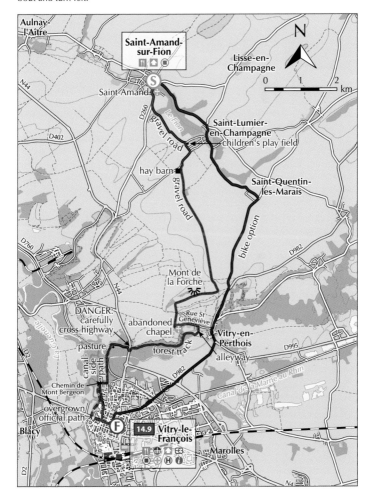

Vast fields stretch to the horizon near Vitry-le-François

The signs point you to an overgrown riverside trail along the Marne, but it is easier simply to continue on this street, Rue de la Contrescarpe, as it continues in the same direction, joining the N4 as a wide arterial and coming to a roundabout at Rue du Pont. Turn left and in three blocks arrive in the center of **Vitry-le-François** at Place d'Armes (3.2km).

(14.9KM) VITRY-LE-FRANÇOIS (ELEV 102M, POP 17,250) 🍽 🌐 🛏 🄲 ⓜ ⊕ Ⓗ 🅘
(1657.1KM)

After the total destruction of the historic town of Vitry-en-Perthois by Emperor Charles V in 1544, the French King Francis I hired architect Girolamo Marini to design and build its replacement. The resulting Renaissance-era city was given the king's name as part of its own. Its primary monuments are the grand, 17th-century **Collegiate Church of Notre-Dame** – often mistaken for a cathedral because of its grand scale – and the **town hall**.

French forces were headquartered in Vitry during the first stages of WWI and later the church served as a field hospital. The 17th-century town hall is best seen from its gardens and reflecting pool. Before WWII the **Gate of the Bridge** was dismantled stone-by-stone to protect it from potential damage. After WWII, when 90% of the town's buildings were again destroyed, the town was rebuilt along its 16th-century plan, the Collegiate Church was repaired, and the Gate of the Bridge, last of the town's Renaissance fortifications, was reassembled.

🏠 **Manoir Francois 1er** 🄾 🄿🅁 🄳🄾 🅁 🄺 🄱🅁 🄳🅁 🄲🅁 🅆 🅂 🅉 5/16, €contact, 1–3 Blvd François I, contact@manoirfrancois1er.com, tel +33 (0)6 73 14 84 00, pool, hot tub, sauna

🏠 **Au Bon Séjour**, €-/51/55/-, Via Romana 170, desvigne@club-internet.fr, tel +33 (0)3 26 74 02 36, www.au-bon-sejour.fr, demi-pension avail at restaurant

STAGE 28

Vitry-le-François to Saint-Remy-en-Bouzemont

Start	Vitry-le-François, Place d'Armes
Finish	Saint-Remy-en-Bouzemont, D58 at D57
Distance	21.1km
Total ascent	213m
Total descent	201m
Difficulty	Moderate
Duration	5½hr
Percentage paved	30%
Lodging	Courdemanges 7.4km, Blaise-sous-Arzillières 13.2km, Saint-Remy 21.1km

A stage of vast fields and vast forests, ending at a remote village tucked into a pleasant valley. The Mont-Moret memorial is a simple monument that takes you back to a bleak moment when the entire area was a desolate battlefield soaked in the blood of young soldiers.

Return on Rue du Pont/**Rue de Paris** past the traffic circle and over the bridge across the Marne. After a small cluster of businesses veer left onto an asphalt **bicycle path** that leads at first through trees. After passing under the railroad tracks, turn left on a gravel road. The road ends and you turn right, cross a pedestrian bridge over La Guenelle stream, and come to the D2 in **Blacy** (**2.8km**, bakery).

Cross the road, check the church's sundial against your watch to see if these things ever work, and at the end of town, turn left (although signs point straight) onto the **gravel road** in the direction of Huiron. Pass the turnoff for a small British and French **WWI cemetery** and come to the D602 in **Glannes** (**2.5km**, bar) and either turn left and

The battle memorial at Mont-Moret stands among the fields above Courdemange

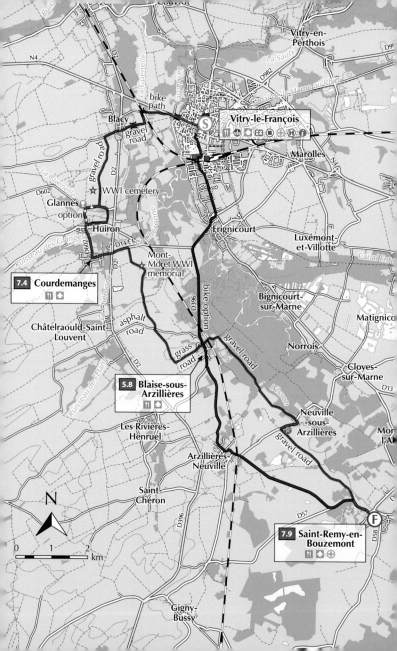

follow signs to make your way around town or simply turn right and follow the D602 across La Petite Guenelle stream where you meet the other route atop a dyke.

Continue on the D602, pass the Church of Saint-Martin in **Huiron** (1.3km, no services) as well as crops and woods before in short order coming to the Grand Rue in **Courdemanges** (0.9km).

(7.4KM) COURDEMANGES (ELEV 108M, POP 466) 🍴 🏠 (1649.7KM)

The First Battle of the Marne leveled the settlement, with only the school building left standing. White wines from the area's **vineyards** have been prized at least since 1773 when the town was already center to 68 hectares of vineyards.

🏠 ▲ **Ferme du Mont-Morêt** Pr Do R Br 6/23, €20 per person, Ferme du Mont Morêt, info@ferme-mont-moret.com, tel +33 (0)7 85 10 46 56, chalets, *gîte*, safari tent, €7 tent site, closed Nov 1–Apr 1

Turn left on the Grand Rue and walk through this pleasant, well-maintained town, coming to the **D2**. Cross the road, now on the D14/E1. Turn right at the sign for the military monument and climb, 600 meters later, to the **Mont-Moret battle memorial** (1.8km, no services).

The **First Battle of the Marne** in 1914 halted the German advance at the expense of tens of thousands of French, British and German lives. Here it is hard not to consider the meaning of the EU flag that flies along with the French flag above the monument as a symbol of European unity and peace.

Continue to the bottom of the hill, and where the road seems to turn right, go straight uphill instead on a grassy road. Cross a narrow, asphalt road and fork left onto a gravel road. Head over the hill and on the opposite side don't miss a left turn onto a **grass road** between two fields that leads to the D396 in the village of **Blaise-sous-Arzillières** (3.9km)

(5.8KM) BLAISE-SOUS-ARZILLIÈRES (ELEV 107M, POP 403) 🍴 🏠 (1643.9KM)

The village's favorite son is Knight Juste de Clermont-d'Amboise (1636–1702) who led his first regiment in battle at the age of 14. He retired at a friary as a bachelor after 20 campaigns.

🏠 **Café de la Place**, 2 Rue du Pont de la Noue, heitzmannfr@wanadoo.fr, tel +33 (0)3 26 72 80 01, (0)6 63 86 89 57

Cross the D396 and afterward the road turns to gravel and curves alongside a tree farm. Before a green bridge, turn right on a gravel road which carries you through

Cyclists take an evening ride through fields near St-Remy-en-Bouzemont

tree farms and crops all the way to **Neuville-sous-Arzillières** (3.8km, no services). The road makes a sharp right curve in town, and you follow it among fields uphill and out of town. At the top of the hill turn left at a **gravel road** with a bench and picnic table beside a tree. This road merges with the **D57** and becomes the D58 at the heart of **Saint-Remy-en-Bouzemont** (4.1km).

(7.9KM) SAINT-REMY-EN-BOUZEMONT (ELEV 114M, POP 603) 🏚 🏛 ⊕
(1636.0KM)

The region was under the ownership in the 17th–19th centuries of the Marquisate of Hamel, and several family members served France in prominent roles. Today's town is an 1836 amalgamation of three villages, giving it the longest official name of any town in France: Saint-Remy-en-Bouzemont-Saint-Genest-et-Isson. It is an official member of the Villes et Villages Fleuris association, which ranks towns and villages from one to four flowers based on the prevalence of blooms (www.villes-et-villages-fleuris.com).

🏚 Logement des Pèlerin 🅾 🅳🅾 🆁 🅺 🆆 1/4 €donation, laurent.ortillon@orange.fr, 14 Grande Rue, tel +33 (0)6 32 27 24 24. Arrive between 4pm and 6pm

STAGE 29
Saint-Remy-en-Bouzemont to Outines

Start	Saint-Remy, D57 at D58
Finish	Outines, town hall
Distance	11.9km
Total ascent	86m
Total descent	63m
Difficulty	Easy
Duration	3hr
Percentage paved	55%
Lodging	Outines 11.9km

A short, isolated stage through woods and near swampy ponds interspersed with farms. The area is a nature preserve and wetland, part of the widespread system of ponds and lakes designed to ease flooding on the Seine and protect Paris. Watch for birds of many species, especially toward the Lac du Der-Chantecoq. The few services on this stretch mean you will rely on your hosts for food.

Continue straight, now on the D58, passing the town hall. After town the road curves through fields at the edge of town; turn left before a **factory**-like building. This road curves right, you cross an asphalt road, then continue through a final neighborhood and head into the fields on what becomes a well-graded road among pastures, hayfields and row crops on fairly flat terrain.

The road turns left and then heads into the woods, emerging at fields to cross a swampy stream before coming to a **farm** (**6.5km**). Fork right just before the farm buildings and come to the start of a barbed wire fence. Keep to the right here, and watch your footing as holes and mounds in the road may be hidden under tall grass.

The doorway of the church at Outines opens out to other half-timber buildings in town (photo: European Association of the Via Francigena ways)

163

At the **end of the fence**, turn right and head around a field before woods and **beehives** ahead. Now heading east, this gravel road continues to an asphalt road where you turn right, passing a gîte on the left (**2.7km, Au Milieu de Nulle Part**, see below). See ahead the sharply pointed spire of the village church of Outines.

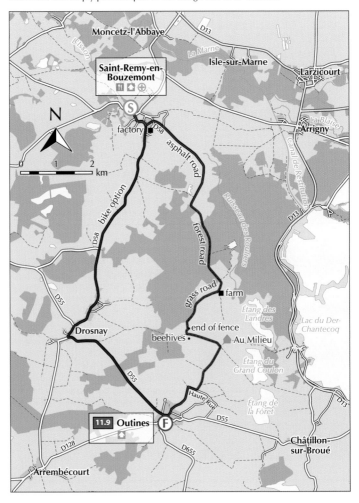

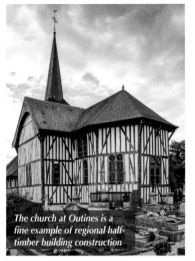

The church at Outines is a fine example of regional half-timber building construction

Some of the posts and beams of the wood church at Outines date from the year 1512

When the road ends, turn right on **Haute Rue** to wind into this town of charming, half-timbered homes and barns and arrive at the D55, church, town hall and war memorial in **Outines** (**2.7km**).

(11.9KM) OUTINES (ELEV 136M, POP 136) 🏛 (1624.1KM)
This quiet agricultural village is best known for its half-timbered homes and in 1970 it received governmental protection against changes to its unique architectural character. The 16th-century **Church of Saint-Nicolas** is the largest half-timber church in the Champagne region, and some of its massive posts and beams date from the year 1512. The interior is well worth viewing for its unique atmosphere and includes a 16th-century statue of St Gond and a 14th-century crucifix.

🏠 **Au Milieu de Nulle Part** ⚙ 🅿 ℝ 🅚 Br Dr Gr ⓢ ⓩ 5/24, €-/60/88/115 locality La Pierre, contact.aumilieudenullepart@gmail.com, tel +33 (0)6 67 36 74 93, treehouse, caravan, and group house, some with kitchen, €12 brkfst

🏠 **Le Courlis**, 10 Place de l'Église, tel +33 (0)6 67 36 74 93 (managed by Au Milieu de Nulle Part with same prices)

STAGE 30
Outines to Montmorency-Beaufort

Start	Outines, town hall
Finish	Montmorency-Beaufort, Rue Principale
Distance	16.5km
Total ascent	81m
Total descent	90m
Difficulty	Easy
Duration	4¼hr
Percentage paved	58%
Lodging	Lentilles 12.5km, Montmorency 16.5km

A short stage of first fields and then forests that could easily be combined with the prior stage into a single day. The high point is the centuries-old half-timber church in Lentilles with echoes of St James. A forest walk through the Réserve Naturelle de l'Étang de la Horre offers calm and quiet.

Turn SE onto the D55 and continue through this town of period half-timber homes. As the D55 curves left, go straight on an **asphalt road**, leading into fields. Go straight when the road turns right, and when it turns left afterward turn right on a grassy road through fields. Come to a small channelized stream, which you cross on a narrow metal **bridge**.

Go straight now between fields until merging to the right with a **gravel road**. This carries you onto the **D56** which then meets the D127 in the hamlet of **Bailly-le-Franc** (**5.2km**, no services), where the barns seem to outnumber the homes. Continue straight on the D56 as it curves toward the forested **Réserve Naturelle de l'Étang de la Horre**.

This **nature reserve**, which centers around the Horre pond, was set aside in the 1990s to serve important migratory routes for birds. It now hosts a diverse population of wildlife, including many species of birds, as well as dragonflies, butterflies and amphibians.

After passing under powerlines, come to signs indicating that the official route turns right onto a dirt road. Shortcut option: Remaining on the quiet D56 is 0.6km shorter than taking the official route. The two routes rejoin at the D56; 100 meters afterward follow signs left onto a **gravel road** leading to the village of **Lentilles** (**7.3km**, 🛑 **Emergency Gîte**, +33 (0)3 25 92 10 72, inquire at mairie).

The 16th-century **Church of Saint-Jacques and Saint-Philippe** is a marvel of woodworking. Note the statue of Saint Jacques the Pilgrim (Saint James/Santiago) above the main portal.

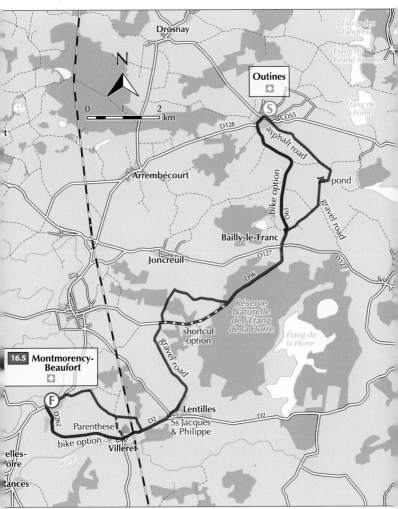

167

The church at Lentilles is another fine example of half-timber construction

At the church, continue straight onto the **D2**. Cross a bridge and turn right just afterward. (Alternatively, go straight on the D2 (bike option on map) for just 400 meters to the village of **Villeret** ⌂ La Parenthese, Rue de la Halte, legillard10@free.fr, tel +33 (0)6 77 19 89 45, (0)3 25 92 11 21, independent caravan.)

Skirt around a field and turn left to cross railroad tracks on a grassy road and come in sight of Montmorency, nestled ahead at the foot of a hill. Merge left with a gravel road leading to the D6/Rue Principale in **Montmorency-Beaufort (4.0km)**.

(16.5KM) MONTMORENCY-BEAUFORT (ELEV 126M, POP 134) ⬚ (1607.6KM)

Beaufort is mentioned in the historic record as early as the 10th century as a property of the family of Broyes. It fell under the dukes of Lancaster during the Hundred Years' War and later the dukes of Burgundy. In the 17th century it was renamed for its owners, the Montmorency-Luxembourg family, and in 1919 the village took its current name. The town is considered to be on the border of two of Champagnes geological areas; 'Wet Champagne' is a marshy region with impermeable soils that are good only for vegetable farming, while conversely the soils of 'Chalk' or 'Dry Champagne' retain too much moisture for viticulture.

⌂ **La Lavandière & Le Studio** 🄾 🄿🅃 🅁 🄺 🄱🅁 🄳🅁 🅂 2/6, €-/-/50/-, 27 Rue Principale, emilie.collombar@gmail.com, tel +33 (0)9 81 11 99 89, (0)6 21 85 49 87, holiday homes. €8 brkfast, €22 dinner available by reserve, spa available, linens provided

STAGE 31
Montmorency-Beaufort to Précy-Saint-Martin

Start	Montmorency-Beaufort, Rue Principale
Finish	Précy-Saint-Martin, town hall
Distance	20.6km
Total ascent	178m
Total descent	180m
Difficulty	Moderate
Duration	5¼hr
Percentage paved	40%
Lodging	Rosnay-l'Hôpital 8.3km, Précy-St-Martin 20.6km

To avoid the asphalt and speeding cars of the D396 highway, which shoots a direct line from Rosnay-l'Hôpital to Brienne-le-Château, the official route instead uses the next Voire River bridge west, at Chalette-sur-Voire, adding 10km to the route. The result is a half-stage from Rosnay to Précy-Saint-Martin followed by another half-stage from there to Brienne. The highlight is the exceptional collection of stained-glass windows at the Church of the Assumption in Rosnay.

The crypt of the church at Rosnay-l'Hôpital dates to the 12th–14th centuries

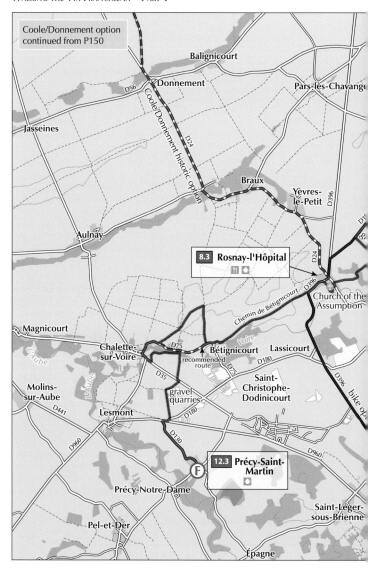

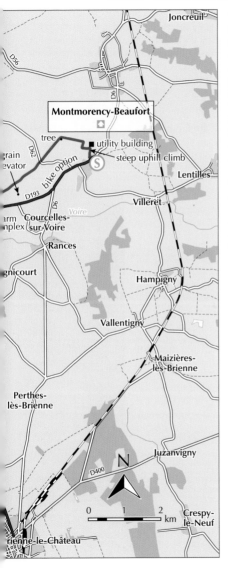

Turn left on the D6 and take the next right, the Rue Haute which climbs to the uphill side of town. Continue until on your right you see a grassy path, which you take very steeply uphill into the woods. The climb is brief; once out of the woods, turn left to pass a **utility building** and then watch carefully for a right turn to cut around the surrounding field. Not long afterward turn left to walk on a farm road into a vast expanse of fields that seemingly stretch for kilometers ahead. Aim for the sole **tree** ahead, and just beyond the tree turn left onto a gravel road.

Cross the **D62** asphalt road and continue across a gravel road that leads to a **grain elevator** on the left, below. Continue to follow the road as it curves left and downhill. Come to the asphalt **D193** (**4.6km**), with an enormous and meticulously maintained farm complex on the left. Turn right and follow the D193 for 500 meters to an unmarked left turn at a **gravel road** (it is also possible to continue and turn left on the D396 'bike option' to enter town) that zigzags through fields and woods to find the D24 at **Rosnay-l'Hôpital** (**3.6km**).

171

(8.3KM) ROSNAY-L'HÔPITAL (ELEV 118M, POP 197) 🔟 🔼 (1599.3KM)

The most notable site in this ancient village is its **Church of Assumption of the Virgin**. Built on two levels, the multi-arched crypt is the oldest section of the building and is dedicated to St Thomas of Canterbury. Upstairs, the 15th–16th-century church has a few traces of 12th-century construction, but its statue of the Virgin of Mercy and its stained-glass windows are of exceptional artistry.

🔺 Gîte d'Etape, rosnaylhopital@wanadoo.fr, tel +33 (0)3 25 92 40 15

🔺 Chambre Chez Mignot 🅾 🇵 🇷 🇧 🇩 1/2, €-/40/-/-, 8 Rue Saint-Georges, jean-philippe.mignot@wanadoo.fr, +33 (0)6 08 74 17 24, demi-pension available, resv req

Turn left onto the D24 and then right on Rue Saint-Georges to find the **Church of the Assumption** (access by contacting the Mignot accommodation). Circle back with the road to find the **D396**, where you veer left to head back into the fields. Just before leaving town, go straight onto **Chemin de Bétignicourt** instead of curving left with the D396. Climb uphill as the road turns to gravel with fields stretching into the distance on the right, and a narrow wood on the left that hides the tiny Voire River. Come to a summit and continue to the D75 in the hamlet of **Bétignicourt** (**4.4km**, no services). Shortcut option: After Bétignicourt the official route detours right onto farm roads to avoid the asphalt D75. Continue on the D75 to save 1.1km.

The two routes rejoin at the D75 where you continue to the D35 in **Chalette-sur-Voire** (**2.4km**, no services). Now turn left on the D35 and cross the **Voire**. The official route soon turns left at a concrete barn to bypass the busy and dangerous D35, skirting around a field and passing a gravel pit before returning to the D35. Turn left and then 50 meters later turn right onto another gravel road. Turn left after the **quarry** ponds and continue to the **D180** asphalt road. Turn right and 50 meters later is the D960, where you turn right in the direction of Troyes. Follow the highway for just 100 meters uphill and turn left onto the **D130** in the direction of 'Précy-Saint-Martin 1,5.' Follow this asphalt road as it enters the town of brick homes and continue past the village church to the town hall (**5.6km**).

15th-century stained glass at the church of Rosnay l'Hôpital shows how people dressed in medieval times

(12.3KM) PRÉCY-SAINT-MARTIN (ELEV 132M, POP 225) 🏠 (1587.0KM)
One of the town's streets bears the name '**Rue de 27 Août 1944**' after the execution here by German troops of 14 civilian hostages as a reprisal for attacks by the French Resistance and advancing American troops. German soldiers also burned the town, including its city hall. Précy-Saint-Martin is recipient of the Croix de Guerre award from the French government.

🏠 **Gîte d'Etape**, Salle des Fêtes, mairie.precy.st.martin@wanadoo.fr, tel +33 (0)3 25 92 44 61, (0)6 09 67 39 75, Mme Vitry

🏠 **Au Fil des Lacs** 🅾 ℗ᵣ ℝ 🅺 ᴮ𝐫 ᴰ𝐫 🆆 🆂 5/12, €-/-/85/95, 6 Rue de la Louvière, aufildeslacs@gmail.com, tel +33 (0)6 80 30 20 26, (0)3 25 27 00 81, €18 dinner, www.aufildeslacs.fr, pool

STAGE 32
Précy-Saint-Martin to Dienville

Start	Précy-Saint-Martin, town hall
Finish	Dienville, Church of Saint-Quentin
Distance	13.4km
Total ascent	137m
Total descent	138m
Difficulty	Easy
Duration	3½hr
Percentage paved	24%
Lodging	Saint-Léger-sous-Brienne 4.3km, Brienne-le-Château 6.8km, Dienville 13.4km

The stage includes a fair amount of time in the woods, with service-rich Brienne-le-Château in the middle and lakeside Dienville at the end.

At the town hall, fork left off the D130 on **Rue des Marronniers**, passing by many half-timber homes in this lovely village. The road turns to gravel and you pass the modern **water tower** at the end of town on the left. Remain on this road through fields and woods and come to the D124 in tiny **Saint-Léger-sous-Brienne** (**4.3km**).

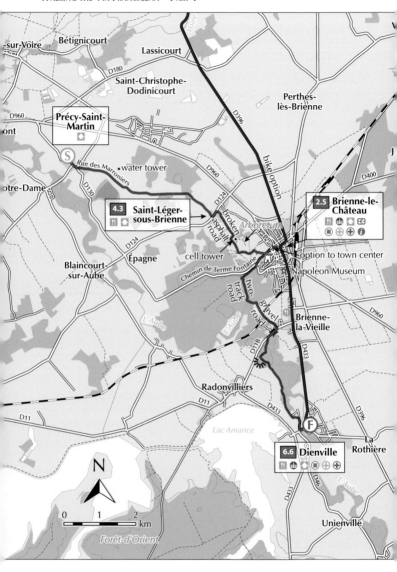

(4.3KM) SAINT-LÉGER-SOUS-BRIENNE (ELEV 130M, POP 387) 🏨 🏛
(1582.7KM)

Once a Gallo-Roman settlement on the Roman Via Agrippa, the town's name was *Requiniaca Cortis*, but with the establishment of a monastery dedicated to St Léger its name was changed in the 11th century. The town's viticulture was abandoned after the phylloxera crisis of the late 19th century when aphids native to America destroyed many of the world's wineries.

🏨 **Air Lane** 🅾 Pf R Bf Df Cf S Z 24/60, €-/70/72/119, Parc d'Activités de l'Aérodrome, air-lane@wanadoo.fr, tel +33 (0)3 25 92 55 55, www.hotel-air-lane.fr, brkfst €10, demi-pension €16, dinner avail only M–Th, located off D960

Turn left, and just after the Church of St-Thibaud turn right onto the next road, Rue de l'Église. In one block, jog right onto a **road of broken asphalt** heading uphill. The road turns right and left through woods and passes a tall **cell tower** on the left. Veer left at another gravel road and then left again as you head downhill to enter the **Arboretum of Brienne-le-Château**. This 0.6 hectare (1.5 acre) forest includes surprising species, such as giant sequoia from North America and araucaria from Chile.

Partway down the hill, turn right onto a gravel path leading through the wood and pass through a metal gate onto a narrow path leading to an asphalt road, the **Chemin de Terme Fontaine (2.5km)**. Straight ahead is the **Château** of Brienne-le-Château. To visit the town, turn left and downhill off the track to come to the town's main street, Rue de Jean Jaurès, in just three blocks. To return to the trail, retrace your steps to this point.

A statue of the young Napoleon Bonaparte stands outside the Hôtel de Ville at Brienne-le-Château

(2.5KM) BRIENNE-LE-CHÂTEAU (ELEV 142M, POP 3473) 🏨 ⊕ 🏧 🄲 ⊙ ⊕ ⊕ 🄸 (1580.2KM)

Most famous of the local nobility was John of Brienne (1170–1237), an important figure in the history of the Crusades who served as King of Jerusalem (1210–25) and Latin Emperor of Constantinople (1229–37), where he was buried in the church of Hagia Sophia. The family's **château** still dominates the town. It stands in the 17th-century form following remodeling by Louis-Marie and Étienne-Charles de Loménie, the latter of whom was finance minister of France in the late 18th century. Today the château serves as a psychiatric hospital which offers occasional visits to the public during the summer months.

The École de Brienne was established here in 1730 and from 1779–84 the young Napoleon Bonaparte lived here and studied military strategy. In December 1813, armies gathered in opposition to Napoleon took Brienne and its castle, but the next month Napoleon regained the city in the Battle of Brienne. The key tourist attraction is the **Musée Napoléon** that occupies the former military school's buildings and has a collection of Napoleonic memorabilia (€9, closed Mondays in season, www.musee-napoleon-brienne.fr). (Train: sadly, the town's train tracks are no longer in use. Bus: www.fluo.eu to Troyes.)

🛏 **Maison Fraternelle du Pèlerin 10** Pr R K Br W S 8/9, €15 min donation p/p, 96 Rue de l'École Militaire, pelerin10MFP@free.fr, tel +33 (0)6 86 97 59 50, +33 (0)6 49 17 70 29, +33(0)6 44 93 26 38, closed 31 Oct–15 Mar

🛏 **Des Voyageurs**, 30 Avenue Pasteur, contact@jl-garnier.fr, tel +33 (0)9 74 56 47 84, (0)3 25 92 83 61, www.restauranthotel-voyageurs.com

Turn right on Chemin de Terme Fontaine and take the first left turn. Immediately turn right and head through the gate on a wide gravel lane between trees, with beautiful views back to the château. Come to an intersection of several gravel roads and take the first left, heading into the woods on a **two-track road**. After a couple of quick turns the road heads straight through the woods, becomes a path, and ends at a wide dirt road.

Turn right, watching for mud, and in 100 meters turn left onto another dirt path, still in the woods and coming alongside a curve of **L'Aube River**. Cross a tiny bridge over a tributary creek as you turn right to leave the woods between pastures. Now cross railroad tracks and continue on a gravel road to the D11B in **Brienne-la-Vielle** (**2.9km**, restaurant).

Once home to the 12th–18th-century Abbey of Basse-Fontaine, the prized relic of **Brienne-la-Vielle**, a finger bone of St John the Baptist, was transferred at the abbey's 19th-century destruction to the town's Church of St Pierre-ès-Liens, which is itself of 12th-century origin. Sigeric likely visited the town as his Stage LXVI 'Breone.'

The Church of Saint-Quentin at Dienville

Turn right and continue on this quiet road across the **bridge over L'Aube**, watching afterward for a marked path on the left. Follow it for a gradual climb through woods, and when it ends at a vast field with a lake ahead in the distance, turn left. Cross under powerlines and emerge from the woods onto a grassy farm road beside fields on your right. Come to scattered homes where the road curves left and turns to asphalt, ending at Rue du Val in **Dienville**. Turn right and come to the D443, where you turn left to arrive at the Church of Saint-Quentin (**3.7km**) with the town's services just afterward.

(6.6KM) DIENVILLE (ELEV 128M, POP 878) 🍴 ⊕ 🛆 ◉ ⊕ ✚ **(1573.6KM)**
The army of Attila the Hun passed through here in 451, and the village was adjacent to the 1814 Battle of La Rothière which led to a retreat to Troyes of Napoleon's army. The town's stone open-air **market** traces its roots to a 1536 charter from King Francis I. Restaurants are mostly lakeside and in good weather a relaxing outdoor lunch or dinner there is a cooling treat. (Bus to Troyes: www. fluo.eu)

▲ ⌂ Le Colombier, campsite €20, glamping, rooms €-/57/-/114, groups, 8 Ave Jean Lanez, lecolombier10@gmail.com, tel +33 (0)3 25 92 23 47, https:// domaine-le-colombier.fr

STAGE 33
Dienville to Dolancourt

Start	Dienville, Church of Saint-Quentin
Finish	Dolancourt, town hall
Distance	20.4km
Total ascent	222m
Total descent	194m
Difficulty	Moderate
Duration	5½hr
Percentage paved	48%
Lodging	Unienville 4.1km, Amance 8.1km, Dolancourt 20.4km

The stage is spent mostly in fields interspersed with occasional woods. After Vauchonvilliers a wide plain opens up, with views for several kilometers ahead. The quiet D46 roadway offers a fast and easy, if hard-surfaced, alternate route and is perfect for cycles. Although Dolancourt is an official stage end, the only lodging there at present is meant for tourists at the Nigloland amusement park, so consider an early end at Amance or a continuation to Bar-sur-Aube.

Pass the church on your left and continue on the D11/Avenue Girard. Fork right on Rue du Moulin and, indeed, pass a large, modern **flour mill** on your right. Just afterward fork right to continue into the fields. Fork left just before the woods that conceal L'Aube River, and walk around the trees until crossing a field to the **D210** asphalt road. Turn right, cross L'Aube, and curve through **Unienville**, passing on your left the Church of Saint-Symphorien and continuing to the next block with its gîte d'etape (**4.1km**).

(4.1KM) UNIENVILLE (ELEV 133M, POP 129) ⬛ (1569.5KM)
Unienville is an agricultural hamlet set at a crossing of roads leading to larger cities in the region and at a critical bridge over the Aube River. The bridge was destroyed by retreating French armies at the start of WWI.

⬢ **Council hostel**, 1/12, €12/-/-/-, 6 Rue Saint-Antoine, mairie-unienville@ wanadoo.fr, tel +33 (0)3 25 92 71 39

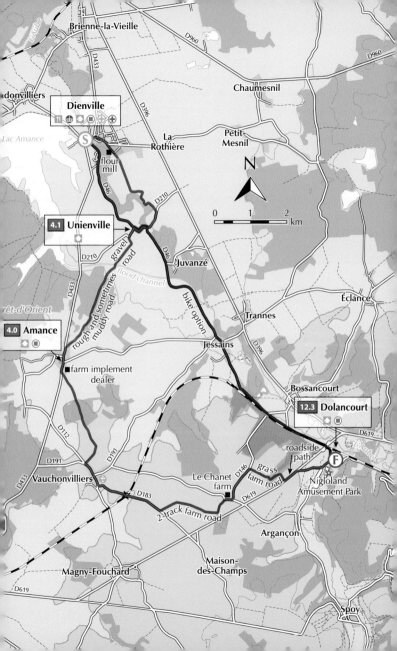

Brienne-la-Vieille

Chaumesnil

donvilliers

Dienville

Petit-Mesnil

La Rothière

Lac Amance

flour mill

N

0 1 2 km

4.1 Unienville

Juvanzé

flood channel

gravel road

Éclance

rêt-d'Orient

4.0 Amance

rough and sometimes muddy road

bike option

Trannes

Jessains

Bossancourt

farm implement dealer

12.3 Dolancourt

D112

D191

roadside path

F

Vauchonvilliers

Le Chanet farm

grass farm road

Nigloland Amusement Park

D183

2-track farm road

D619

Argançon

Magny-Fouchard

Maison-des-Champs

Spoy

Morning light over rows of trees near Unienville

Turn left after the *gîte* onto Rue de la Croix/D210, but as the road takes a right turn, fork left instead onto **gravel**. Pass a barn and fork right with the road, heading toward the flood channel. Cross the **channel** and afterward fork right, heading into the woods. The road now becomes rough and sometimes muddy as it climbs gradually. Coming out of the woods at a field, fork right and follow this road ahead to the noisy D443 highway and *gîte* d'etape on the north edge of **Amance** (**4.0km**).

(4.0KM) AMANCE (ELEV 159M, POP 253) 🏕 ⊚ (1565.5KM)
Three hamlets were combined in the 12th century to create this tiny village, which at one time was surrounded by ramparts. A small foundation of a tower dated 1478 stands at Ferrand Square. In this town of khaki-colored stone and stucco homes there are several Renaissance-era homes listed as historic monuments. The 18th-century **Saint-Laurent Church** features prized stained-glass windows. (Bus to Troyes: www.fluo.eu)

🏠 **Council hostel**, Place R Pietremont, commune-amance@wanadoo.fr, tel +33 (0)7 69 46 70 78, (0)3 25 41 41 87, Mme Fevre

Turn left and pass the *mairie*. As you leave town, fork left after a **farm implement dealership** and follow this road through fields, a large wood, and to the D191/D112 in the village of **Vauchonvilliers** (**3.6km**). Turn left and follow the road through this sparse village and continue straight onto Rue d'Église when the D191 forks to the left before the **Church of Saint-Pierre et Saint-Paul**. Just 150 meters after the church, fork left onto the **D183** where expansive views of farmland open to the south.

Cross a bridge over railroad tracks and continue through the wide expanse of fields. Fork left onto a **two-track farm road**, which curves right. After the curve, turn left onto a gravel road that leads to a large cluster of white farm buildings, where just afterward is a hamlet called **Le Chanet** (**4.8km**). Veer right at the sole stop sign at the D144 and one block later at the edge of town turn left onto the **D146** in the direction of Bossancourt. When you've made your way to the top of the gentle rise, turn right on a **grassy farm road** that winds downhill through woods toward the **D619** highway.

Now see ahead and to your left the tower of the **Nigloland amusement park** in Dolancourt. Opened in 1987, Nigloland welcomes 500,000 visitors each year and includes 39 major rides (www.nigloland.com).

Just before the highway, turn left onto a roadside path, then cross the highway and head down the driveway toward the amusement park. After the park entrance come to the town hall in **Dolancourt** (**3.9km**).

(12.3KM) DOLANCOURT (ELEV 160M, POP 153) 🏕 ⊚ (1553.2KM)
Despite being dominated by neighboring Nigloland, the village manages to retain a certain quiet and charm. Evidence shows a settlement here in Gallo-Roman times and sections of Roman pavement have been uncovered. In the 12th century the town was on the lands of the Dolancourt family. (Bus to Troyes: www.fluo.eu)

🏠 **Moulin du Landion**, 4/8, €-/-/87/-, 5 Rue St-Léger, contact@moulindulandion. com, tel +33 (0)3 25 27 92 17

A ferris wheel of Nigloland stands out among vineyards and trees at Dolancourt

STAGE 34
Dolancourt to Baroville

Start	Dolancourt, town hall
Finish	Baroville, town hall
Distance	18.5km
Total ascent	458m
Total descent	393m
Difficulty	Moderate
Duration	5hr
Percentage paved	23%
Lodging	Bar-sur-Aube 12.2km, Baroville 18.5km

The official route climbs steeply on forest pathways behind Nigloland, then spends time in woods and fields before descending to Bar-sur-Aube. An easy and quick alternative is the quiet, asphalt D46 that runs along the valley floor and spans the distance in about four fewer kilometers. Another very steep climb on the official route after Bar-sur-Aube offers a remarkable view of the Aube Valley, but those in a hurry for the stage end at Baroville may opt for easy and quiet asphalt roads through Fontaine. After Bar-sur-Aube the next supermarket is 38km away in Châteauvillain – or Bricon if you choose the Blessonville option.

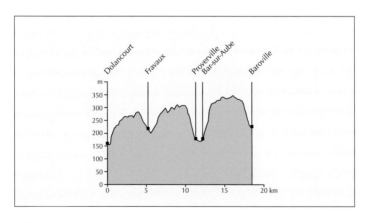

Continue past the town hall on the D46 which forks right and crosses the tiny Landion River. When the road turns sharply left at a traffic circle after town, instead cross the street and take a narrow **path steeply uphill** into the woods. The path ends at a gravel road which you follow to the right, continuing uphill into the fields. The road curves back into the woods, where you pass shooting platforms used during hunting season.

At the top of the hill, turn left on another **gravel road**, following it through the woods and back into fields on the other side. Skirt around a **farmhouse** and continue on through the surrounding fields. The road ends at a T-junction, where you turn left to continue in the same direction on the **D113** asphalt road. Turn right at a **tree farm** onto

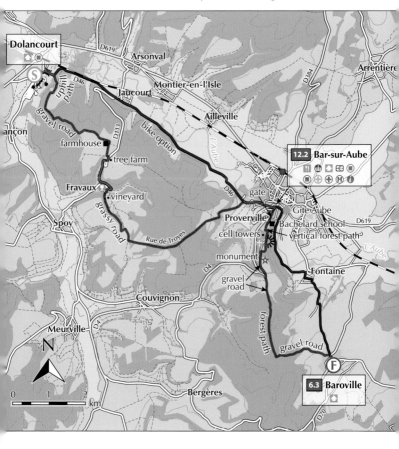

183

a grassy road heading downhill to cut the loop off the D113 and then join the road to circle around the north side of the village of **Fravaux** (5.5km, bar), which you enter at its Rue Principale on the village's east side.

Take the first left, just before the town hall, heading uphill. Pass a large **vineyard** on the left, and when the gravel road curves left, go straight on a **grassy road** to bisect this narrow margin of trees. Turn left on the other side and pick up another road as it curves around a field. Turn left at the next gravel road, where you begin to see views of the town ahead. This road becomes **Rue de Troyes** and will carry you through woods, fields, and vineyards before its end at the D46 in **Proverville** (5.8km).

Turn right on the D46, which becomes the Grande Rue in Proverville and soon afterward Rue Romagon as it crosses the boundary to Bar-sur-Aube. The D46 ends at the D4/Foute de Couvignon, where you fork right and continue one block to Rue Pierre Brossolette on the south bank of the Aube in **Bar-sur-Aube** (0.9km). A right turn here continues the main route; alternatively, to head to the center city, turn left, cross the river and continue five blocks to Rue Nationale.

(12.2KM) BAR-SUR-AUBE (ELEV 168M, POP 5387) ⊞ ⊕ ⌂ Ⓒ ⊙ ⊙ ⊕ ⊕ ⊞ ❶ (1541.0KM)

Undoubtedly Sigeric's visit in 990 at Stage LXV 'Bar' included a stop at the Sainte-Germain shrine on the Côte des Bar, the ridge above this charming riverside town. Its position near prosperous Champagne fairs and the eminent Clairvaux Abbey gave it a high point of importance in the Middle Ages. The primary remnant of this era is the 12th-century **Church of Saint-Pierre**, with its unusual wooden porch, or 'halloy' likely used then as a market. The colorful **town hall** fills the buildings of the 17th-century convent at Rue d'Aube and Rue Nationale. (Bus: www.postauto.ch and www.fluo.eu)

⌂ **Apartement 4 Pièces** Ⓓⓞ Ⓡ Ⓚ 3/8, €10/-/-/-, 13 Rue du Collège, jmfsainton@ yahoo.fr, tel +33 (0)3 25 27 24 25 (tourist office), res by phone only weekdays except Wed, closed Oct 15–Apr 15

⌂ **Les Oiseaux du Tartre**, €-/50/60/75, 11 Rue de l'Europe, catminh10@hotmail. fr, tel +33 (0)6 22 53 76 08, https://catminh10.wixsite.com/oiseaux-du-tartre

⌂ **De la Pomme d'Or**, €-/-/57/-, 79 Faubourg de Belfort, www. hoteldelapommedor.com, tel +33 (0)9 70 35 19 09, cont brkfst €6

Turn right and uphill on Rue Pierre Brossolette, passing through the pedestrian gates and quickly gaining elevation first on a pedestrian and cycle path and then on an automobile road. Pass a **school** and when the pavement ends continue straight uphill on gravel. Follow signs that direct you left after a fence and follow the traverse along the fence line until a right turn leads you very steeply up a tricky and **vertical forest path** which will certainly test the tread on your soles.

The city hall at Bar-sur-Aube was once a convent

Once at the top of Colline Sainte-Germaine, leave the woods for a clearing near a barn and two tall **cell/radio towers**. Come to a lovely **viewpoint** over the Aube Valley, adjacent to the chapel of Sainte-Germaine. According to legend, Germaine, a young maiden and devoted virgin, was martyred after refusing the advances of Attila the Hun at this site in AD451.

Keeping the meadow and farm buildings on your right, continue along the ridge, and when the meadow comes to an end veer right and pick up a gravel road. Pass a **monument to Sainte-Germaine** and afterward pass through a field and take the first fork left onto gravel when the road makes a right turn, heading slightly uphill. Cross under power lines and enter the woods, recently thinned by logging. After the logged area the path turns into a tranquil **forest walk** among young deciduous trees.

At an intersection, turn left in the direction of Baroville, where the path becomes a road that becomes steep as it nears town. Join a road leading right and downhill. Come to the first street in town, Rue de Couvignon, and turn left to come to the D70, where a right turn leads to the town hall and the Church of Saint-Etienne in **Baroville** (**6.3km**, water, benches).

(6.3KM) BAROVILLE (ELEV 220M, POP 313) 🏠 (1534.6KM)
The village is mentioned in 1095 under the name Basnoville and was under the aegis of Châlons and then Langres. Over 200 hectares of **vineyards** serve 50 bustling wineries, and the town itself is tucked into a fold among vineyard-covered hills.

🏠 Champagne Urbaine, 4 Rue de la Côté Sandrey, www.champagne-urbain.fr, tel +33 (0)3 25 27 00 36, closed during grape harvest

STAGE 35
Baroville to Orges

Start	Baroville, town hall
Finish	Orges, Dhuy River
Distance	26.9km
Total ascent	473m
Total descent	478m
Difficulty	Moderately hard
Duration	7hr
Percentage paved	42%
Lodging	Clairvaux/Ville-sous-la-Ferté 8.6km, Cirfontaines 19.2km, Orges 26.9km

A few forested hills and valleys separate Baroville from Clairvaux, site of the famous medieval monastery. A swampy forest and climb follow Clairvaux, making for slow going in wet weather. After Aizanville the Blessonville option becomes available which bypasses Orges and Châteauvillain, making a direct line for Richebourg and saving 7.2km. Both options vary between forests and wide fields and both can be glorious in good weather.

Keep the Church of St-Etienne on your right and continue through town on Rue des Pressoirs. Pass the *gîte*, and as the asphalt road turns left instead go straight uphill among the **vineyards** on a wide gravel road. At the top of the hill continue straight, heading into a small valley with row crops at the bottom, vineyards on the right, and a wooded ridge straight ahead. As the uphill begins, fork left to head straight into and through the woods.

Back out into the fields, at the summit see the town of Arconville in the distance to the right. Continue straight as the road leads downhill to a valley in the woods. Cross through a wide **green metal gate** and pick up a wide gravel road, the **Sommiere des Moines** (Monks' Bed-Base), which continues in the same straight line up the next hill.

A couple takes a walk through vineyards after Baroville

186

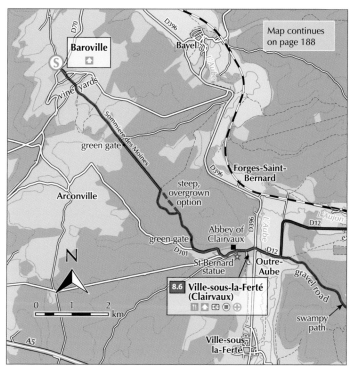

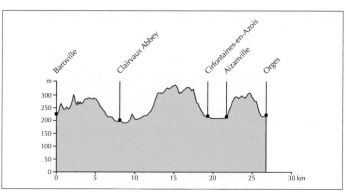

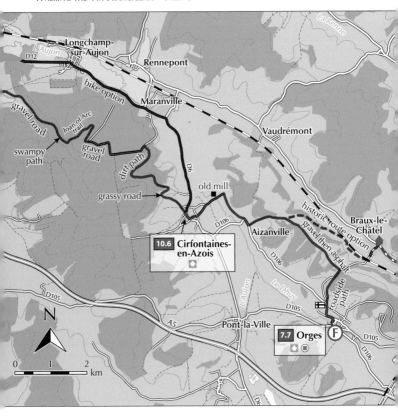

The signs point to a right turn after the summit, onto the Route Forestière de Poule Grive (Forest Route of the Thrush Hen). While it is possible to shortcut straight ahead and steeply downhill at this intersection, the recommended route to the right is safer, better maintained, and just 300 meters longer. Curve downhill with the road and come to the bottom of the shortcut where you take the right fork, following the signs downhill.

Near the bottom, go through another **green metal gate** and turn left on the asphalt **D101** into a narrow valley. As you follow the road into town it curves right to follow alongside a tall stone wall. Continue to follow the wall until you come to the main entrance of the **Abbey of Clairvaux** (**8.1km**, gift shop, restrooms, stamp. No photos allowed), used since the French Revolution as a high-security prison.

At just 25 years old but already showing great promise, a young priest, Bernard of Fontaine-lès-Dijon, was sent in 1115 to establish a Cistercian abbey in this small valley he named 'Clairvaux.' From here he became one of the major figures of the medieval Catholic church, where his mystical writings were a counterbalance to the prevailing scholasticism of his contemporaries. He was canonized just 21 years after his death by Pope Alexander III as **St Bernard of Clairvaux** and his writings and sermons are considered classics of Christian spirituality to this day. Dante Alighieri honored him as last of the guides in Paradise in his *Divine Comedy*, and hymns attributed to St Bernard are still sung in churches. A statue of St Bernard of Clairvaux overlooks the former abbey from the hillside above.

Just 500 meters later come to the D396 and the small cluster of homes that is the village of Clairvaux in the municipality of **Ville-sous-la-Ferté** (0.5km).

(8.6KM) CLAIRVAUX/VILLE-SOUS-LA-FERTÉ (ELEV 190M, POP 1077)
🏨 🔲 🄴 ◉ ⊕ (1526.1KM)

By 1780 there were only 36 monks left at the **Abbey of Clairvaux**, and in the French Revolution they were dispersed, the property was nationalized, and the abbey grounds were attached to this nearby village. In 1804, Napoleon ordered the abbey transformed into a penitentiary. During WWII French Resistance fighters were imprisoned here and 21 were executed. (Bus: www.postauto.ch)

🏠 **Hôtel-Restaurant de l'Abbaye**, €-/55/-/-, 19 Route de Dijon, hrabbaye-clairvaux@orange.fr, tel +33 (0)3 25 27 80 12, https://hotel-restaurant-abbaye.fr, demi-pension avail

Cross the D396 highway and continue on the **D12** in the direction of Châteauvillain through the village of Outre-Aube. Once out in the fields the road turns left, while the route instead goes straight on a **gravel road** heading uphill through fields. As you climb, the path enters woods, where you may encounter severe mud in wet weather. At a left turn uphill on the **Joan of Arc Trail** leave the swampy path behind.

The **GR703/Joan of Arc Trail** commemorates the saint's 1429 passage from Vaucouleurs to Chinon to spur King Charles V to expel the English from France. During her trip she stayed overnight at Clairvaux, which has a plaque commemorating the visit's 500th anniversary.

In 900 meters watch carefully for a sign leading to a sharp right turn onto a wide dirt trail, followed by a right turn onto a wide grassy road, still in the woods. You have now left the Aube Department of France and entered the Haute-Marne. At a clearing, this road meets a **gravel road** where you turn left. Stay on this road as it turns first sharply right and then left.

After the road turns to asphalt to head to the villages of Maranville and Irceville, turn right instead onto a wide **dirt path** that now doubles back into the woods. The road loops around as it heads downhill, with numbered hunting blinds along the way. It ends at a gravel road where you turn left, continuing downhill into the Aujon Valley. Emerge from the woods and turn right on a **grassy road** that winds down among fields to the D6 at the village of **Cirfontaines** (**10.6km**, bread vending machine).

(10.6KM) CIRFONTAINES-EN-AZOIS (ELEV 215M, POP 191) 🗺 (1515.5KM)

Bus: www.postauto.ch, www.sncf.com

🏠 **Host Family Marcillet**, 7 Gr Grande Rue, tel +33 (0)6 76 20 67 55

'Voie Historique' – direct route to Richebourg (17.9km)

At the plaza in Cirfontaines, find signs for the 'Voie Historique' – so named since Sigeric stayed at Blessonville, which he listed as LXIV 'Blaecuile.' The route diverges from the official Via Francigena/GR145 after the next village and leads from there somewhat more directly to Richebourg, bypassing Châteauvillain and its services and saving about 7km while not offering any particular scenic advantages. Accommodation is available at **Braux-le-Châtel** (🏠 **Host Family Herrero**, 25 Grand Rue, +33 (0)3 25 03 93 89, 🏠 **Host Family Pelte**, 18 Grand Rue, +33 (0)3 25 31 61 12), **Blessonville** at the pilgrim house (+33 (0)6 22 78 90 95), Bugniéres (+33 (0)6 77 16 91 84), and Marac (+33 (0)6 76 91 15 20) and Bricon (🏠 **Hostel**, 3 Rue du Leclerc, +33 (0)7 89 53 83 29). The small grocery store in **Bricon** is the last grocery until Langres (closed Mondays and daily 12–3pm), and the bustling L'Europe Bar/Restaurant offers refreshment at the edge of town.

Main route

Pass the *mairie* and then the church on your left and take the next left. Fork left at the town's *lavarie* (wash fountain) and cross to the narrow woods which conceal the Aujon River. Cross the river, pass the **old mill**, and turn right when the road ends. Arrive at the D106 in **Aizanville** (**2.4km**, no services). After the Church of Saint-Georges, follow signs that direct you left and uphill on a gravel road that leads steeply to the ridge top.

At the top, come to the historic route option (**1.3km**; see above). Either turn right to stay on the official route GR145 to Orges and Châteauvillain or go straight to head toward Braux-le-Châtel visible in the distance. On the official route, the road descends and turns to asphalt before it meets the Braux-Orges road. Either turn right to take the road or go forward 10 meters and turn right to catch the comfortable and serene path that follows the road. The path becomes a farm track as it emerges into the fields, then you join the D106 before the **cemetery**. Follow the D106 through **Orges**, meeting the D105 at the Dhuy River (**4.0km**).

A field of flax soaks in the sun above Aizanville

(7.7KM) ORGES (ELEV 216M, POP 375) 🏠 ◉ **(1507.8KM)**
The town's name translates as 'barley.' The existence of its mill can be traced to 1321 and since 1903 it has been used as a factory for production of silk flowers used in decoration. The mill's paddle wheel still drives 19th-century machinery and the **flower mill** grounds host weddings, diners, and overnight guests (from €70, https://moulindelafleuristerie.fr). (Bus: www.postauto.ch)

🛏 Le Moulin de la Fleuristerie, 3/7, €-/-/69/-, 4 Chemin de la Fleuristerie, accueil@moulindelafleuristerie.fr, tel +33 (0)7 82 21 21 23, (0)6 22 10 89 48, demi-pension avail, book on website – at the time of writing the promo code is VF2022

STAGE 36
Orges to Richebourg

Start	Orges, Dhuy River
Finish	Richebourg, D102 at D10
Distance	18.8km
Total ascent	212m
Total descent	83m
Difficulty	Easy
Duration	5hr
Percentage paved	21%
Lodging	Châteauvillain 5.4km, Richebourg 18.8km

Although pilgrims may choose to walk the Blessonville route to save a couple of hours, Châteauvillain is an interesting and historic town that earns its place on the Via Francigena by providing a wealth of services to pilgrims and offering the last supermarket until Langres, about 83km away.

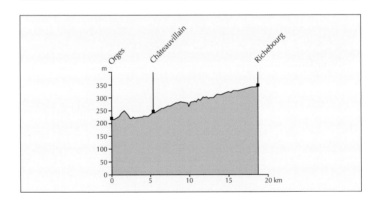

Cross the river and turn left, still on the D106, but one block after the stop sign, turn right. After farm buildings the road turns to **gravel** in the fields and heads for a gap between two low, forested hills. Cross under the **A5 motorway** and go straight on an asphalt road to the edge of the village of Marmesse, where you join with the D207.

An old tower from Châteauvillain's medieval walls is visible in one of its homes

Continue through fields until you come to the former train tracks, which you cross and in 200 meters come to the D65 across from the cemetery at the northern fringe of **Châteauvillain** (5.4km). The route turns here, but if you would like to enjoy the town's services and sights, walk straight ahead on Rue de Chaumont to come to the town hall and center in 900 meters.

(5.4KM) CHÂTEAUVILLAIN (ELEV 239M, POP 1689) 🏨 ⊕ 🏠 🄫 ⊕ ⊕ 𝒊 (1502.4KM)

The city was built in the 11th century around the **Castrum Villanum**, a fortification of the House of Châtillon, and retains about 20 towers, including the 45m castle keep with 5m-thick walls. Its **Porte Madame** city gate dates from the 12th–14th century. The town has 5km of picturesque narrow streets and walkways.

⛺ Castels Lodges 🄾 🄿𝔱 🅁 🄺 🄶𝔯 🅆 🅂 5/15, €-/50/70/100, Rue Penthièvre, castels.lodges@gmail.com, tel +33 (0)6 11 61 87 32

Turn east onto **Rue Gravière** (Gravel Pit Street), keeping the cemetery on your right, and head again into the fields. The road turns to gravel and aims at a forest ahead, turning right 100 meters shy and ending at an **asphalt road**. Turn left here and follow this road as it turns left into the woods, part of the French Parc National de Forêts. The 560 sq km park was established as France's 11th national park in 2019 and is dedicated to its vast forests and their inhabitants.

Once on the uphill side of a dip, turn right on a **wide dirt path**, still in the woods, with sounds of the A5 motorway to your left. The path ends at another dirt path, where you turn right. Cross a grassy road and then a cleared **fire break** to reach a two-track road on the opposite side. Watch here for evidence of rutting boars.

> **Caution:** While boars have an excellent sense of smell, they are very near-sighted, may not see or hear your approach and may not smell you if you are downwind. If you see fresh signs of boars, such as rutting marks in the path, watch carefully and make noise so you do not surprise them. Once surprised, they will run away. Never approach a boar, which can be extremely dangerous if cornered or when separated from its piglets.

After a **clearing**, the sloppy two-track road becomes a neat and well-maintained gravel track. When this road meets another **gravel road** in a wide curve, turn left and continue through the woods. Turn right at the **'D'Orleans' route** and continue almost perfectly straight for the next 4km, going straight even though the road itself turns right, and finally coming to a **white gate** just before the D102 roadway where the Blessonville option rejoins. Turn right on the D102 to come just across the first field to the D10 in **Richebourg (13.4km)**.

(13.4KM) RICHEBOURG (ELEV 343M, POP 278) 🏠 (1489.0KM)
Richebourg is one of 59 municipalities located in the 242,148-hectare **National Forest Park**. The region's rocky soil makes its woodlands unsuitable for agriculture and in 2019 they were gathered together as a park by the French government to preserve their ecosystems.

🏠 La Maison Renaud, 3 Domaine d'Orchamps, la.maison.renaud@wanadoo.fr, tel +33 (0)3 25 31 05 46, (0)6 75 94 40 49

Cyclists roll into Richebourg

STAGE 37
Richebourg to Faverolles

Start	Richebourg, D102 at D10
Finish	Faverolles, D256 at Rue Côtes de l'Église
Distance	17.8km (includes one 2.3km shortcut, but not another optional shortcut saving a further 2.1km)
Total ascent	258m
Total descent	233m
Difficulty	Easy
Duration	4¾hr
Percentage paved	89%
Lodging	Mormant 6.8km, Leffonds 10.4km, Faverolles 17.8km

Between Richebourg and Leffonds the Francigena stewards have worked hard to keep walkers on soft surfaces, but those who don't mind asphalt underfoot can walk the quiet road first to Mormant and then on past Leffonds.

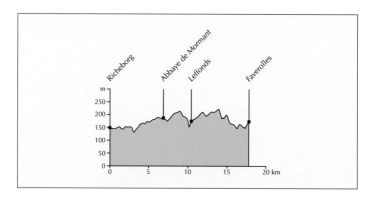

Cross the D10 and continue on the **D102**/Rue de la Levée de César toward Leffonds, heading out into the fields. Come to an option (**1.4km**). The official route turns south to pass through the Val des Dames Forest, taking a south and then southwest route, at first through fields and then through woods. Follow signage to arrive at Mormant

*Cyclists enjoy a quiet road through farmland after Richebourg
(photo: European Association of the Via Francigena ways)*

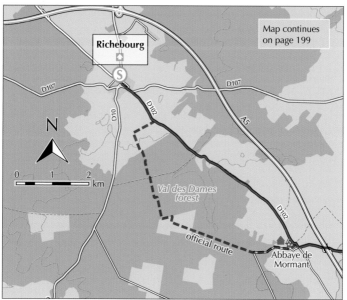

Map continues
on page 199

Abbaye de Mormant once housed pilgrims on the way to Rome and Jerusalem

Abbey from the west. Recommended shortcut: Especially in wet weather it is recommended to remain on the quiet, asphalt D102 to save 2.3km. Continue on the D102 as it comes to the **Mormant Abbey** (5.5km ♠ Gîte de l'Abbaye O Pr R K Br Dr W S 3/11, €-/20/40/60, 14 Rue de l'Abbaye Hameau de Mormant, a.michelot52@yahoo.fr, tel +33 (0)6 79 01 33 53, €5 brkfst, €15 demi-pension.

> First mention of the **Abbaye de Mormant** is in the 12th century, and over its long history it passed from Augustinian hands to become a commandery of the Templars and Hospitallers. From ancient times the site served as a hospital for travelers before its destruction in the Hundred Years' War. It was repaired by the Hospitallers but became an agricultural compound in the French Revolution and ultimately fell into disrepair.

The D102 now curves around the abbey site and heads east. Cross the **A5** motorway and continue on the D102 into Leffonds. Once in town, a path at the Sointures stream cuts off a loop of the road and you head uphill on the other side, back on the D102, to arrive at the D154 in **Leffonds** (3.6km).

(10.4KM) LEFFONDS (ELEV 368M, POP 345) 🏔 (1478.6KM)
This village is sometimes called 'Leffonds-la-Haute' which helps differentiate it from the village of 'Leffond' on the Francigena near Champlitte.

♠ La Cressonnière O Pr R Br Dr W S 4/8, €-/30/60/90, 21 Rue de la Cressonnière, dominique.begny@gmail.com, tel +33 (0)6 75 32 72 43, (0)6 44 73 09 20, brkfst incl, €25 demi-pension. Lodging in comfortable caravan. Dogs, donkeys, horses welcome.

Shortcut option

The official GR145 route here turns right on the D154/Rue de l'Église to walk a circuitous route through fields and woods before rejoining the D102. Save 2.1km by simply continuing on the quiet D102 to rejoin the official route.

Main route

After a **paddock** on the D102, turn left onto a **gravel road** that heads through another wood and emerges into a field just before the **D143** asphalt road. Cross the road and continue, now on the **Rue du Château**, into town. Cross the Suize stream and either stay on this road, now the D256, or take any of the left turns to arrive at the main road of the town, the Rue Côtes de l'Église in **Faverolles** (**7.3km**).

> **(7.3KM) FAVEROLLES** (ELEV 369M, POP 118) 🏛 **(1471.3KM)**
>
> An impressive mausoleum, built in the first century AD along the Roman road, was discovered here in the 1970s. Although the site had been used as a stone quarry since the Middle Ages it still yielded important archeological finds, many of which are contained in the **Musée Archeologique** set in the village's old post office (€3.50, https://atelierarcheologiquefaverolles.fr).
>
> 🏠 **Council hostel**, 1 Chemin de Chirey, mairie-faverolles@wanadoor.fr, tel +33 (0)3 25 30 39 08

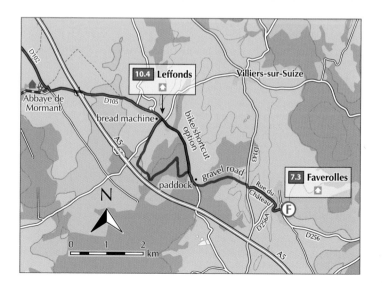

STAGE 38

Faverolles to Langres

Start	Faverolles, D256 at Rue Côtes de l'Église
Finish	Langres, Place Diderot
Distance	21.0km
Total ascent	367m
Total descent	267m
Difficulty	Moderately hard
Duration	5½hr
Percentage paved	60%
Lodging	Saint-Ciergues 12.0km, Perrancey 14.8km, Langres 21.0km

A stage of woods and fields, punctuated by the crossing of the Lac de la Mouche dam and a steep climb up to one of the route's most charming towns. There are few things more relaxing than sipping a cup of tea in Place Diderot in the heart of beautiful Langres on a sunny day; while the view from the Tour Piquante atop the town's walls is surely one of the great vistas of the Via Francigena.

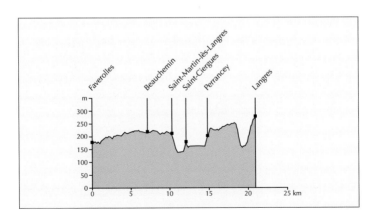

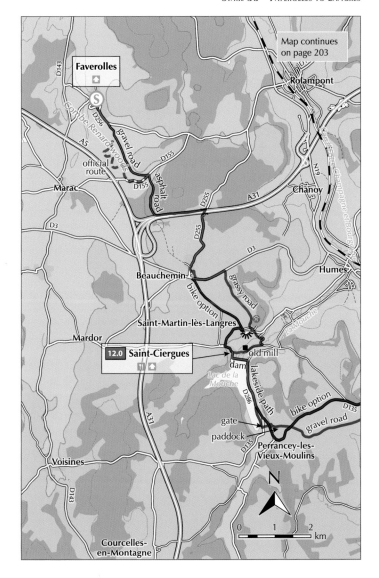

Map continues
on page 203

Faverolles

Rolampont

D143

D256

Combe Renard woods

gravel road

A5

official route

D155

D155

asphalt road

D255

Marac

D3

Chanoy

N19

A31

D3

D255

Humes

La Mouche

Beauchemin

grassy road

bike option

Saint-Martin-lès-Langres

Mardor

12.0 Saint-Ciergues

old mill

dam

lakeside path

Lac de la Mouche

D286

bike option

D135

gravel road

gate

paddock

D135

Perrancey-les-Vieux-Moulins

A31

Voisines

N

D143

0   1   2
km

Courcelles-en-Montagne

Continue on the D256. Follow it out of town and then fork right on the Chemin de Beauchemin. In 500 meters come to an option. Recommended shortcut option: The official route turns right to walk through the Combe Renard woods before coming to the D155. You can stay on this gravel road to save 1.1km. Come to the **D155** where the official route rejoins. Cross the road and go straight and uphill toward the woods on the **asphalt road** to the other side, where the road turns left to follow alongside the **A31/E54** motorway. Continue until the road ends at the **D255** and turn right to cross under the highway. Follow the D255 to the Grand Rue of the tiny village of **Beauchemin** (**7.0km**, no services).

Turn left on the Grand Rue and either continue to the D3 at the end of town, or follow signs to the next road, which also leads to the D3. Turn left to walk on this roadway without benefit of sidewalks, noting on your far right the twin towers of the cathedral at Langres. Turn right onto a **grassy road** before woods, and continue through fields, passing a park with picnic tables. When the road ends, turn left into the village of **Saint-Martin-lès-Langres** (**3.2km**).

Head through the village and cross the D286 onto Rue des Charrières, where you catch your first glimpses of the Lac de la Mouche reservoir. Continue down the very steep hill toward the concrete dam of the reservoir, passing an **old mill** and crossing the river on a low stone bridge. Come to an asphalt road, turn right and walk steeply up to the D286/Rue du Lac in **Saint-Ciergues** (**1.8km**, restaurant closed Wed).

(12.0KM) SAINT-CIERGUES (ELEV 372M, POP 189) 🍴 🛏 **(1459.3KM)**
The village lost a third of its land with late 19th-century construction of La Mouche dam, but the result is the 97-hectare **Lac de la Mouche**. The town's **Church of St-Cyr-et-Sainte-Julitte** dates from the 13th–17th centuries.

🏠 **Host Family Grandclerc**, 1 Rue des Roises, elisabeth.garnier0157@orange.fr, tel +33 (0)3 25 84 82 54, (0)6 52 82 17 85

Turn left, take the shortcut steps down to the **dam**, and walk atop the dam 400 meters to the other side of the valley, enjoying views of the lake to the right and countryside to the left. Now turn right to walk alongside the lake, first on a path by the road and then on a path that follows the Mouche River upstream from the reservoir. When the path turns right to cross the river, instead turn left and walk through a **gate** to cross the asphalt D135. Walk up the steep hill, coming to the Grand Rue in the village of **Perrancey-les-Vieux-Moulins** (**2.8km**, 🏠 Domaine de Montauban, 4/13, €-/29/54/-, 3 Route de Montauban, karine.leroykl@gmail.com, tel +33 (0)6 75 98 73 75, (0)3 25 88 12 61, brkfst €8, apartments).

Turn right and then take an immediate left to continue up the hill on Chemin de Champ Segre. The road turns to a grassy path as you walk beyond and around a large white house before continuing up the hill. Pass a **paddock** and meet a gravel road, where you turn right to come once more to the D135.

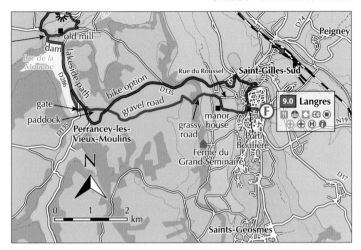

Cross the D135, with fields on your left and woods and meadows on your right. Soon veer left onto a **gravel road** that continues through long fields with scattered woods, slowly climbing. The road finally turns left and ends at a gravel road running alongside a pasture fence. Turn right and continue to climb. As you come alongside woods in 300 meters, turn left on a **grassy road**, leading under trees. The road becomes a wide dirt and gravel path as it now descends.

The Lac de la Liez is visible in the distance from the Tour Piquante on the walls of Langres

As views of the ramparts of Langres open up just across a narrow valley the road descends steeply, turning to an asphalt street, the **Rue du Chanoine Roussel**. Cross La Bonnelle stream at the bottom of the valley, turn right and follow this road past a **manor house** as it curves left and then steeply uphill. After a steep climb you come alongside the N19 highway. Look for a steep ramp that takes you up to the road, which you cross at a crosswalk. Enter the old city through **Port Boulière** and walk up Rue Boulière to find Place Diderot at the center of **Langres** (6.2km).

(9.0KM) LANGRES (ELEV 472M, POP 8653) 🏨 ⊕ 🏧 🍴 🅲 ⓜ ⊕ ⊕ Ⓗ ❶ **(1450.3KM)** Inarguably one of the gems of the Via Francigena, Langres is a hilltop town that retains its defensive **walls** and its historic character. Walk around the walls for spectacular views of the surrounding countryside. Walk inside the walls and enjoy a well-preserved village filled with medieval and Renaissance-era buildings.

This limestone promontory was settled by the Gallic Lingones tribe; the Romans fortified it with stone walls and called it *Andemantunum*, using the fortress to protect the crossing of a dozen Roman roads. Although it was overrun in subsequent invasions, the town prospered in the Middle Ages as its powerful diocese dominated the regions of Champagne, Burgundy and Franche-Comté. Bishops of Langres were dukes and peers of France. In the 17th century the ramparts were remodeled by Sébastian le Prestre de Vauban into their present contours, which share design characteristics with other area fortresses by Vauban. Among the more elaborate city gates is the **Porte des Moulins** on the city's south side. The 2000-year-old **Roman triumphal arch** on the west side was incorporated into the walls as a defensive tower and is the town's oldest structure.

Langres was birthplace of Denis Diderot (1713–84), eminent Enlightenment philosopher and editor-in-chief of the famous *Encyclopedia*, and Jeanne Mance (1606–1722), co-founder of the city of Montreal, Canada. The town features two museums, the **Maison des Lumières Denis Diderot** and the **Musée d'Art et d'Histoire** (€7 for both, closed Mondays in season, www.musees-langres.fr).

🏠 **Ferme du Grand Seminaire** Ⓞ 🅿ⓡ Ⓡ 🅱ⓡ 🅳ⓡ 🆆 🆂 2/4, €-/20/-/-, 160 Chemin du Séminaire, Faubourg du Buzon, gisele.peter@wanadoo.fr, tel +33 90)6 69 47 21 42, (0)3 25 87 27 26, incl breakfast, dinner avail on req

🏠 **Ferme Sainte-Anne**, 9/30, €33/-/55/77, 380 Chemins de la Ferme Saint-Anne, contact@gite-sainteanne.fr, tel +33 (0)3 25 88 45 14, (0)6 03 08 29 77, https://gite-sainteanne.fr/en, brkfst €8, discount with credential, tents €3, linens avail

🏠 **Presbytery Home**, €12/-/-/-, 1 bis Rue Aubert, paroissedelangres@orange.fr, tel +33 (0)3 25 87 11 48

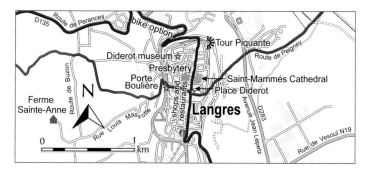

STAGE 39

Langres to Chalindrey

Start	Langres, Place Diderot
Finish	Chalindrey, Ave de la Gare at Rue de Mulhouse
Distance	24.8km
Total ascent	161m
Total descent	300m
Difficulty	Moderate
Duration	6¼hr
Percentage paved	43%
Lodging	Culmont 23.4km, Chalindrey 24.8km

The D17 is the shortest route between Langres and Chalindrey, but it makes for a lackluster and occasionally perilous walk. Instead, the GR145/VF official route heads north to walk around the peaceful Lac de la Liez reservoir. Besides safety, another benefit of the official route is the intriguing and historic Fort Fermier at Montlandon. Beware of an unkempt forest walk before Culmont, which may necessitate taking the road from Montlandon through Torcenay.

Cross Rue Diderot and head downhill on Rue du Grand Cloître to pass through the city gate and down the auto roads Grand Rue de Ss Murs and Côte des Trois Rois to the valley below. After crossing the **D283** you are soon among pastures and rolling hills on the **Route de Peigney**. Come to the **Marne River**, here the Canal Entre

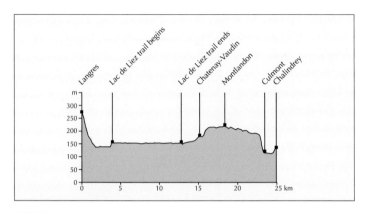

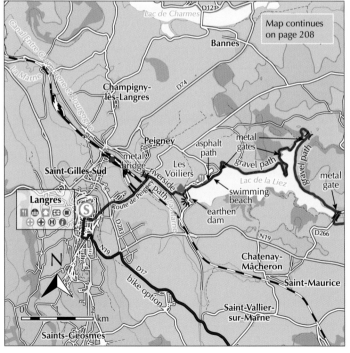

Champagne et Bourgogne, and take a metal bridge to the left that allows you to cross the canal and turn right to continue on the canal-side asphalt path.

> Headwaters of the 514km **Marne River** are just a few kilometers south of this point. The waterway is one of the main tributaries of the Seine and it gives its name to four French departments, plus the First and Second Battles of the Marne, fought in 1914 and 1918 respectively. The river is heavily channelized, with most of the canals built in the 19th century, although one – the oldest canal in France – was built in 1235.

Just before the next bridge turn left and follow signs to a path and gravel road that leads to the top of the earthen dam where you find beautiful views back to Langres. Now take the **asphalt path** that runs along the shoreline of the lake and follow it as it passes a green metal gate, turns to gravel and becomes a very pleasant walk in the lakeside woods. After a green **metal gate** take a gravel road through pastures and then continue on a path through the wetlands at the head of the lake.

Finally at the head of the lake, cross a modest **bridge** over the tiny Suane River. Go around another green **metal gate** and find yourself on a wide **gravel path**, now heading south on the lake's eastern shore. At the lake's eastern end, pass a final **gate** where the gravel road turns to asphalt among scattered homes and ends at the **D266** asphalt road (**12.8km**).

Forested pathways lead around Lac de Liez

Turn right and follow the road across the **Liez River bridge**, forking left after the bridge onto a gravel road between a pasture and field that follows the Liez River's south bank, gradually ascending. When the road turns left, fork right instead to arrive at the **D188** asphalt road, where you turn right to enter the village of **Chatenay-Vaudin** (**2.3km**, no services).

Just before the last house of town, fork left on an **asphalt road** leading among pastures. The road turns to gravel; when it takes a sharp left, go straight onto a **grassy farm road** heading toward the top of the hill. The road ends at the **D51**, just before a tempting but dangerous shortcut. Resist the temptation to take the busy N19/E54 south, and instead resign yourself to turning left for a much safer and potentially very interesting loop through Montlandon and its fort. Turn left and come to the entrance of **Fort Fermier**/Fort Montlandon (**2.7km**).

Look carefully to the left as you walk toward **Montlandon** and see the partially subterranean Fort Fermier, built in the 1880s as a line of defense for France's eastern borders. The fort could hold 360 soldiers, plus armaments and horses. Today it is revitalized by two couples as a farm (www.facebook.com/LeFortFermier).

Continue on the D51 into **Montlandon** proper and turn right after the WWI monument to return on the **Rue du Tennis** to the N19. Cross the road onto the D307 and in 400 meters come to signs pointing you to the right and into the woods.

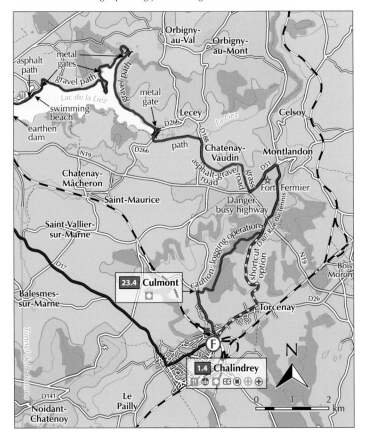

Pilgrims take a tour through Fort Fermier at Montlandon (photo: European Association of the Via Francigena ways)

Shortcut and caution
In 2021 a logging operation rendered the official route through the woods at least temporarily impenetrable. To avoid this walk and also save 250 meters, continue straight on the D307 to come in just 2.5km to the village of **Torcenay**, from which you can proceed to **Chalindrey** on the D26. Since Torcenay is the first village on the next stage it is possible to bypass Chalindrey by taking this shortcut, although Chalindrey offers the most services until Champlitte.

Official route
Follow the logging road through the woods and, if it is still impenetrable, return to the D307 and continue from there to Torcenay as described above. Otherwise, continue on the logging road to arrive at an asphalt road where you turn right and follow the road downhill to the D125F in **Culmont** (**5.6km**).

(23.4KM) CULMONT (ELEV 313M, POP 580) 🔼 (**1426.9KM**)
The town was founded in the late 18th century and shares a train station with nearby Chalindrey.

🛏 **La Val Arbin**, €15/-/-/-, 19 Rue du Haut, levalarbin@gmail.com, tel +33 (0)3 25 88 50 34, equestrian farm, brkfst €6, poss of dinner snack

🛏 **À la Source du Saolon**, €-/35/50/60, 9 Rue du Haut, alasourcedusaolon@ gmail.com, tel +33 (0)3 25 88 91 61, price incl brkfst, dinner €15

Turn left on the D125F and follow it through town. Come to the end of the D125F at Rue du Sault below the Culmont-Chalindrey **train station**. Turn left on Avenue de la Gare and in one block find Rue De Mulhouse (**1.4km**). Turn right and go under the tracks to find the main services of **Chalindrey** on the Rue de la République.

(1.4KM) CHALINDREY (ELEV 330M, POP 2654) 🏨 ⊕ 🛏 🄲 ◉ ⊕ ⊕ (1425.5KM)
According to local legend, the devil, nicknamed Foulletot, lived on a nearby hill and presided in rituals with local witches and wizards. In a famous 1598 trial one of its inhabitants, Clément Rabiet, was declared a sorcerer. The trial and execution earned the town the name of 'Land of Witches.' In late October each year Chalindrey holds a Witches' Festival (www.fetedessorcieres.fr). In the 19th century Chalindrey became a railroad hub, which led to its destruction in WWII in a series of bombing raids.

🛏 Au Pied du Cognelot ⓞ ℗ℝ ℝ 𝔹𝕣 𝔻𝕣 𝕎 𝕊 rooms/beds, €-/40/50/-, 10 Rue de l'Hôtel de Ville, parodi.bruno@orange.fr, tel +33 (0)6 76 77 76 25, https://aupieducognelot.com, demi-pension avail

STAGE 40
Chalindrey to Coublanc

Start	Chalindrey, Ave de la Gare at Rue de Mulhouse
Finish	Coublanc, WWI monument
Distance	23.7km
Total ascent	372m
Total descent	448m
Difficulty	Moderately hard
Duration	6¼hr
Percentage paved	52%
Lodging	Grandchamp (on option at 14.2km), Coublanc 23.7km

The official route chooses beautiful forests rather than easy and direct asphalt roads, but in wet weather the forest trails can be tricky. If you're pressed for time or tired of forests, as much as 5.0km can be saved in asphalt shortcuts.

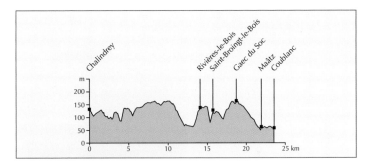

A wooden bridge crosses a small stream after Torcenay

Walk uphill on the **D26**/Rue de Mulhouse to the Rue du Maquis, just one block before the central square of **Torcenay** (**1.4km**). Turn right here, just after the non-drinkable fountain. This takes you through a neighborhood of suburban-style homes. Walk downhill and pass under the **railroad tracks**, curving right along the stream. Cross a narrow concrete **bridge** over the Salon River (here just a stream) and follow a path that begins to climb into Bussières-lés-Belmont National Forest, where you'll find yourself for much of the day.

When the path ends at a dirt road, turn right and follow it as it becomes a path leading back down to the Salon. Cross the river on a long **bridge** and continue on the narrow trail on the opposite side, watching carefully for signs that send you left and right as you zigzag your way up the hill. In wet weather be prepared to climb some steep and slippery banks.

Finally come to a dirt **logging road** where you turn left. Shortly after turn right onto a **wide gravel road**. Pass a large clearing on your left. Signs point you left alongside the clearing, but it's shorter and easier to skip the left turn. Continue until the road ends at the **D125C**, where you turn left and join the D125C shortcut option. Soon turn off the D125C onto an **asphalt road** that will carry you for the next 3km through the woods. When the road ends at another **asphalt road**, turn right to descend to the **D136**, where you turn left to come to the hamlet of **Grosse-Sauve** (**8.3km**, no services).

The site of **Grosse-Sauve** dates from Roman times when it was a stopover for travelers to and from Rome. Destroyed after the fall of Rome, by the ninth century the site was rebuilt by monks, who established an abbey here, dedicated to Saint-Nicolas. Their immense Gothic church was destroyed in the 18th century, but the choir area still stands among the farm buildings. Legends say that the devil visits the area every seven years to dance under an old tree nearby, 'Le Chêne Macabré,' which is visible from the road.

This structure is all that remains of a large church at Grosse-Sauve, destroyed in the 18th century

Turn right before the buildings and continue on asphalt back into the woods, passing a sign for the **chapel of Notre-Dame** 800 meters to the right. Emerge from the woods into fields and walk among the farm buildings of Montfricon, a tiny farm settlement. See also toward the SW the next village. The road turns to **gravel** and heads downhill through fields, turning left at an asphalt road, which curves right to cross the **Resaigne stream**.

Grandchamp shortcut/wet-weather option

To save time and the possibility of walking on muddy and difficult trails, particularly in winter, turn left in the direction of **Grandchamp** (⌂ La Vallée Verte ⊙ Pᶠ R Bᶠ Dᶠ Cᶠ W 5/12, €-/80/90/120, 8 Rue du Cul de Sac, contact@lavalleeverte.eu, tel +33 (0)6 59 81 45 64, (0)7 60 08 51 69, €28 dinner avail) to join the D122, which can connect you to **Maâtz** via the bike option on asphalt, saving 5km.

Main route

Head steeply uphill to the D17 in **Rivières-le-Bois** (**4.4km**, no services). Turn right and continue through town. Just after the WWI monument, turn left on a narrow lane between two homes. Fork left and uphill, following signs to a **two-track farm road** at the first pasture. The road heads into the woods and goes steeply downhill, becoming a wide path. Go straight and cross a **bridge** at the bottom of the vale, heading uphill on the grassy margin between two barbed-wire fences.

Turn left at a stone picnic shelter (**1.7km**) just before **Saint-Broingt-le-Bois** and traverse the hillside above the village on a grassy path. The path turns right to arrive at the **D122** asphalt road at the edge of town, where you turn left. After a left curve, turn right onto a **gravel road** toward the wooded ridge. The road climbs through woods to a plateau covered in fields. After the **Gaec du Soc livestock ranch**, fork left to continue

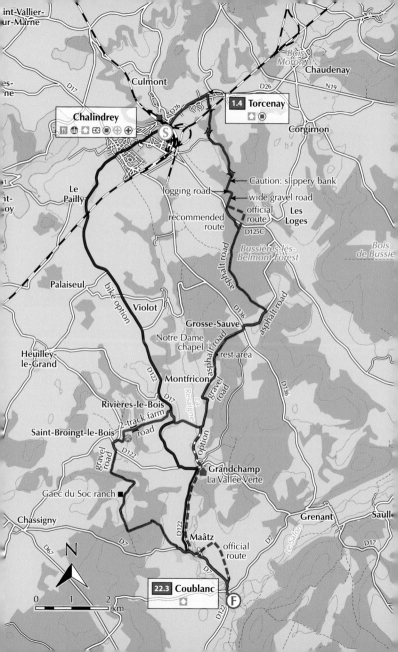

Chalindrey

1.4 Torcenay

Culmont

Saint-Vallier-sur-Marne

Chaudenay

Corgirnon

Caution: slippery bank

logging road

wide gravel road

official route

Le Pailly

recommended route

Les Loges

Bussières-lès-Belmont Forest

Bois de Bussié

Palaiseul

bike option

Violot

Grosse-Sauve

Notre Dame chapel

rest area

Heuilley-le-Grand

Montfricon

Rivières-le-Bois

2-track farm road

Saint-Broingt-le-Bois

gravel road

bike option

Grandchamp
La Vallée Verte

Gaec du Soc ranch

Chassigny

Grenant

Saulx

N

0 1 2 km

Maâtz

official route

22.3 Coublanc

F

The view over Maâtz toward Coublanc

south, heading back into the woods. Soon the road turns left and becomes a path which at its end zigzags out of the woods into fields to descend to the **D7** roadway. From the path you can see beyond Maâtz to the stage end at Coublanc.

Turn left to pass the D122 from Grandchamp, cross the Resaigne stream and come to the church and walled cemetery of **Maâtz** (**6.3km**, no services). Continue out of town on the D7 and, if you prefer to keep off asphalt, follow signs to take the left turn through fields on the official route outside town. Otherwise, continue on the quiet **D7** and, once in town, go straight onto the D122 to the WWI monument at the heart of **Coublanc** (**1.6km**).

(22.3KM) COUBLANC (ELEV 244M, POP 118)  (1401.8KM)

Documents confirm the existence of Coublanc in the 12th century when it was host to a priory. An ancient legend tells of the lord of the castle who, after returning from the Third Crusade in pilgrim garb, was not received into his own home until he presented his ring to his wife, who was scheduled to be married to another man that same day. (Bus: www.viamobigo.fr)

🏠 **Le Domaine de la Réserve**, 5/14, €-/85/100/-, 15 Route d'Arcinges, www.ledomainedelareserve.fr/contact-chambres-hote-coublanc, tel +33 (0)3 85 25 88 51, luxury spa, pool, massages, sauna, demi-pension avail, 17th-century house

SECTION 4:
BOURGOGNE-
FRANCHE-COMTÉ

The slow and easy climb up the Loue River Valley is framed by steep hills on both sides (Stage 47)

Section 4 overview

The terrain begins to change after Langres in the Haute Saône and Doubs departments of the Bourgogne-Franche-Comté region. Still agricultural, the fields begin to be replaced by pastures, and the pastures are interspersed among larger forests. Once in the Loue Valley, where granite bluffs framed by forests stand sentinel above the green valley floor, the rolling farmlands of France are behind, to be replaced by the ridges and valleys of the Jura Mountains, gateway to Switzerland.

The village of Les-Hôpitaux-Neufs is nestled in the hills of the Bief Valley (Stage 49)

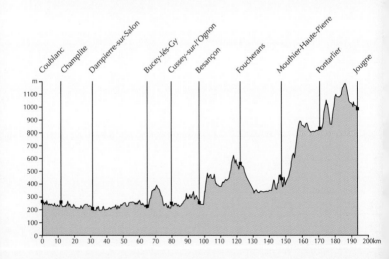

STAGE 41

Coublanc to Champlitte

Start	Coublanc, WWI monument
Finish	Champlitte, town hall
Distance	11.7km
Total ascent	151m
Total descent	156m
Difficulty	Easy
Duration	3hr
Percentage paved	41%
Lodging	Leffond 3.8km, Champlitte 11.7km

The current route finds farm roads and village streets to keep walkers off the D17 to Champlitte, and the result is a pleasant and short stage. However, in order to bring pilgrims to the château at the entry to Champlitte the route will be moved to the D17 from at least Leffond. Either way is pleasant, since the D17 is a very quiet road, and both tracks follow the green and rural Salon River.

A stone archway leads to the old mill after Leffond

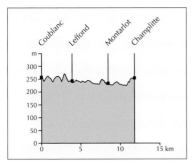

Pass the WWI monument on your right and continue on Le Village east of the D122 through town. Cross the Salon River and continue among older homes behind tall stone walls. The road comes to farm buildings where you turn right to head through another farm and then out into fields on a **two-track farm road**. Cross the Salon again and continue a slow climb with the Salon on your right and woods on your left. When it ends, turn right, cross

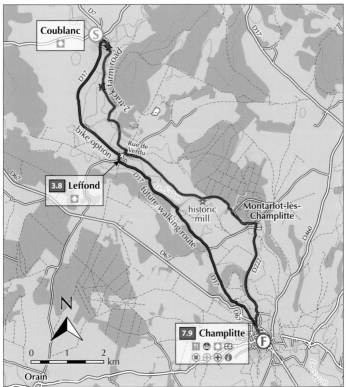

fields, and then turn left before the river. The road ends and you turn right to come in one block to the Salon bridge in **Leffond** (3.8km).

(3.8KM) LEFFOND (ELEV 235M, POP <50) ⬚ (1398.0KM)
The church's helmet-shaped **bell tower** was remodeled in 1788 and includes a carillon from 1946. (Bus: www.viamobigo.fr)

🏠 Accueil Pèlerin Associatif Ⓞ Ⓓⓞ Ⓡ Ⓚ Ⓑⓡ Ⓓⓡ Ⓢ 1/4, €18/-/-/-, 3 Rue des Bordes, bernard.gautheron777@orange.fr, tel +33 (0)7 85 21 41 73, (0)3 84 67 69 09, €28 demi-pension,

🏠 Chambre en Bordure de Rivière Ⓞ Ⓟⓡ Ⓡ Ⓑⓡ Ⓓⓡ Ⓦ Ⓢ 2/5, €-/25/40/60, 10 Rue de Verdu, ellev@orange.fr, tel +33 (0)6 65 08 95 48, €25 demi-pension

Turn left on **Rue de Verdu** before the bridge and continue through town and out to the fields. Pass a beautiful and historic **mill** (2.6km) and begin to climb to a traverse on the hillside as a curve in the river pushes the road north. As it descends, the road joins an asphalt road and then another as it curves left into the village of **Montarlot-lès-Champlitte** (2.0km). Turn right to cross the Salon River on the D222's multi-arched bridge, follow the road until it merges with the D67 (groceries) and continue left past the château to the town hall in **Champlitte** (3.3km).

(7.9KM) CHAMPLITTE (ELEV 248M, POP 1848) 🍴 ⊕ ⬚ Ⓒ ◉ ⊕ ⊕ ❶ (1390.1KM)
Champlitte's roots extend to a Gallo-Roman town at this site, and in the Middle Ages a fortified castle stood atop the hill with the village in the valley below. By the 15th century Champlitte was host to three monasteries and the **castle** had been rebuilt with a moat and sturdy walls, remnants of which can be seen in the Annonciades and Charles-Quint towers. A fire completely destroyed the medieval castle in 1751 and its current appearance dates from a late 18th-century reconstruction. In 1825 the municipality purchased the building and uses it as its **Museum of Popular Arts and Traditions** which gives an overview of rural life and farm practices (€5, open daily in summer, closed Mon/Tue otherwise). The **Via Francigena's French offices** are located in the municipal facility adjacent to the château. (Bus. www.viamobigo.fr)

🏠 Accueil Pèlerin Communal Ⓞ Ⓓⓞ Ⓡ Ⓚ Ⓑⓡ Ⓓⓡ Ⓒⓕ Ⓢ 1/4, €18/-/-/-, Rue de l'Église, gite@mairie-champlitte.fr, tel +33 (0)3 84 67 64 10, (0)6 49 40 22 66, group *gîte* avail for up to 43 people

🏠 Hotel du Donjon, €-/45/-/-, 46 Rue de la République, www.hotel-restaurant-du-donjon.com, tel +33 (0)3 84 67 66 95, brkfst €7

STAGE 42

Champlitte to Dampierre-sur-Salon

Start	Champlitte, town hall
Finish	Dampierre-sur-Salon, Rue des Charmottes at D70
Distance	19.5km
Total ascent	227m
Total descent	275m
Difficulty	Moderate
Duration	5hr
Percentage paved	51%
Lodging	Dampierre-sur-Salon 19.5km

The Salon Valley is your host once again on this stage of gently hilly farmlands and pasturelands, with peek-a-boo views to the river throughout the day. There are no services until Dampierre so plan on carrying ample food and water.

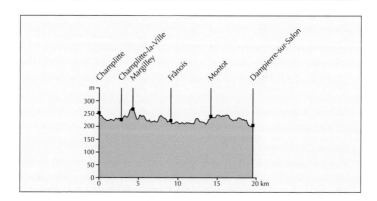

Continue past the town hall and turn left at any of the next three streets to find the D460/Avenue de la Brèche. Waiting until the third left takes you by Boulangerie Feichtinger, an excellent bakery. Follow the D460 as it crosses the **Salon**, then the D17/Route de Champlitte-la-Ville which you follow one block before turning left. Shortcut option: If the D17 is quiet, save 600 meters by continuing on it to Champlitte-la-Ville. Here the official route circumnavigates two fields before returning to the D17 at **Champlitte-la-Ville** (**2.8km**, no services).

The Church of Saint-Christophe stands at the center of Champlitte

Keep the church on your left as you head through town and uphill on the **D103**, arriving very soon to the village of **Margilley** (**1.5km**, no services). The town's wash house is a good example of such structures built throughout Europe in the 17th–19th centuries for the washing of clothes. Once in town, either turn right following the signs or turn right at the WWI monument to head south, downhill, and out of town into fields. Keep the tiny, meandering Salon on your right, following signs toward the woods on the left.

Come to the woods, but stay in the fields until finally crossing a long, narrow field into the woods. Emerge to the fields again very soon, where the road turns to asphalt and then ends. Take either fork ahead, enjoying views to Neuvelle-lès-Champlitte to the right, and continue past the cemetery to the D36 in **Frânois** (**4.7km**, no services). Turn right on the D36, cross the river, and when the road curves right at an intersection, turn left onto an **asphalt alley**. It soon becomes a gravel road that skirts along the Salon in the middle of the valley.

After a **factory building**, turn left onto the D289, but turn right on a gravel road just before re-crossing the river. Take the next fork left to cross fields and woods to the **D158**, which you briefly follow to the left before continuing in the same direction to the first road of the next town. Turn left to come to the D290/Grand Rue in **Montot** (**4.9km**, no services).

Curve to the right in the village, then continue past the **cemetery** and when the road curves left, instead go straight, making a straight shot into the fields. When this road ends at an asphalt road turn left, noting Dampierre, now on your right. At the end of this road, turn right onto **En Chenoz** and come to the D70 at the Rue des Charmottes in **Dampierre-sur-Salon** (**5.5km**). Most of the town's services are left and across the river bridges, beginning in about 500 meters (bakery, groceries).

Champlitte

19.5 Dampierre-sur-Salon

Roche-et-Raucourt

Autet

La Saône

Courtesoult-et-Gatey

Larret

bike option

En Chenoz

Rue des Charmottes

Delain

Denèvre

D36

Montot

D290

Achey

D158

Fraîois

D289

factory

gravel road

gravel road

asphalt alley

Champlitte-la-Ville

Margilley

bike option

Neuvelle-lès-Champlitte

bike option

Écuelle

Ovrières

Vars

shortcut bike option

Le Salon

N

0   1   2 km

(19.5KM) DAMPIERRE-SUR-SALON (ELEV 199M, POP 1276)
🍴 ⊕ ⌂ 🅒 ⊛ ⊕ 𝒊 (1370.6KM)

The town was a holding of the Dampierre family until the 14th century, and has long been tied to metal fabrication. It continues that heritage in a large and busy metal factory. It is birthplace of Charles Couyba (1866–1930) who managed to hold down prominent national political appointments while writing poetry like the *Chansons Rouge* under the pen name Maurice Boukay. Two channels of the Salon sluice through Dampierre, and most of its services are between their two bridges. Pilgrims will most likely remember Dampierre as the town with the incongruous steel and glass hotel (now closed) set among 300-year old stone buildings. (Bus: www.viamobigo.fr)

🛏 **Council hostel**, 1/4, €Donation, Place de l'Hôtel de Ville, mairie@dampierresursalon.fr, tel +33 (0)7 86 00 53 27

🛏 **Au Bon Vivant** 🄾 🄿🅛 🄳🄾 🅁 🄺 🄱🅛 🄳🅛 🅦 🅂 4/14, €14/65/80/90, 22 Rue des Orgevaux, christophe@desre.net, tel +33 (0)6 21 16 34 57, (0)9 80 59 81 82, brkfst incl, €23 dinner by reserv

STAGE 43
Dampierre-sur-Salon to Bucey-lès-Gy

Start	Dampierre-sur-Salon, Rue des Charmottes at D70
Finish	Bucey-lès-Gy, D185 at Rue de l'Europe
Distance	33.9km
Total ascent	382m
Total descent	368m
Difficulty	Hard (duration)
Duration	8¾hr
Percentage paved	82%
Lodging	Seveux 8.7km, Bucey-lès-Gy 33.9km

Tunnels, canals, and forests mark this soft, beautiful, and somewhat long stage. The viewpoint above the tunnel of the Savoyeux Canal before Seveux offers one of the most elegant vistas of the Via Francigena, and the asphalt road through the forest before Montbleuse is lovely, quiet and green.

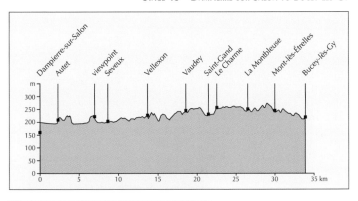

Mist rises from the pastures below Autet on an autumn morning

Back at the D70 and Rue des Charmottes, cross the road and continue on what is now called the **Rue de la Grande Ligne** as it makes its way down the Salon valley. See to the left the church steeple in the next village, and when the road ends, turn left to cross the Salon River for the final time, and come to the D2 in **Autet** (2.2km, no services). Jog right one block and continue uphill with the church on your left, now on **Vignes des Rues**. Merge with the D69 from the right and, just after the Colly-Bombled **factory**, turn right.

This **gravel road** wraps around a field, plunges steeply in a wood (bikers beware), crosses under the railroad tracks in a claustrophobic tunnel, crosses a narrow channel on a steel and wood **bridge**, then turns left to join a paved path that follows the **Saône River** upstream.

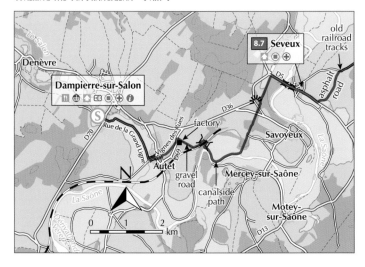

The **Saône** is one of the major tributaries of the Rhône River, which it joins in Lyon. In the next days the route crosses l'Ognon and the Doubs, both tributaries of the Saône.

Come to a lock structure and turn left to continue alongside a canal. While the canal continues through a tunnel, take the ramp and steps above the tunnel to a viewpoint, then continue on the canal's right side. Turn right at the next road, the **D5**, and follow it across the Saône's two channels into the town of **Seveux** (**6.5km**).

(8.7KM) SEVEUX-MOTEY (ELEV 198M, POP 482) 🏠 ◉ ⊕ (1361.9KM)

Sigeric noted his visit here as 'LXI Sefui,' which along with the presence of the nearby **Château de Ray** confirms its medieval origins. In 2019 Seveux was administratively joined with its neighbor, Motey. (Bus: www.viamobigo.fr)

🏠 **Gîte Rêve**, 1/2, €30/-/40/-, 1 Place de la Fourlotte, roger.varraut@orange.fr, tel +33 (0)6 06 87 00 13, https://gitereve.wixsite.com/gite-reve, two guest houses and one room with double bed. Pool, brkfst and dinner available

Continue on the D5/Grand Rue and watch for a left turn on a narrow **asphalt road** leading to fields behind the village. When the road ends, turn right at a narrow asphalt lane to cross the **disused rail tracks** and continue left in the fields, keeping the woods on your right.

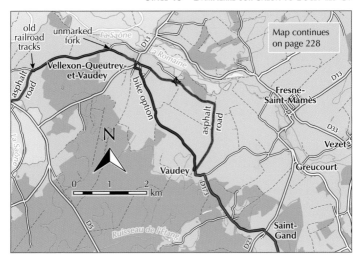

On the hillside to the left is the **Château de Ray**, an 18th-century structure built on the foundations of a powerful 10th-century castle. After 33 generations' ownership by the same noble family line the castle was given in 2015 to the Haute-Saône department (guided tours available: +33 (0)3 84 95 77 37 chateauderay@haute-saone.fr).

At an **unmarked fork** as you near the next village go right and soon arrive at the D13 in **Vellexon-Queutrey-et-Vaudey** (**5.1km**, no services). Cross the road and continue uphill. The road curves right to catch a **bridge**, after which you turn left, keeping the woods on your left. This road finally ends at an **asphalt road** where you turn right and soon see the greenhouses of the next village drawing near.

Arrive in tiny **Vaudey** (**4.6km**, no services) and turn left on the **D173** to curve with it through the village and out the opposite side in the direction of Saint-Gand. Follow the quiet asphalt D173 over a low wooded ridge to arrive in **Saint-Gand** (**3.0km**, no services). Continue into the cluster of homes and barns called **Le Charme** (**1.1km**, no services) where you turn right off the D173 in the direction of Les Frondey. After a large pasture fork left in the direction of La Montbleuse and walk on a fairly level **asphalt road** through a lovely forest. When you emerge into the fields, arrive in **La Montbleuse** (**4.2km**, no services).

Head straight through town and back into the fields, passing a children's play area with picnic tables before arriving in **Mont-lès-Étrelles** (**2.0km**, no services). Head to the bottom of the hill in the hamlet and turn left to find a path that makes its way clockwise around the Church of the Nativity of Notre-Dame. The church is

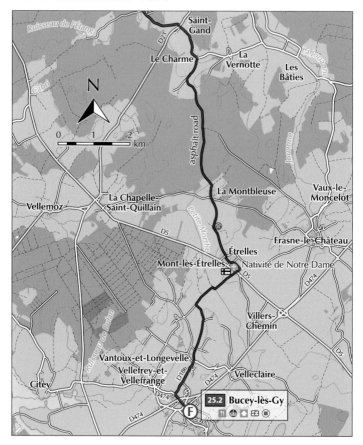

noted for its ornate marble and gilt altarpiece, unusual in the area and fabricated by itinerant Italian craftsmen in the 1730s. After the church, cross the D5 onto an asphalt road. Pass the **cemetery** on your right and cross into a wide valley of fields and farms. Partway across the fields, make a sharp left to come to the hamlet of **Vantoux-et-Longevelle** (**3.8km**, no services).

Continue straight through the hamlet as the road becomes the D186, which comes to an end at the D185 on the NW edge of **Bucey-lès-Gy**. Turn left, cross the D474 highway (café, grocery, picnic tables), and continue two blocks to the heart of town at the D12/Rue de l'Europe (**1.4km**).

(25.2KM) BUCEY-LÈS-GY (ELEV 213M, POP 610) 🏠 ⊕ 🏪 ℂ ◉ **(1336.7KM)**
Although its roots are medieval, many of Bucey's older buildings were destroyed
in wars of the 16th–17th centuries. The town was long part of the estate of the
Abbey of Corneux, part of the network of abbeys under the aegis of the Abbey of
St Martin in Laon. For this reason the area is known as 'Terre Saint-Martin.' Wine
has long been produced here, and **vineyards** abound on south-facing hillsides.
(Bus: www.viamobigo.fr)

🏠 Monts de Gy Pr Do R K Br Dr W S Z 4/12, €-/20/40/60, 7 Chemin des
   Écoliers, patrimoine70700@gmail.com, tel +33 (0)3 84 32 88 34, (0)7 82 52
   94 98, €5 brkfst, €19 demi-pension, meals by res, book >24hr adv, closed
   Nov 15–Mar 1

🏠 Chez les Domdoms, 1/3, €28/pp, 14 Rue des Esterlins, lesdomdoms@orange.
   fr, tel +33 (0)6 41 13 13 44, (0)3 84 32 95 33

STAGE 44
Bucey-lès-Gy to Cussey-sur-l'Ognon

Start	Bucey-lès-Gy, D12/Rue de l'Europe
Finish	Cussey-sur-l'Ognon, town hall
Distance	14.6km
Total ascent	278m
Total descent	250m
Difficulty	Easy
Duration	4hr
Percentage paved	63%
Lodging	Montboillon 10.4km, Cussey-sur-l'Ognon 14.6km

Enjoy a long climb on asphalt through the forest after Bucey-lès-Gy, but after
the asphalt ends the route in wet weather can be a morass of mud, mire and
mosquitoes. Afterward it's rolling hills on asphalt roads among fields into
Cussey-sur-l'Ognon.

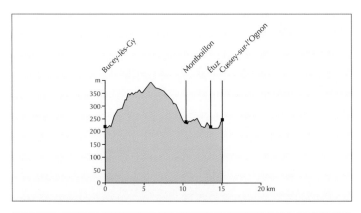

A farm road leads into the woods between Bucey-lès-Gy and Montboillon

At the D12/Rue de l'Europe veer right to take Rue du Canal through town, passing markers that direct you right onto the Camino de Santiago heading through nearby Gy. On the far side of town fork left to continue on Chemin des Écoliers, then two blocks later fork right onto **Rue de Folle** and begin to climb.

Arrive at a plateau covered in fields, then continue across a wooded ridge to a second plateau. As you continue downhill on the second plateau, turn left onto a **gravel road** (a right turn goes to Saint-Maurice) and begin a long walk through the forests of the Vallon de Fontenelay Nature Reserve.

Continue straight when an asphalt road takes off to the right, and then go right at the next fork. When the road makes a curve to the left, go straight onto a wide and **grassy path**, still in the woods. Come to a large cul-de-sac (picnic tables) and continue now on **asphalt** through the woods and wind with the road down into **Montboillon** (**10.4km**).

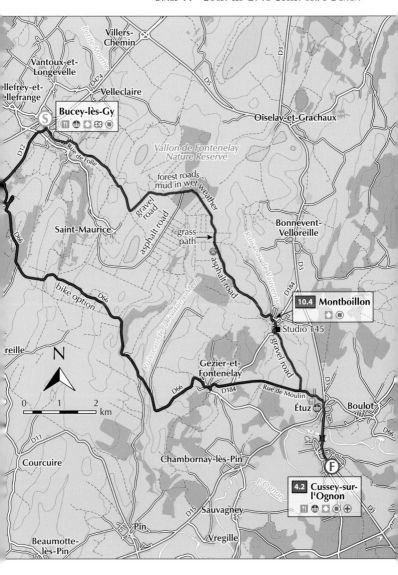

(10.4KM) MONTBOILLON (ELEV 232M, POP 263) ▲ ◉ (1326.3KM)
The hamlet sits at the joining of three valleys, not far from the Roman road that connected Besançon and Langres. (Bus: www.viamobigo.fr)

⌂ **Studio 145**, 6 Rue du Tremblois, tel +33 (0)3 84 32 44 62, (0)6 76 70 69 84

At the town's *lavoir*, turn right on Rue du Moulin, if it is not overgrown and impassible, and walk through the back side of town along the stream. Otherwise, continue past the *mairie* and turn right on the D184 to continue to the south side of the village, diverting briefly on a side street to pass the **Studio 145** gîte. Fork left just afterward on Rue du Tremblois which turns to gravel and heads into the fields. The road ends at the **Rue du Moulin** and you turn left to head uphill through suburban homes to the D3/Grand Rue in **Étuz** (**3.1km**, grocery, restaurant).

Turn right to follow the D3 across **l'Ognon River**. Either continue straight at the next fork on Rue du Village, or curve through town on the D1/Grand Rue. The two rejoin at the town hall on Rue de Besançon in **Cussey-sur-l'Ognon** (**1.1km**).

(4.2KM) CUSSEY-SUR-L'OGNON (ELEV 226M, POP 1029) �\|⅟ ⊕ ▲ ◉ ⊕
(1322.1KM)
The village appears in records beginning in 967 as 'Cussiacus,' and in Sigeric's 990 visit he called it 'LX Cuscei.' Both names derive from the Celtic word *cus* (rock). The Romans built a **bridge** here to cross the Ognon, and a **castle** soon followed to protect the bridge. In an 1870 battle of the Franco-Prussian War the Prussians were unable to take the bridge and proceed beyond. (Bus: www.via-mobigo.fr) Contact city hall for local host families: mairiedecusseysurlognon@orange.fr, +33 (0)3 81 57 78 62.

The quiet D1 road leads into Cussey-sur-l'Ognon

STAGE 45
Cussey-sur-l'Ognon to Besançon

Start	Cussey-sur-l'Ognon, town hall
Finish	Besançon, Pont Battant
Distance	17.8km
Total ascent	256m
Total descent	254m
Difficulty	Moderate
Duration	4¾hr
Percentage paved	68%
Lodging	Besançon 17.8km

A stage of woods, parks, and suburbs, with two memorable climbs and a couple of other notable ascents tossed in as you put the flatlands of France permanently in the rearview mirror. If you've walked from Bucey-lès-Gy you may find comfort in skipping the largest ridges by taking the train from the TGV station into Besançon proper, which allows more time for either an aperitif at a relaxed lunch inside La Boucle, a visit to the Victor Hugo birthplace museum, an inspection of the Roman Porte Noire, or moments of contemplation in the beautiful cathedral – or all the above in this very lovely and sophisticated regional capital set beside the Jura Mountains.

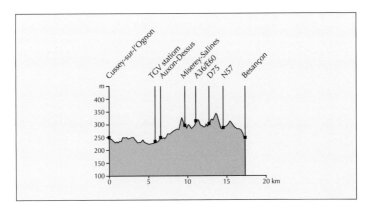

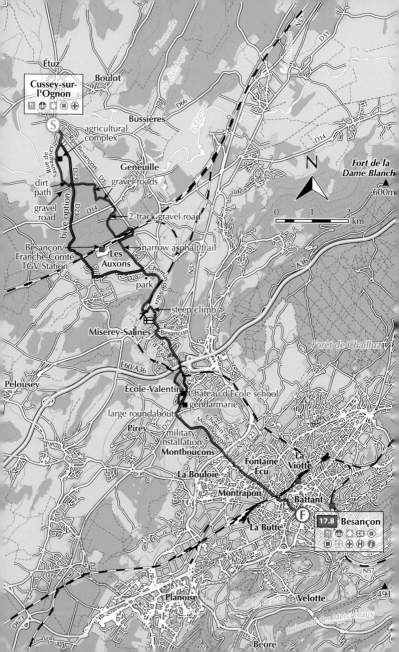

Cussey-sur-
l'Ognon

S

Étuz

BOULOT

Bussières

agricultural
complex

Geneuille

Rue de Sauvagney

Rue Besançon

D230

D14

gravel roads

dirt
path

bike option

gravel
road

2-track gravel road

Besançon/
Franche-Comté
TGV Station

Les
Auxons

narrow asphalt trail

D287

Chemin de Saux

park

steep climb

Miserey-Salines

Rue de
Besançon

N57

Pelousey

E60/A36

La Tournaille

Rie du Maroy

D66

L'Ognon

D14

Fort de la
Dame Blanch

600m

N

0   1   2
|___|___|___|___| km

A36

N57

D31

Forêt de Chailluz

École-Valentin

Château d'École school
gendarmerie

large roundabout

Pirey

military
installation

Montboucons

La Bouloie

Chemin de Montboucon

D323

Montrapon

Fontaine
Écu

La
Viotte

Battant

F

17.8 Besançon

La Butte

Planoise

Velotte

N57

491

Beure

Le Doubs

Ruisseau des Mercureaux

From the town hall, continue on the D1/Rue Besançon and fork right immediately onto the D230. When the D230 curves left, go straight onto **Rue de Sauvagney** instead, heading downhill through a neighborhood and continuing as you are again in the fields. Fork left after an agricultural complex and begin uphill through fields, heading toward a wooded ridge.

The road ends and you turn left onto a narrow **dirt path**, which ends 200 meters later at a **gravel road**, where you turn left. Still in the woods, cross another asphalt road and almost immediately go left onto a path that continues east. As you near the sounds of the D1 beyond, turn right and the path becomes a gravel road. Take a new path on the left, then fork right onto a gravel road. This leads to the **D14** roadway, which you cross to continue on a **two-track gravel road**.

Pass a reservoir on your right, followed by a gravel road which ends at the fences of the TGV rail tracks across from the Gare Besançon Franche-Comté TGV station. Turn left to cross over the **tracks** and then right afterward to walk toward the station alongside the access road. Come to a **narrow asphalt trail** before the TGV station's first parking lot (**5.9km**).

> The **station** is 1.1km directly ahead, has a café and WC, and has connections to the entire French TGV and regular rail system, including hourly trains for the 15-minute €5 ride to Besançon Viotte station, which is near the route at the entrance to the city.

Turn left onto the asphalt trail which heads through woods and then becomes a street in the Besançon suburb of **Les Auxons**. Cross the D287 to come to the *mairie*, and then turn right after the church to walk through a park, finding the **Chemin de Vaux**, a narrow asphalt road leading uphill. The road curves right and then becomes a wide path below rail tracks, continuing its ascent through woods. Cross a **bridge** over the tracks and turn left to go around a field to climb a very steep ridge between pastures. Turn right to pass a **cemetery**, going left afterward and downhill on Rue de l'Ancien Couvent, where few signs remain of the ancient convent.

Arrive at the D5/**Rue de Besançon** in suburban **Miserey-Salines** (**4.2km**, no services), where you turn right, passing the village church, and in two blocks turn left on **Rue d'Ecole** to continue downhill. This street heads down to the bottom of town and then back up on the other side, ending on the back side of a large supermarket. Across Rue des Salines is a friendly hamburger restaurant, and uphill beyond that is the **E60/A36 motorway**, which you pass under.

Almost at the top of the hill, turn right onto a wide pathway for pedestrians that heads into the woods for your last sylvan encounter before urban Besançon. Cross a gravel path, go through a pedestrian gate, and go left and downhill toward the historic *lavoir*. Walk over the low retaining wall to catch a path leading through a narrow field below the **Château d'École school**. Come to an asphalt street and turn left, winding your way toward a roundabout with the D108 across from the **Gendarmerie Nationale**.

Continue right on the D108 and at the **large roundabout** that follows take the second left in the direction of Besançon, heading uphill on a wide asphalt road that passes a **military installation**. You now stay almost continually straight all the way into central Besançon, first on **Chemin des Montboucons**, where you cross the N57/E23 motorway and pass through the technology neighborhood of Besançon.

After crossing above the train tracks come to a traffic ellipse where you go two blocks left to pass through a gap in the old city's outer walls to the right. Come in just one block to a three-way intersection and take the second right onto Rue des Frères Mercier through an old neighborhood of

Pedestrian return to the Besançon's streets after a brief rain shower

closely spaced buildings, many with street-level shops and restaurants. At the bottom of the hill you have arrived at Église Sainte-Madeleine and, just beyond, the Doubs River and **Pont Battant** (**7.6km**). Besançon's old quarter, 'La Boucle,' with its shops and plazas is just beyond, along with the cathedral and, above everything, the historic citadel.

(17.8KM) BESANÇON (ELEV 242M, POP 128,426) 🛏 🚊 🛌 🄲 🍴 ⊛ ⊕ ⊕ 🄷 ℹ
(1304.3KM)

The Francigena's topography changes dramatically at Besançon, which is located at the junction of the wide plains and rolling hills of France's agricultural regions and the Jura Mountains, the craggy bulwark between France and Switzerland. The old town is crowded into a loop or *boucle* (buckle) of the Doubs River, and above it all is a stone citadel designed to provide an impenetrable defense of France's eastern flank. Julius Caesar called the city '*Vesontionem*' in his Gallic Wars, and noted it was the largest Celtic settlement in the area. The Romans built an amphitheater here, as well as city walls, of which the AD175 **Porte Noire** gate is all that remains. The city fell first to the Burgundians and then to the Franks in late antiquity. It was part of the kingdom of Upper Burgundy when Sigeric visited here ('LIX Bysiceon'), and later was part of the Habsburg Empire. Besançon was conquered in 1674 by the army of Louis IV, who commissioned architect and military strategist Sébastien Vauban to construct its battlements in order to ensure it would remain in French hands.

Among Besançon's famous sons and daughters are Auguste and Louis Lumière, inventors of the film projector, and esteemed author Victor Hugo (1802–85) of *Les Misérables* and *The Hunchback of Notre Dame* fame. Besançon expanded in the mid 20th century and its suburbs spread mostly toward its west side, but its charm remains within La Boucle. Any sampling of the city's delights should include a walk across the Pont Battant, a relaxed stroll among the shops of the Grande-Rue, and then a sidewalk coffee in one of the many squares. A walk further uphill to the SE takes you to Castan Square, the birthplace of Victor Hugo (https://maisonvictorhugo.besancon.fr/en/), the site of the beautiful **Cathedral of Saint-Jean and the Roman Porte Noire**. (Bus: www.viamobigo.fr; train through Viotte station to link to France's nearby TGV network: www.sncf.com)

⌂ **Maison Mazagran**, 1/2, €25/-/-/-, 64 Chemin de Mazagran, maisonmazagran@free.fr, tel +33 (0)6 87 78 68 45, brkfst €7, pool in season, no meals

⌂ **Espace Grammont**, €-/27/-/-, 20 Rue de Megevand, accueil-cd@ centrediocesain-besancon.fr, tel +33 (0)3 81 25 17 17, www. espacegrammont.fr, brkfst, €2, demi-pension €11, diocesan retreat house, call in the morning for a space that evening

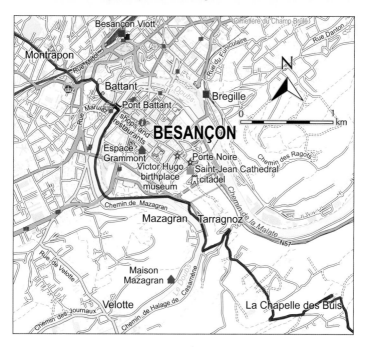

STAGE 46
Besançon to Foucherans

Start	Besançon, Pont Battant
Finish	Foucherans, town hall
Distance	25.7km
Total ascent	696m
Total descent	380m
Difficulty	Moderately hard
Duration	7hr
Percentage paved	56%
Lodging	Saône 14.0km, Foucherans 25.7km

The stage begins with an easy riverside walk around La Boucle, and then after one colossal climb you are catching your breath while enjoying the views over Besançon from La Chapelle des Buis and the Monument de la Libération. After a quick descent the route leads on gravel roads through marshes and woods to tiny Foucherans.

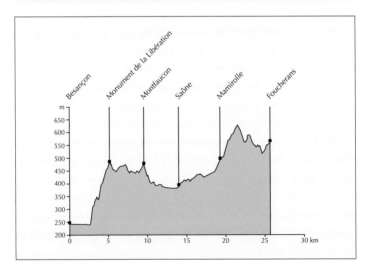

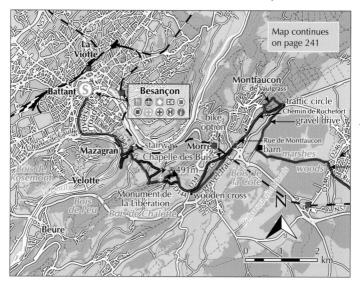

Cross the Pont Battant over the Doubs River and immediately turn right onto the **riverside road**. Head down to the riverside path and follow it around Le Boucle through parks and alongside battlement towers, passing under first the **D683**, then the Boulevard Charles de Gaulle. At the south side, the path comes alongside the D683; soon afterward turn right onto a narrow bridge.

Pass alongside a lock system and then continue on a bike path alongside the roadway. After a pedestrian bridge that crosses to the right over the river, watch for signs pointing you left, across the road, to a very steep asphalt road heading up the steep ridge. The road ends and you continue up a long **stairway** that leads to the next road, where you turn left and then switchback right to follow the road uphill. From here you can now see the back side of the citadel walls.

Follow signs uphill toward La Chapelle des Buis on the roadway or on the shortcut paths and stairways that cut off the long auto road loop. Arrive at the **chapel** itself to enjoy excellent views and a tour of the structure (**4.7km**). The village, named for the 17th-century chapel and the boxwood (buis) that covers the mountainside, was a sanctuary for resistance against secularization in the French Revolution. ⌂ **La Chapelle des Buis**, €Donation, 89 Chemin de la Chapelle des Buis, franciscainsdesbuis@gmail.com, tel +33 (0)3 81 81 33 25, www.chapelledesbuis.org/via-francigena.

After the chapel it's possible to follow the D144 roadway downhill, though it's much more interesting and inspiring to turn left and follow signs up through the woods to the viewpoint and church at the **Monument de la Libération** (**0.4km**).

During WWII the Archbishop of Besançon promised to build a **chapel** if the city was not ravaged by bombing. True to his word when the city was spared, in 1949 this crypt chapel and monumental statue of the Virgin and child were dedicated on the site of 19th-century battlements. The solitude and spectacular views make the viewpoint a favorite of local citizens.

After viewing the monument, return to the driveway and take a path to the left that descends steeply before finding a gentler gravel path that merges onto the **D144**. Go left on the roadway, heading downhill. At the next intersection fork right onto a gravel track beside a **wooden cross** and then fork left onto a wide path to begin a fairly flat traverse of the ridge in a NE direction under trees.

Keep straight along the top of this low ridge, crossing a gully and again finding the ridgetop path. The path becomes a farm driveway before it joins a road from the right. When the road ends, turn right on **Rue de Montfaucon**. The route ultimately lies directly across the valley, but the maze of busy arterials makes it necessary to continue NE

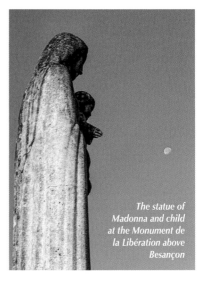

The statue of Madonna and child at the Monument de la Libération above Besançon

into the lower neighborhoods of **Montfaucon** before doubling back on the valley's opposite side. Continue left as this street comes to the D146 and then immediately fork right onto **Chemin de Rochefort** (bread vending machine).

When the road ends, make a sharp left to go uphill, where after a home on the right you see two trailheads. Take the first trail, marked '**Chemin de Vaulgras**,' leading downhill. The path curves right and descends among deep ruts until coming out of the woods at a **traffic circle**. Keep the roundabout on your left as you cross two roads, turning right after the second to find a **gravel drive** running parallel to the roadway.

Now on the east side of the valley, follow this road among pastures and fields. After passing the farm buildings of a small settlement, turn left to cross the fields and enter the **marshes and woods** beyond. In season, the local wildlife don camouflage gear with orange vests and line up in shelters along this road to be warily observed by the marsh's avian residents. The road turns to asphalt and then ends at Rue de la Fontaine in **Saône (8.9km)**.

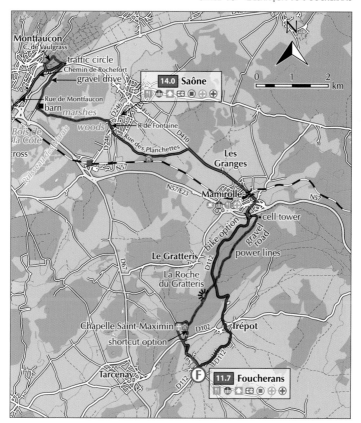

(14.0KM) SAÔNE (ELEV 391M, POP 2838) 🍴 ⊕ 🛏 🅲 ◉ ⊕ ⊕ **(1290.3KM)**
The name 'Saône' comes from the Celtic *sag* (sacred) and *onna* (water) and refers
to the waters of the marsh that were said to disappear suddenly at divine will. The
marsh contains remnants of the Roman road likely used by Caesar, Sigeric, and
many others to travel to Besançon and beyond.

🏠 **Les Marais**, 5/12, €-/55/60/-, 4 Grande-Rue, brasserielesmarais@laposte.net,
   tel +33 (0)3 81 55 70 64, www.le-comtois-les-marais-saone.fr

Turn right here and soon cross the **D246**/Avenue de la Gare onto **Rue des Planchettes**, which curves SE and uphill out of town into the fields. The asphalt road nestles up against the woods as it curves left, then ends at the **D410**, where you turn right. Pass through the hamlet of **Les Granges** and continue on to cross under the train tracks, continue up a flight of steps and come to the end of the road in **Mamirolle** (**5.2km**, groceries, restaurants, pharmacy, train). ⌂ Au Doubs Cocon Fleuri ▣ ▣ ▣ ▣ ▣2/4, €60/person incl brkfst, 36 Grand Rue, Florence.berthalamy@orange.fr, tel +33 (0)6 16 96 26 32, (0)6 26 02 52, dinner tray €12.

Turn right onto the D112/Rue de l'Église, which passes the Church of Saint-Pierre, before curving left to cross over the **N57/E23 motorway**. Just after the motorway, turn left and go uphill on Chemin du Mont, turning right just before a **cell tower** onto a gravel road that climbs the ridge steeply at first and then becomes a serene and beautiful forested path. After crossing the motorway it is also possible simply to continue on the quiet D112 to avoid the steep climb.

Cross under **powerlines** and descend to the familiar **D112** road, which you cross to continue on the path. Come to an optional viewpoint at **La Roche du Gratteris** for a scenic overlook to the valley you've just crossed, or continue on the path until it ends at a road. A left turn allows a slightly quicker entry to Foucherans, but a right turn carries you on a loop across the field to the 18th-century **Chapel of Saint-Maximin** (picnic tables), a quiet hermitage tucked between the field and forest.

> Pilgrimage to this site, dedicated to **Saint-Maximin of Trier**, began sometime after his death in AD346. According to legend, Maximin's pack animal was killed by a bear, who the saint then tamed as the pack animal's replacement to carry his pack to Rome. With the decline in pilgrimage in the 18th century the chapel was demolished and the disputed relics of the saint were transferred to the Foucherans church. It was rebuilt in 1866 and renovated in 1995.

Either route heads south to the **D102**, which you cross to pass the church and gîte, then end at the D112 and town hall in **Foucherans** (**6.5km**).

(11.7KM) FOUCHERANS (ELEV 559M, POP 343) ▣ ⊕ ▣ ▣ ◉ ⊕ ⊕ (1278.6KM)
Along with its proximity to the St Maximin Chapel, the area is home to **dolmen stones** set in the woods and likely part of pre-Roman spiritual practice. (Bus: www.viamobigo.fr)

⌂ Gîte d'Etape de Foucherans 25 ▣ ▣ ▣ ▣ ▣ ▣ 3/14, €20/20/40/60, 16 Rue de l'Église, gite.etape.foucherans25@gmail.com, tel +33 (0)6 84 27 04 67, closed Nov–Mar, group rates, €3 brkfst

STAGE 47

Foucherans to Mouthier-Haute-Pierre

Start	Foucherans, town hall
Finish	Mouthier-Haute-Pierre, Church of Saint-Laurent
Distance	25.5km
Total ascent	297m
Total descent	423m
Difficulty	Moderate
Duration	6¾hr
Percentage paved	67%
Lodging	Ornans 11.5km, Montgesoye 15.7km, Vuillafans 19.1km, Lods 23.2km, Mouthier-Haute-Pierre 25.5km

A former railroad route brings you down into the lovely Loue River valley, whose granite bluffs among forested ridges offer delightful vistas. The area is justifiably loved by weekend auto tourists, which means the route offers plentiful tourist-oriented services. Note that options for food and lodging gradually decrease as the valley slowly climbs toward the river's mountainous source. While history buffs may grumble, the Francigena can be excused for departing Sigeric's itinerary here, since the archbishop traveled on a less-scenic route through Nods (now Les Premiers-Sapins) as his stage 'LVIII Nos.'

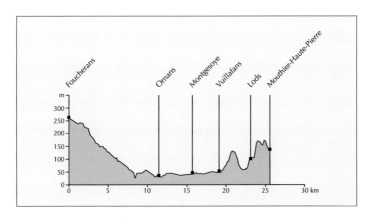

Turn right onto the D112/Rue de la Mairie, and then make an immediate left onto Rue de Bonnevaux, heading toward the village **church**. Continue downhill and out of town, forking right onto an asphalt road after a pasture. After the driveway of a **large farm**, fork left. This road now heads gradually downhill among wide pastures with distant views to the low ridges ahead.

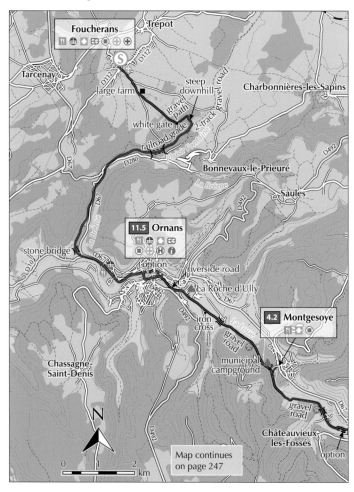

Map continues on page 247

Come to the forest, which you enter after passing through a **white gate**. In 250 meters turn left onto a wide and straight **gravel path**, which dips down a steep hill, then make a hard right turn to continue downhill more gradually. At a **two-track road**, turn right to begin a long traverse of the ridge above the north bank of the Plaisir Fontaine stream. Because of the very easy grade you soon realize you are on an old **railroad grade**, heading gradually downhill. Pass through a 180-meter-long tunnel as you curve right, now in the Brême River valley.

Cross the **D280** roadway and then the **D67**, heading gradually downhill on this scenic and gentle descent. Cross over a monumental, tall **stone bridge** just before the confluence of the Brême and Loue rivers, and continue on the railroad right-of-way alongside the D67 to a roundabout among big-box retail stores at the edge of Ornans (**9.3km**, groceries, restaurant). Cross the road to continue on the left side of the D67, which you can follow directly to the D492 in central **Ornans** (**2.1km**). By forking left off the D492 onto Rue des Chazeaux you can save a few meters and miss a blind curve in the road. However, the official route skips central Ornans by turning right on Avenue Général de Gaulle to cross the Loue and then turns left to take the **D492** along the south side of the river.

(11.5KM) ORNANS (ELEV 328M, POP 4385) 🍴 ⊕ 🛏 🄲 ⊚ ⊕ 🄷 ❶ **(1267.1KM)**
Ornans is the largest town of the recreational and touristic Loue Valley and one of its most scenic. Houses set virtually in the river and its location in Franche-Comté earn it the nickname 'Comtoise Venice.' River activities like whitewater sports and fishing are key in the local economy. The painter Gustave Courbet (1819–77) was born here, and his birthplace houses the **Gustave Courbet Departmental Museum** and nearly 50 of his works, many depicting local scenes (€6, off-season closed Tues, www.musee-courbet.fr). (Bus: www.viamobigo.fr)

🛏 L'Atelier du Peintre `Pr` `R` `Br` `Dr` `W` `S` 3/7, €-/60/80/-, 37 Place Courbet, latelierdupeintrornans@gmail.com, tel +33 (0)6 33 69 64 99, brkfst €8, demi-pension €20, closed Jan/Feb

🛏 Au Sanglier qui Fume `Pr` `Do` `R` `K` `Br` `Dr` `S` `Z` 3/6, €15/15/30/45, 5 Chemin dit de la Tuilerie, padramonesdu25@gmail.com, tel +33 (0)7 71 62 35 80, (0)9 87 88 52 28, €5 brkfst, demi-pension €25, shuttle to/from path, closed Nov–Mar

🛏 La Table de Gustave, €-/63/86/-, seasonal, 11 Rue Jacques Gervais, reservation@latabledegustave.fr, tel +33 (0)3 21 27 15 02, brkfst €10

From the D67 and the D492 in central Ornans, go south across the Loue River bridge where the official route rejoins and turn left to continue on the **riverside road**. The rest of the stage continues up the scenic Loue Valley, marked by limestone cliffs set amid forests on either side, with green pastures and fields along the river. Continue out

A graceful stone bridge spans the Loue River at Montgesoye

of town, overlooking a campground on the left, and forking left at an **iron cross**. When this asphalt road turns left, go straight instead onto a **gravel road** where you cross a stream and begin to climb almost imperceptibly.

A curve of the river below forces the road to hug the woods and mountainside; before coming to the next town, pass a campsite, join a narrow asphalt road and come to a bridge leading left and across the river into the village of **Montgesoye (4.2km)**.

(4.2KM) MONTGESOYE (ELEV 340M, POP 472) 🍴 🏕 ◉ (1262.9KM)

Records indicate establishment of the Châteauvieux (old castle) near Vuillafans at the end of the ninth century, and from there the Lords of Montgesoye exercised their dominion over the entire Loue Valley. (Bus: www.viamobigo.fr)

🏠 **Host Family Souvet**, 6 Rue de la Cascade, souvet.laurence@orange.fr, tel +33 (0)6 07 15 34 75, (0)3 81 62 14 87

Continue, back on the east side of the river, where the road soon turns to gravel as it continues up the valley. The road branches into two separate tracks, with the left better maintained for wet weather, and then curves south to pass a small park (picnic tables) and cross the Raffenot creek and enter a neighborhood of red-roofed homes on the outskirts of Vuillafans. Although it is possible to continue straight at Rue de la Gare

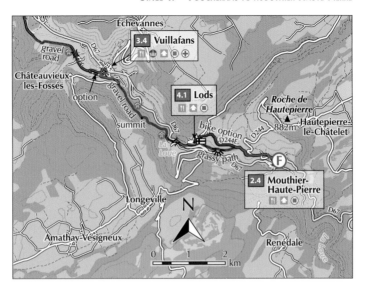

and skip the center of town, the services make it worthwhile to fork left onto Chemin les Chenevières and cross the Loue into the center of town, where you turn right on the D67 to come in one block to the Church of the Assumption in **Vuillafans (3.4km)**.

(3.4KM) VUILLAFANS (ELEV 347M, POP 695) (1259.5KM)

Once a major wine center, **vineyards** were removed during the phylloxera crisis of the 1800s. The current vines have been replanted only in the last 40 years. The town's 13th-century **Châteauneuf** stood above town and across the river from Châteauvieux and its ruins are visible from the D27 highway. (Bus: www. viamobigo.fr)

⌂ **Hostel de la Tuffière**, 10/35, from €52, 1 Chemin de Montgesoye, latuffiere2@wanadoo.fr, tel +33 (0)3 81 60 96 76, (0)6 16 61 81 78, www. latuffiere.com, incl demi-pension

⌂ Accueil Pèlerin **Pr R Br Dr W S** 2/4, €contact, 1 Rue Saint-Claude, solangecardeur@orange.fr, tel +33 (0)6 79 27 31 54, (0)3 81 60 91 42, demi-pension €30

Return to the south bank of the Loue by turning left to cross the old stone bridge, and veer right onto Rue Saint-Claude to find Rue de la Gare. Cross the street and fork left onto the D27/Rue du Vieux Château, which climbs gradually with views back toward town. When the road makes a hairpin right turn, go straight onto a **gravel road** heading more steeply uphill through the woods. This mountain-bike route climbs through the woods, passing a rest area and then coming to a **summit** before heading back toward the valley floor.

Pass a campground to the sounds of cascading water, and then turn left to cross the river on a metal **bridge** and right on the D67 on the opposite bank. Fork left soon afterward and head steeply uphill on a narrow asphalt road, passing the town's **cemetery** on your left. Come to the D32/Route d'Athose in **Lods** (4.1km).

(4.1KM) LODS (ELEV 400M, POP 283) 🍴 🏕 ⊚ **(1255.4KM)**
Houses cling to the mountainside in this tiny, ancient village closely associated with production of wines in past centuries. (Bus: www.viamobigo.fr)

🏠 **Hotel de France**, 1 Place de Pezard, www.hoteldefrancelods.com, tel +33 (0)3 81 60 95 29, demi-pension avail

Turn right on the D32 in this charming village of stone homes and then turn left onto Rue de l'Eglise. The domed, limestone, 18th-century church has an elaborate golden altarpiece and carved pulpit. Just after the church, turn right on a narrow lane that quickly becomes a **grassy path** along the terraced mountainside. The path turns to gravel and steeply ascends to a **viewpoint** with a sweeping view of the valley and mountains beyond.

When the path ends at the **D244E** paved road, turn right to begin the descent to Mouthier, which is nestled at the base of dramatic gray and yellow limestone cliffs. Fork left on the Rue Pavée once in town to come to the tall-steepled Church of Saint-Laurent in **Mouthier-Haute-Pierre** (2.4km).

The Church of Saint-Laurent in Mouthier-Haute-Pierre

(2.4KM) MOUTHIER-HAUTE-PIERRE (ELEV 432M, POP 358) 🍴 🏠 ◉
(1253.0KM)

Mouthier is at the upper end of the Loue Valley and serves as end of the stage not because of its services, which are thin, but because it is a threshold to what comes next – the steep climb to the river's source and then the plateau above. The town's name derives from its history as site of a monastery, cited in records as early as 870. It is a meticulously well-maintained and picturesque village, worthy of a quiet evening stroll. The 14th-century **Church of St-Laurent** is made even more photogenic by its backdrop: a sheer, granite cliff. (Bus: www.viamobigo.fr)

🔺 **Gîte La Vigneronne** ◉ Pr R Br Dr S 3/5, €-/35/60/-, 26 Grande Rue, r.lebris@orange.fr, tel +33 (0)6 79 53 10 28, demi-pension €20 or brkfst €5 with 48hr notice

🔺 **La Cascade Hotel/Restaurant**, 18/30, €-/-/78/130, 4 Route des Gorges de Nouailles, hotellacascade@wanadoo.fr, +33 (0)3 81 60 95 30, www.hotel-lacascade.fr

STAGE 48
Mouthier-Haute-Pierre to Pontarlier

Start	Mouthier-Haute-Pierre, Church of Saint-Laurent
Finish	Pontarlier, Rue de la Gare at Rue de la République
Distance	23.7km
Total ascent	679m
Total descent	279m
Difficulty	Hard (terrain and climb)
Duration	6½hr
Percentage paved	60%
Lodging	Ouhans 8.1km, Pontarlier 23.7km

The unforgettable 200m climb on forest paths alongside the cascading Loue to its source is one of the Via Francigena's most beautiful experiences. Just afterward is the austere Chapelle Notre-Dame at Ouhans, set on a mound among the hills. A wide farm valley in the throes of industrialization greets you before Doubs and Pontarlier. Foot gear with a good grip is important on the forest path.

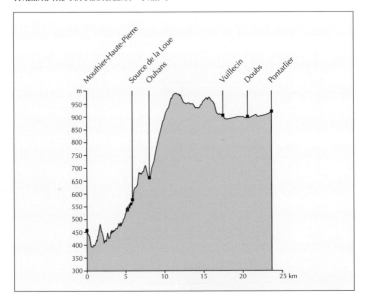

Head downhill from the church on Rue du Chapite and arrive at the D67. Turn left and immediately fork right at the small store and post office, heading downhill. As the street curves left, take the stairway to the right, and then merge left onto the asphalt Rue des Moulins. Looking to the terrain ahead you can see the saddle between two sides of the valley; crossing it is the next goal. Come alongside the Loue and pass an old **watermill**.

Pass through a gate (picnic tables) and continue uphill on the wide gravel path that climbs in switchbacks. Come to a road which you follow downhill to cross to a **hydroelectric facility** with large sluice pipes above. Cross a bridge beyond the generator facility and then begin a long climb up the opposite

A forest path leads uphill toward the Source de la Loue

250

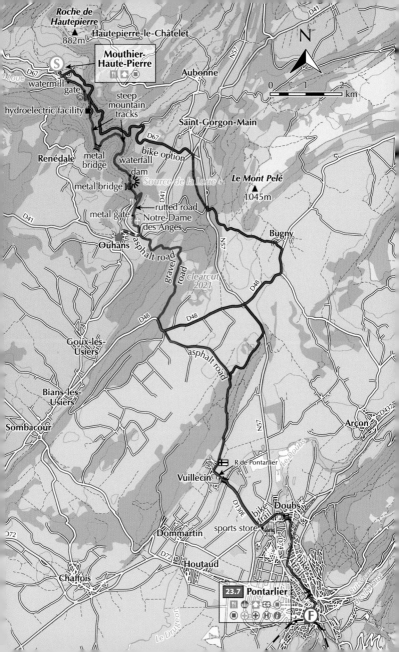

N

0   1   2
km

Roche de Hautepierre
▲ 882m

Hautepierre-le-Châtelet

Mouthier-Haute-Pierre

S

watermill
gate

steep
mountain
tracks

hydroelectric facility ■

Aubonne

Saint-Gorgon-Main

D67

bike option

Le Mont Pelé
▲ 1045m

Renédale

metal
bridge

waterfall
dam

Source de la Loue

metal bridge

D41

rutted road

Notre-Dame
des Anges

metal gate

Ouhans

asphalt road

gravel
road

*clearcut
2021*

Bugny

D48

D41

D48

D48

asphalt road

Goux-les-Usiers

Bians-les-Usiers

Sombacour

N57

Arçon

D437

R de Pontarlier

Vuillecin

bike
trail

Doubs

sports store

D72

D72

D130E

Dommartin

Houtaud

Chaffois

23.7 **Pontarlier**

F

D72

N57

N57

N57

bank of the river. The trail is a **steep mountain track** over roots and rocky outcroppings where surefootedness and agility are critical.

Come to the dam and powerhouse at the foot of a dramatic, horseshoe-shaped cliff of 150m in height. The headwaters of the Loue River spring from the base of the cliff and begin their descent toward the Rhône River and ultimately the Mediterranean Sea. Take the sidewalk uphill, which you realize as you walk serves double duty as a floodway when necessary for cascading waters from above. Spaced along the left are small refuge stations in case of sudden inundation. Soon come to parking lot, gift shop and café at Chalet de la Loue (**6.4km**, closed Dec, Jan, Feb).

Continue climbing on the path behind the café where you fork right, heading to Notre-Dame des Anges. Soon turn right on a **rutted road** that carries you through the woods and, after a **metal gate**, out into the fields. To the right is the village of Ouhans, and, on the low, grassy hill ahead is the 10-sided neo-Gothic chapel of **Notre-Dame des Anges**, which you can reach either by cutting across the field or continuing straight on the road.

> The **chapel** was completed in 1875 in gratitude for preservation of the nearby village. Inside, each wall is adorned with the statue of an angel, while over the wall opposite the entry there is a statue of the Virgin Mary.

Continue south, coming to the **D41** roadway (**1.6km**). A right turn here would take you in 600 meters to Ouhans (🏠 **Host Family Salomon**, €30/-/-/-, 9 Rue des Fuves, jean.salomon@orange.fr tel +33 (0)6 48 74 18 09, €5 linens). To continue on the main route, cross the D41 and go straight on an **asphalt road** among pastures. When the road goes left, continue straight up the hill toward woods, which you enter for a long, sustained climb on asphalt.

Pass through another pasture and when the road curves left, fork right onto **gravel** to continue the ascent through an extensive logging operation, with areas that were clearcut in 2021. Arrive at the **D48** roadway (**3.9km**) and turn left, finally reaching the summit. Follow the quiet D48 downhill and as you emerge from the woods arrive at an intersection with two roads. Take the second left that leads between two broad meadows toward the forested ridge on the opposite side.

Remain on the **asphalt road** as you climb through the woods. On the way down, see the town of Vuillecin straight ahead, Lake Le Moray to your immediate left, and the tall steeple of the Church of the Assumption in Doubs across the fields on your far left. Continue straight, passing the **cemetery** on your left, and arrive at Rue de Pontarlier in **Vuillecin** (**5.5km**, no services).

Turn left, pass the town hall (bread vending machine) and cross Le Drudgeon, a channelized stream at the valley floor. Continue now on the sidewalk-free **D130E** to cross this wide valley with a uneasy mix of pastures, farm buildings and factories. Come to an immense roundabout across from a shopping center (sports store, restaurants, groceries) which you follow clockwise to cross the E23/N57 and pick up a **bike lane** along the D130. Continue across the D74 onto the Rue du Petit Saint-Claude

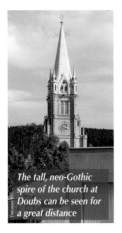

The tall, neo-Gothic spire of the church at Doubs can be seen for a great distance

and either continue across the Doubs River to a right turn on the Rue de l'Église, or follow the signs to turn right at the Rue du Puits and cross the Doubs on a pedestrian bridge to the Rue de l'Église, skipping the monumental church in **Doubs** (3.1km, restaurants, bar, bakery).

Turn right on Rue de l'Église and follow it to the Rue de la Chaussée, where you turn right to continue on sidewalks and then a **bike trail** as the road loosely follows the course of the Doubs. Curve left to pass a soccer pitch and turn right to cross the next bridge over the Doubs to continue following the river on the opposite bank. Curve toward downtown on the Rue de la Fontaine, which becomes Quai du Petit Cours before ending at the D437/Rue de la Gare. Turn right to arrive at Rue de la République in the center of **Pontarlier** in two blocks (3.1km).

(23.7KM) PONTARLIER (ELEV 828M, POP 20,313) 🍴 �] 🏠 🏧 ⊚ ⊙ ⊕ ⊕ 🏥 ⓘ
(1229.3KM)

Pontarlier lies on the ancient road between Orbe and Besançon, so it is little wonder that Sigeric stopped here in 990 as Stage 'LVII Punterlin.' The town was built by Gauls at this important location on the Doubs River, foot of the easiest climb over the Jura Mountains until other roads through the mountains were built in the 17th century. Pontarlier's economy in the 19th century was based on the production of the liquor absinthe, developed here by Henri Louis Pernod in 1805. At one time its 20 **distilleries** employed over 3000 people. Due to concerns about the liquor's safety (as well as complaints by the wine industry), 'the Green Fairy' was banned in France and other countries and was only reintroduced in 2001. Pontarlier also appears in Victor Hugo's *Les Misérables* as the city to which Jean Valjean was to report after his parole. Today the city's center is the eight-block Rue de la République, which begins at the **Port Saint-Pierre** and ends at the river. A 15th-century mansion houses the **Municipal Museum** which hosts exhibits about the city's history, its prized beverage, and pieces of art including a self-portrait of Gustave Courbet (€4.20, 2 Place d'Arçon, +33 (0)3 81 38 82 16). (Bus: www.viamobigo.fr)

🛏 **Auberge de Jeunesse** 〚Pr〛〚Do〛〚R〛〚K〛〚Bf〛〚Dr〛〚Cf〛〚S〛〚Z〛 23/80, €25/41/55/71 21 Rue Marpaud, pontarlier@hifrance.org, tel +33 (0)3 81 39 06 57, www.hifrance. org/auberge-de-jeunesse/pontarlier.html, brkfst €6, closed early Nov

🛏 **La Maison d'À Côté** 〚O〛〚Pr〛〚R〛〚Cf〛〚W〛〚S〛 2/4, €-/85/100/115 11 Rue Jules Mathez, arlette.laude@orange.fr, tel +33 (0)6 87 84 09 11, www.lamaison-da-cote.fr

STAGE 49
Pontarlier to Jougne

Start	Pontarlier, Rue de la République
Finish	Jougne, town hall
Distance	23.1km
Total ascent	641m
Total descent	494m
Difficulty	Moderately hard (climb)
Duration	6¼hr
Percentage paved	50%
Lodging	La Cluse-et-Mijoux 6.4km, Les Fourgs 12.4km, Jougne 23.1km

Outside Pontarlier it is easy to grumble that another mountain walk is required due to the narrow valley floor being filled by a modern highway. This time, however, there is a big payoff with spectacular views from two successive lookouts of the amazing Fort de Joux. Afterward, a walk over the ridge brings you to ski-centric Les Fourgs and on to the beginning of the Orbe Valley. After your arrival at Les Fourgs you have two route options – the primary route through Jougne and the Gorge de l'Orbe, or the route variant through Sainte-Croix (see 'Stage 49–50 variant').

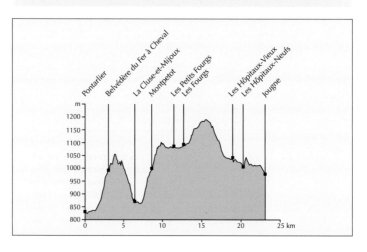

*A quick climb after Pontarlier reveals the lush
Doubs Valley, with Fort de Joux on the ridge above*

Turn left on Rue de la République and continue through central Pontarlier, crossing the Doubs River. Now on the **D74**, at the roundabout after the hospital turn left in the direction of Le Larmont, which puts you on a quiet lane heading to the tall ridge ahead. The road curves south through a line of trees and switchbacks to the left; instead, leave the road here and take a **gravel road** heading up the wooded ridge.

Continue to what seems like a summit, where you turn right on a gravel road among pastures. Come to the option of a viewpoint 40 meters off the trail at **Belvédère du Fer à Cheval** (Horseshoe Lookout; **3.0km**) where you can enjoy your first views across the gorge to the Fort de Joux.

In the 11th century the Lords of Joux rebuilt the former wooden **fortress** on this strategic promontory above the Doubs River, using stone to strengthen it as a redoubt to protect their lands. It was purchased in 1454 by the Duke of Burgundy who transformed it into a border fort which then variously passed into Austrian and French hands. The Austrians captured it from the French in 1814, but back in French hands by the late 19th century it was remodeled to its current form and became part of the Maginot Line protecting France from German invasion. It was also used as a prison, but currently it houses exhibits of rare 18th–20th-century weapons and, at 147m, one of the deepest hand-dug wells in France.

Fort de Joux served as a key defense of France against invaders approaching from the Jura Mountains

Return to the trail to continue east now. At a gravel road turn right to descend to the ruins of Fort Malher set on a cliff at the end of the ridge. Be certain to take the walkway around to the opposite side for astounding views of the Fort de Joux and surrounding region. Come to a **metal gate** with a clever latch system that also serves as an intelligence test (the author failed), then switchback down the mountainside. Take a stairway to the left of the church to arrive at the D67B in **La Cluse-et-Mijoux** (3.4km).

(6.4KM) LA-CLUSE-ET-MIJOUX (ELEV 866M, POP 1171) 🏨 🏠 🄲 ◉ ⊕ ⊕
(1222.9KM)
This gorge bottleneck allowed collection of tolls on the salt and iron that flowed from the north, and spices, rice, and silk that flowed from the south. The town is closely linked to the forts that dominate its twin mountains. Other routes after the 17th century decreased its importance, and the town came to rely on agriculture – first grain and then livestock. The historic **distillery** of the Sons of Emile Pernot (not to be confused with Henri-Louis Pernod) has been resident in the town since 2009 and operates guided tours of its production facility (see http://en.emilepernot.fr). (Bus: www.postauto.ch)

🏠 Auberge du Château de Joux, €-/-/85/105, 127 le Franbourg, RN 57, aubergeduchateaudejoux@gmail.com, tel +33 (0)3 81 69 40 41, €12, restaurant on premises

Turn left on the D67B in the direction of Neuchatel and two blocks later, after a large barn, turn right onto Val du Fort and curve behind homes to cross under the railroad tracks. Continue through marshy pastures on a gravel road heading up

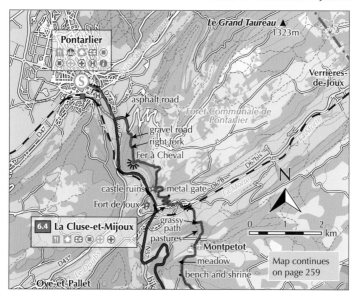

A small shrine in the woods welcomes visitors to Les Petits Fourgs

the wooded ridge. The road becomes a clearly marked, **grassy pathway** as it heads uphill in the woods among rocks and sometimes in mud.

Pass through woods to another **pasture**, after which you pass through a metal gate into a third pasture. Cross a road to come to a chapel in the hamlet of **Montpetot** (2.2km, 🏠 gîte). Take the second left after the chapel (water fountain) and continue through a pasture into the woods atop the ridge, first on a gravel road and, after a barbed-wire gate, on a path. Come to a spacious green **meadow** at the summit, where you keep left to meet a gravel road. Ignore the signs pointing you left and continue straight, once again into the woods.

Pass a **shrine and bench** and afterward come to fields in a wide and high

257

valley, with the town of Les Petits Fourgs to the left (⌂ accommodation). The road ends at a barn where you turn right, onto an asphalt road. Come to the D6 highway at a petrol station (picnic tables, local products market across the highway) and follow it left to arrive in 900 meters just a block below the parish church in central **Les Fourgs** (3.8km).

(6.0KM) LES FOURGS (ELEV 1083M, POP 1345) ▯ ⊕ ▯ ▯ ❶ (1216.9KM)

Meaning 'The Forks' in low-Latin, this village sits in a high valley, with widely spaced agricultural and recreational buildings built in a red-roofed chalet style.

⌂ Au Charnet **O Pt R K Br Dr W S** 2/3, €-/25/50/-, 8 Rue des Buclés, Brigitte. vurpillot@free.fr, tel +33 (0)6 71 60 27 50, shuttle to/from path, brkfst incl, €20 demi-pension

⌂ Accueil Pèlerin **O Pt R K Br Dr W S Z** 1/3, €-/26/52/75, 78 Grande Rue, tiss25@hotmail.fr, tel +33 (0)7 85 29 94 00, (0)3 81 69 50 54

As you near the end of town, turn right on **Rue des Côtes** and head uphill toward a ski run in a clearing of the forested ridge. The road continues among summer pastures and winter Nordic ski slopes scattered among woods. Still on asphalt, come to a **summit** at 1200m elevation in the forest and begin more steeply downhill.

Near the bottom of the hill, enter La Seigne Valley and pass La Beridole farm. Signs point you left, off asphalt, to continue on Nordic ski runs, but it's shorter to continue on the road directly into the village. Come to the valley floor at the village of **Les Hôpitaux-Vieux** (6.5km, bakery, picnic tables, ⌂ Host Family Cordereix, 3/4, €20/-/-/-, 1 Chemin des Coudrettes, francoisecordereix@hotmail.fr, tel +33 (0)7 70 99 35 56, (0)3 81 49 00 29, brkfst incl, pilgrim plate €10).

Documents describe the establishment of a leprosy hospital at **Les Hôpitaux-Vieux** in 1282 on what had been a stop on the Roman road. The village was completely destroyed in 1639 during the Thirty Years' War. Today the village hosts a winter network of 100km of Nordic ski trails and in the summer the biathlon stadium is used for roller-skating and roller-skiing.

Pass through the village on Rue de la Seigne, which merges with the D9 to cross under the N57/E23 motorway. Either continue straight on the roadway through the town of **Les Hôpitaux-Neufs** to Jougne, or watch carefully for a left turn after the first building on the left which leads to the official track that goes uphill on a **grassy path** to an asphalt road beside the motorway. When the road turns right, continue alongside the highway on a gravel path leading into woods.

Turn left to cross the N57/E23 in a tunnel and emerge at a roundabout, where you continue on the N57/E23/Route des Alpes. Fork left onto the Grande de Faubourg/ **Grande Rue** (grocery on right), passing the village church and coming to the town hall when the street ends at the D423 in **Jougne** (4.2km).

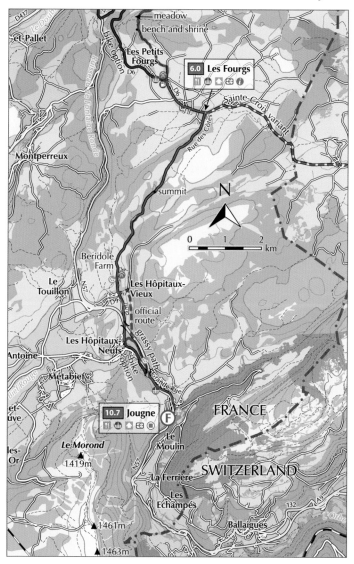

(10.7KM) JOUGNE (ELEV 974M, POP 1839) 🍴 ⊕ 🛏 🅴 ⊛ (1206.2KM)
Records show a 13th-century castle built to enforce tolls along this primary
route between Orbe and Pontarlier. The medieval village was destroyed in 15th
and 16th-century wars, with few remnants except in street names like 'Rue du
Château.' Although a rail line came to Jougne thanks to a 1.6km tunnel built in
1872, the tunnel was destroyed in 1940 to prevent rail traffic to Switzerland.
Marshal Philippe Pétain, hero of Verdun in WWI and scandalous leader of Vichy
France in WWII, was extradited to France at the Swiss border near here on April
26, 1945. There is scholarly debate as to whether Jougne and its neighboring
village of La Ferrière are Sigeric's 'LVI Antifern' or whether the name refers to the
improbably distant town of Yverdon-les-Bains. (Bus: www.postauto.ch)

🔺 **Host Family Paget** Pr R Br Dr S Z 2/4, €30 per person, 6 Rue de la Loge,
paget.daniele@orange.fr, tel +33 (0)6 35 90 88 48, (0)3 81 49 07 82, price
incl brkfst, €10 dinner by reserve, closed weekends, please reserve by email
15 days prior, reception from 4pm

🔺 **La Couronne** Pr R Br Dr Cf S 10/33, €-/85/109/128, 6 Rue de l'Église,
lacouronnejougne@free.fr, tel +33 (0)3 81 49 10 50, €10 brkfst, €35
demi-pension

An archway frames the village church of Jougne

SECTION 5:
SWITZERLAND – VAUD

After Éclépens the track follows a bicycle/pedestrian trail along a channel (Stage 51)

Section 5 overview

The Canton of Vaud is in Romandy, the French-speaking region of Switzerland. Here the slopes of the Jura Mountains descend to the Swiss Plateau, centered at Lac Léman – Lake Geneva in English. The lofty, snow-covered peaks of the French and Swiss Alps dominate views across the glimmering lake, whose shores are populated by tourists, wine growers, and Swiss residents, relaxing in one of their own country's most beautiful regions.

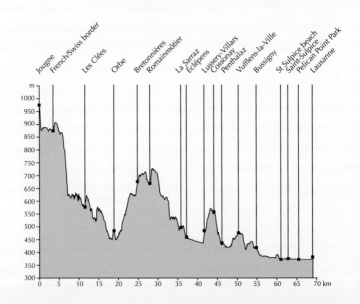

STAGE 50
Jougne to Orbe

Start	Jougne, town hall
Finish	Orbe, Place du Marché
Distance	19.0km
Total ascent	208m
Total descent	696m
Difficulty	Moderately hard (terrain)
Duration	5hr
Percentage paved	48%
Lodging	Orbe 19.0km

Only a few kilometers remain of France before crossing its peaceful and easy-to-miss border with Switzerland. Here the currency changes from euros (€) to Swiss Francs (CHF) and other subtle changes emerge (like the *mairie* is now the *maison de commune*), although French is still the language of this region. Switzerland greets you with a very lovely and memorable walk in the Gorge de l'Orbe, below the limestone cliffs hewed out over millennia. The town of Orbe is well organized and crisp in the delightfully Swiss manner, with a castle at its center.

A simple stone monument marks the border between France and Switzerland

Turn left after the town hall and church and just after a picnic table and gravel road fork right to a path and stairway that quickly descends into the Jougnena Gorge, arriving soon at the **Chapel of Saint-Maurice**. This 12th-century chapel is the last vestige of a ninth-century abbey founded at the site. The interior retains some of its Gothic-era columnar capitals. Cross the road at the bottom of the hill then cross the Jougnena stream and pass a **soccer pitch** of the villages of Le Moulin and Les Maillots which nestle below tall limestone cliffs. Pass through the village of **Les Echampés** (no services), continuing straight toward farm buildings in a large pasture. The road turns to gravel; just before the farm buildings, pass a small stone **monument** on the left that marks the France-Switzerland border (**3.4km**).

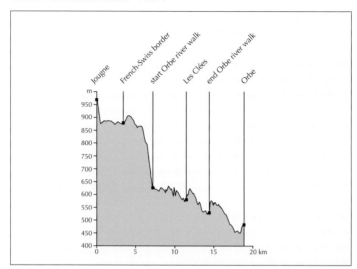

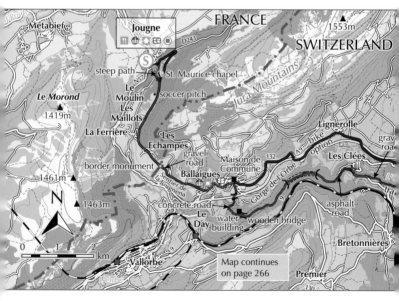

Map continues on page 266

The route is here called **'Sentier de la Jougnena'** and markings for the Via Francigena disappear. Head through pastures and woods as you curve onto the Grand-Rue of your first Swiss town, **Ballaigues** (**2.5km**, groceries, café, ATM).

> Euros are often accepted in Switzerland, but change is always given in CHF (Swiss francs). You may want to withdraw Swiss francs at this town's ATM for a good exchange rate.

Just before the *maison de commune*, turn right on a narrow asphalt lane heading downhill where it becomes a two-track grass road. Join an asphalt roadway that continues downhill to cross under the E23/A9 viaduct. After the motorway, take a two-track road leading right and into the woods. Pass a meadow where you pass through a metal turnstile gate before descending further into woods.

Cross a **concrete road** and continue downhill on the steep and narrow path. At the bottom, instead of turning right onto a gravel road, take the second trail left that continues to descend into the Orbe River gorge natural reserve, with tall limestone cliffs on the left. Turn left onto a wide path that carries you past a **water utility building** then across the Orbe River on a **wooden bridge** (**1.3km**).

Moss covers rocks in the riverbed at the start of the Gorge de l'Orbe

Now begins some of the most beautiful and interesting forest walking on the entire Via Francigena as you make your way down the **Gorge de l'Orbe** on pathways, cliff-side walkways, and through hand-hewn tunnels, all under the umbrella of trees with the music of the river rising from below and soft pine needles underfoot. At various forks, always choose the path closest to the river to stay on track.

After a time, the path becomes an **asphalt road** and rises to a bridge across the river to the village of **Les Clées** (**4.3km**, restaurant), where it is well worth the climb into town to enjoy lunch. Otherwise, turn right and connect on a path to the roadway below, where you turn right. Follow the roadway for a short time before going straight onto a **gravel road** before the first pasture.

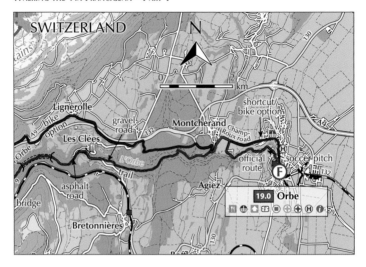

The road descends and becomes a single-track trail with the river now far below. Come to a sign that gives you the option of the Rive Gauche (left bank). Cross the blue-railing bridge to the left bank and climb the path on a steep trail of rocks and tree roots. At a wider trail, turn right, following the trail along limestone cliffs on the left with occasional caves. At a fork in the trail, stay on the river side, keeping a small reservoir on your left.

Follow signs to the parking area and turn right on the asphalt road beyond. The road ends at the two-lane **Champ-Roux road**, where you turn right, noting signs for the Via Francigena that show the Sainte-Croix variant has rejoined here. Now catch your first glimpses of the town of Orbe to the right. At the next road you come to a choice.

Recommended shortcut option
You can return down to the gorge and then climb back up into Orbe or make a simpler, flatter, and 400 meters shorter entry to Orbe by continuing straight ahead on Champ-Roux to turn right at the roundabout and continuing to the Place du Marché in central **Orbe** from the north.

Official route
On the longer route, turn right onto a narrow asphalt road that cuts across fields and pastures before crossing the river and spilling out to a **soccer pitch** below the city. Cross the river once more and climb steeply into town, passing the road to the train station and turning left at Rue de la Poste to arrive, in two blocks, at Place du Marché in **Orbe** (**7.5km**).

Buildings on the Grand-Rue of Orbe

(19.0KM) ORBE (ELEV 477M, POP 5132) 🔢 ⊕ 🛏 🄵 ⊙ ⊕ ⊕ ⊕ 🅘 (1187.2KM)
This settlement of the Helvetii people of Gaul was known as *Urba* in Roman
times, and the mosaic floors of a lavish Roman villa nearby (www.pro-urba.ch/
mosaiques) show its prosperity in ancient times. In the Middle Ages a castle was
built here along with a bridge to span the Orbe River and its round **tower** is visible today in the center city. Orbe is home to a research factory of the Nestlé
company, and 15% of the company's products are produced here. A 52m-high
chimney is preserved from a former chocolate factory. (Bus: www.travys.ch;
trains: www.sbb.ch to Cossonay, Lausanne, and many stops along the Francigena
until Orsières.)

🛖 Cosy & Calme ⊙ 🄿 🅁 1/2, CHF-/80/80/- Route du Signal 8, valerie.
   destribois@gmail.com, tel +41 (0)78 803 77 73, http://hebergement-orbe.ch

🛖 Catholic Church Rectory, 1/2, CHFDonation, Chemin de la Dame 1,
   paroisse.orbe@cath-vd.ch, tel +41 (0)24 441 32 90, (0)79 595 20 63

🛖 ▲ Camping TCS le Signal 🅁 🄺 🄶 🅆 2–4 person bungalows, CHFsee www.
   tcs.ch, Route du Signal 9, camping.orbe@tcs.ch, tel +41 (0)24 441 38 57,
   closed Nov–Mar

STAGE 49–50 VARIANT

Les Fourgs to Orbe via Sainte-Croix

Start	Les Fourgs, D6 at Rue des Côtes
Finish	Orbe, Champ-Roux
Distance	27.3km
Total ascent	324m
Total descent	928m
Difficulty	Moderately hard
Duration	7¼hr
Percentage paved	60%
Lodging	Douanes 3.0km, L'Auberson 4.2km, Sainte-Croix 9.5km, Orbe 27.3km

Although it once served as the official Via Francigena route and has its own advantages, the beautiful Gorge de l'Orbe on the Jougne route makes this route a second choice. This route is a negligible 600 meters longer, has slightly more asphalt, but has memorable Alpine views and vineyard walks.

Although signs near Les Petits-Fourgs would have you skip Les Fourgs, instead continue on the D6 into town and, when the Jougne route (see Stages 49–50) branches right at Rue des Côtes, go straight, continuing on the **D6**. When you descend out of the woods arrive at the Douane (customs) **checkpoint (3.0km**, hostel, restaurant) for truckers. 🔺 La Grand'Borne, 🅿 🅳ℴ 🆁 🅺 🅱ℓ 🅳ℓ 🅶ℓ 🅦 🆂 🆉 23/61, CHF36/60/70/-, Route de la Grand-Borne, info@lagrandborne.ch, tel +41 (0)24 454 13 51, at the border, closed Wed, brkfst CHF8, dinner avail only on weekends. Turn left just afterward and cross through a paddock, take farm roads through a large farm and then return to the highway in the village of **L'Auberson (1.2km**, 🔺 Famille Cornaz 🅾 🅳ℴ 🆁 🅺 🅱ℓ 🆂 1/6, €20/-/-/-, Route de Culliairy 14, thaiscornaz@yahoo.fr, tel +41 (0)76 822 51 06, €5 brkfst).

Turn left on the Grand-Rue and after the last house on the right, fork right, heading toward into a small valley where, on the opposite side, you can see a road traversing the hillside which is the route into Sainte-Croix, just over the ridge. Descend to the first main street, Avenue de Neuchâtel, and turn right. Follow the road as it snakes downhill, becoming Rue de France before it arrives at the Avenue de la Gare at the center of **Sainte-Croix (5.3km)**.

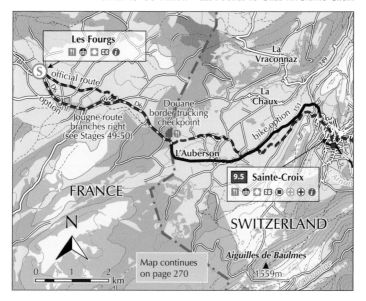

(9.5KM) SAINTE-CROIX (ELEV 1069M, POP 4400) 🍴 ⊕ 🏠 🏧 ⊙ ⊕ ⊕ 🛈
(1205.3KM)

The town's church of the Holy Cross was a pilgrimage destination in its own right in the Middle Ages. In the 18th century it became a watchmaking center and in the late 19th century local factories produced phonographs, cameras, typewriters and radios. (Train: www.sbb.ch)

🛏 **Calme et Vue** ⊙ Pr R K Br W S 2/2, CHF-/55/85/-, Monts-des-Cerfs 749, gloormiel@gmail.com, tel +41 (0)79 523 49 24, https://bnb.ch/fr/calme-et-vue-2899, brkfst incl, between L'Auberson and Ste-Croix

Cross Avenue de la Gare, turn left at the next street and then right on Rue Neuve, which becomes the aptly named Avenue des Alpes, given the stunning views to the French Alps and Lake Neuchâtel. A series of sometimes-steep roadside paths and short-cuts now lead you down the mountain, crossing back and forth over the Granges-la-Côte road with options to walk on an old Roman road until you arrive at the village of **Vuiteboeuf**.

Off the mountain slope now, the route makes a SW turn toward Orbe. As this happens, you can enjoy views of the Alps and Lake Neuchâtel in good weather. Make

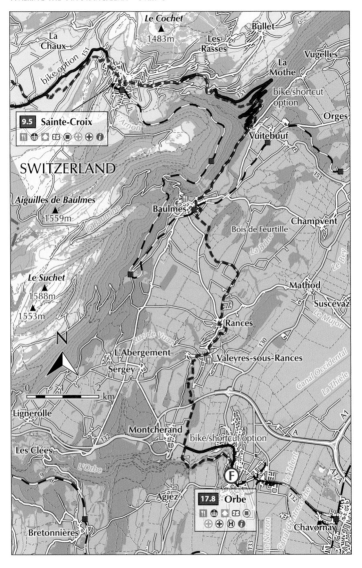

your way, following signs, to the community library and there pick up the Route du Pied de la Côte that will carry you along the mountainside to the next village, **Baulmes** (**8.8km**, restaurants, train). Follow signs that lead you along the edge of town to just before the **train station** where you turn left and begin a zigzag pattern through fields, keeping you off the main street to arrive in **Rances** (**4.3km**). Now you are in the midst of vineyards where it is not uncommon to hear the loud crack of gunshot blanks fired to ward off birds.

Take the Chemin de l'Abbaye to **Valeyres-sous-Rances** (**1.3km**, restaurant) and then head south on vineyard roads, following signs to cross under the A9/E23 roadway to arrive at the Champ-Roux road and the Jougne route. You can either turn left here for a shortcut into Orbe or follow signs down to the Orbe River from which you climb back into central **Orbe** (see Stage 50 for more details).

STAGE 51
Orbe to Cossonay

Start	Orbe, Place du Marché
Finish	Cossonay, town hall
Distance	25.6km
Total ascent	520m
Total descent	439m
Difficulty	Moderately hard
Duration	6¾hr
Percentage paved	40%
Lodging	Romainmôtier 9.1km, Éclépens 18.4km, Cossonay 25.6km

The route seems to flirt momentarily with a return to the Gorge de l'Orbe but instead carries us to the medieval Swiss town of Romainmôtier, tucked into a valley and forgotten by time until it was recently discovered by tourists who have not yet spoiled it. Few cities can compete for charm, but a few blocks of central Cossonay do their best.

From Place du Marché go west on Rue de la Poste, turn right on Rue de Terreaux, and then head down the staircase in 200 meters to Rue de la Gare. Cross the river bridge and continue left between the soccer pitches to reach a fork at a **wooden hut/**

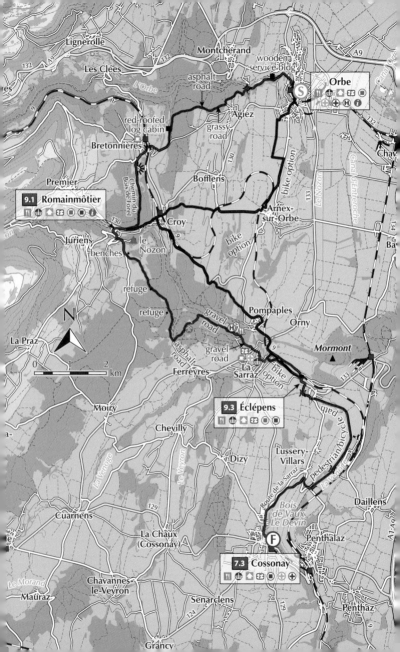

Ligerolle

Les Clées

Montcherand

wooden service bldg

Orbe **S**

asphalt road

Agiez

L'Orbe

red-roofed log cabin

Bretonnières

grassy road

Chav

bike option

Le Nozon

Canal d'Entreroche

Premier

Bofflens

9.1 Romainmôtier

Arnex-sur-Orbe

Croy

Juriens

benches

le Nozon

bike option

La Praz

refuge

refuge

N

Ba

Pompaples

Orny

Mormont

gravel road

0   1   2
km

asphalt road

gravel road

Ferreyres

La Sarraz

bike option

9.3 Éclépens

Moiry

Chevilly

pedestrian/bicycle path

Lussery-Villars

Dizy

la Venoge

le Veyron

Cuarnens

Route de la Sarraz

Daillens

Bois de Vaux Le Devin

Penthalaz

La Chaux (Cossonay)

F

7.3 Cossonay

Le Morand

Chavannes-le-Veyron

Senarclens

Penthaz

Maûraz

Grancy

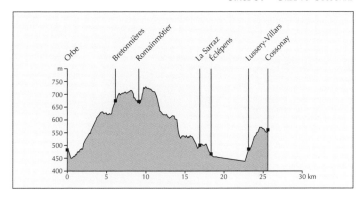

service building. Fork left toward a white farmhouse and pick up a gravel road through pastures and then woods. Cross a **bridge** over a tributary stream and turn left in the direction of Bretonnières.

The route follows a gravel road above the village of Agiez

Climb a narrow dirt path up the hill alongside the stream and soon fork right to cross another path and continue uphill, leaving the sounds of the stream behind you. At the edge of the woods, follow signs right onto a two-track gravel road heading uphill that curves around the vineyard and the village of **Agiez**. Before coming to the village, fork right onto a **grassy road** that becomes a path as it climbs the hillside. Come to an **asphalt road** and turn right, continuing uphill.

The road turns to gravel; follow signs to fork right onto a path continuing uphill. Don't miss a right turn leading downhill by a **red-roofed log cabin**. Just afterward turn left on a concrete lane leading to a road at the edge of fields. Turn right and then right again to cut off the loop of the road, then cross under the highway and rail tracks into **Bretonnières** (**6.2km**, café/restaurant opens daily at 9am).

273

Continue straight through town, heading uphill and forking left toward woods onto **Chemin du Bois de Forel**. Look ahead to see views of the Alps and Lake Neuchâtel in the far distance. The road turns to gravel as it enters the deciduous forest and curves down to cross the Rue de Vaulion where it descends to become the Rue du Bourg of scenically beautiful **Romainmôtier** (**2.9km**).

(9.1KM) ROMAINMÔTIER (ELEV 666M, POP 533) 🍴 ⊕ 🏨 🏧 ⊙ ⊙ ⓘ
(1178.1KM)

Saint Romain founded this **monastery** of the Brothers of Jura in the fifth century, making it the oldest monastery in Switzerland. By the sixth century it was restored in the movement led by Irish monk St Colomban, and then became part of the Cluny network of monasteries in the 10th century. Its current building holds some marks of its Romanesque roots in the 11th century, but a 20th-century renovation is responsible for its current form. In 1536 during the Reformation the abbey's monks were dispersed or converted to Protestantism, and today its congregation is part of the Reformed Church of Switzerland. On the Via Francigena it is the first major Protestant building since Canterbury and Dover. (Bus: www.postauto.ch)

🛏 L'Ermitage, 2/6, CHF-/60/90/115, Rue du Bourg 9 (to left at 1st fl), ermitage. romainmotier@gmail.com, tel +41 (0)79 535 88 04

▲ Camping Le Nozon 🄿 🅁 🄱 🅆 7/14, CHF35/per person, CHF10 linens, CHF13 brkfst, domstreit@bluewin.ch, Route du Signal 2, tel +41 (0)24 453 13 70, https://campingromainmotier.wordpress.com, chalets, bungalows and caravans, pool, closed 1 Nov–31 Mar, resv by web or phone only

The road curves around through the medieval village and out on the other side. As it switches back to the right, walk through a parking lot to find an asphalt road that heads up the hill. Come to an asphalt road with **Le Nozon campground** on your left and turn left to follow this road among pastures. Fork left after a pair of benches and right after crossing under powerlines as you head gradually downhill.

The asphalt ends and you fork directly into the woods on gravel, staying straight to pass a **first** and a **second** large-group municipal refuge set into the woods. This lovely path through the woods finally ends at an **asphalt**

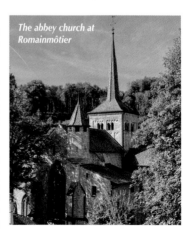

The abbey church at Romainmôtier

Views of the French Alps above Lussery-Villars

road before a pasture. Turn left and in 150 meters turn left again onto a gravel road. Continue in the woods and turn left before a covered picnic area where the trail begins to descend quickly. The path ends after a steep descent to a **gravel road**, where you turn right. This pleasant road, still in the woods, ends at an asphalt road before a **hospital** complex (café).

Turn right, heading along the parking area, and then fork right onto the asphalt Chemin de Buis. As this road curves uphill, turn left onto a **gravel road** in the direction of La Sarraz. Pass through some small housing compounds and then a caravan park (restaurant). Follow this pedestrian trail downhill, as it becomes a street and ends at the Route de Ferreyres (groceries). Turn left, cross the bridge, and in two blocks come to the main street of the old part of **La Sarraz** (**7.6km**, ATM, café, pharmacy).

Turn left and at the next street, Avenue de la Gare, turn right. Take the crosswalk and after the greenhouse turn left to climb steps and find a road that follows along to the right, above the train tracks. Fork right to remain just above the tracks. After a terraced vineyard the road turns, crosses the tracks, and curves left into central **Éclépens** (**1.6km**).

(9.3KM) ÉCLÉPENS (ELEV 461M, POP 1219) 🍴 ⊕ 🏠 🅵 ⦿ ⦿ (1168.8KM)

Listed as 'Sclependingus' in 814 and 'Sclepens' in 1147, Éclépens is listed among the Inventory of Swiss Heritage Sites in part due to an Iron Age archeological site nearby. The town was founded on the banks of the Venoge stream, which will accompany you all the way to Lac Léman. (Bus: www.postauto.ch)

🛏 **Auberge Communale**, 9/17, CHF-/70/120/-, Rue du Village 1, info@auberge-eclepens.ch, tel +41 (0)21 866 72 01, www.auberge-eclepens.ch, restaurant, closed Sun–Mon

Turn right on a narrow asphalt road before the town hall, and in about 300 meters cross the Venoge River, turning left afterward to a **pedestrian/bicycle trail** running along its course. Follow this trail along fields, punctuated by the occasional cotton-wood tree, for the next nearly 4km until it crosses a **bridge** and comes to an asphalt road. Turn right, cross another bridge, and then continue on a series of gravel shortcuts that lead to a left on the **Route de la Sarraz**. Now head downhill into the old city. Fork left onto Petite Rue, and then turn right on Rue du Temple to come to the town hall in **Cossonay** (**7.3km**).

(7.3KM) COSSONAY (ELEV 561M, POP 2795) 🏨 ⊕ 🏧 🄵 ◉ ⊕ ⊕ (1161.5KM)
Earliest records list the village of Cochoniacum here in 1096. By 1228 it appears in records as Cossonai. An abbey was founded here in the 13th century, and a fire completely consumed Cossonay in the 14th. Although the Venoge River served mills to grind grain from nearby farms from the 16th century onward, in the 20th century the town took its place as a commuter town of nearby Lausanne. (Bus: www.postauto.ch; train accessible via funicular to Cossonay-Penthalaz station, www.sbb.ch)

Consult online resources for lodging, continue to Bussigny, or consider taking the train to Lausanne and returning by train to complete the stage.

Medieval charm is just a block off the busy main street of Cossonay

STAGE 52
Cossonay to Lausanne

Start	Cossonay, town hall
Finish	Lausanne, Château d'Ouchy
Distance	24.9km
Total ascent	153m
Total descent	331m
Difficulty	Moderate
Duration	6½hr
Percentage paved	42%
Lodging	Bussigny 10.7km, Lausanne 24.9km

The route essentially follows the course of the Venoge stream as it makes its way downhill to Lac Léman; however, the way is not simple and requires close attention to signage. Once at the lake, enjoy views of the Alps as you follow lakeside paths and roads through posh suburbs and parks into cosmopolitan Lausanne.

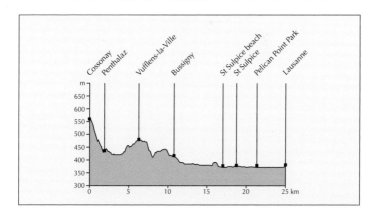

First it is necessary to get off the ridge and below Cossonay to arrive at Penthalaz. Pass the town hall and the Temple de Cossonay and continue two blocks to the Route d'Etangs to follow the sidewalk on the right side where, after a wall, you cross the busy street to find a somewhat isolated path that heads down the ridge through woods to

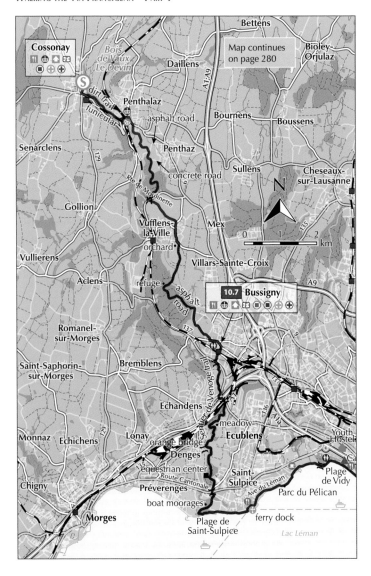

Cossonay

S

Bois de Vaux Le Devin

Daillens

dirt trail

funicular

Penthalaz

asphalt road

Bettens

Bioley-Orjulaz

Map continues on page 280

Bournens

Boussens

Senarclens

129

Rte de Moulinette

Penthaz

concrete road

Sullens

Cheseaux-sur-Lausanne

Gollion

Vufflens-la-Ville

orchard

Mex

135

N

0   1   2
km

Vullierens

Aclens

refuge

asphalt road

Villars-Sainte-Croix

10.7 Bussigny

A9

127

Romanel-sur-Morges

Bremblens

Saint-Saphorin-sur-Morges

Echandens

Cordon de Venoge Trail

meadow

Ecublens

A1a

136

137

Youth Hostel

Monnaz   Echichens

Lonay

orange bridge

129

Denges

equestrian center

135

Route Cantonale

Préverenges

boat moorages

Chigny

Morges

Saint-Sulpice

Ave du Léman

Plage de Saint-Sulpice

ferry dock

Plage de Vidy

Parc du Pélican

Ca

Lac Léman

the Cossonay-Penthalaz **train station**. Funicular option: It is also possible to follow signs across the Route d'Etangs to the nearby Cossonay-Ville station, where a funicular descends to the train station in 6 minutes for CHF2.40.

Arriving at the train station, cross the tracks on the auto bridge and turn right at the roundabout. Pass a bakery and just afterward turn right on an asphalt road going downhill into a park system where you follow along the Venoge stream, continuing downhill. The road curves to the left and ends. Turn right, continuing downhill and aiming for a well-hidden trail that begins in a parking lot and heads left into the woods. Follow alongside the Venoge, then cross an **asphalt road** to join a **concrete road** that curves around the edge of two large fields.

At the end of the fields head into the woods, where you follow a path that crosses the Venoge, gradually climbing, and then fork right onto a gravel road that ends at a narrow asphalt road with a large two-lane highway to the left. Turn left and cross the highway on a **bridge**. Now you are among fields that slope downhill toward Lac Léman and the French Alps ahead in the distance. When the road ends, turn right and walk through the suburban settlement of **Vufflens-la-Ville** (**6.4km**, no services).

As you leave town and return to fields, turn right after an **orchard** in the direction of a refuge and continue through fields and back into the woods. Follow the paved road under powerlines and then, on gravel, continue to an **asphalt road**, enjoying occasional views toward the Alps. Turn left on the asphalt road and as you come out of the woods, turn right before the first neighborhood of homes. Turn left into another neighborhood of new homes and make your way downhill to Rue Saint-Germain, where you turn left to arrive at the Hôtel de Ville in **Bussigny** (**4.2km**).

(10.7KM) BUSSIGNY (ELEV 417M, POP 8930) ▯ ⊕ ☐ ⓕ ⊙ ◎ ⊕ ⊕ (1150.8KM)
Originally two separate hamlets, Bussigny and Saint-Germain, all that is left of the latter is Rue Saint-Germain. With the growth of Lausanne in the 20th century it became something of a Lausanne suburb. (Bus: www.postauto.ch; train: www.sbb.ch)

🛏 **Ibis Budget Bussigny** ⓞ 𝗣𝗿 𝗥 𝗕𝗿 𝗚 𝗦 𝗭 CHF-/-/114/-, Rue de Industrie 67, h7599@accor.com, tel +41 (0)21 706 53 53, https://all.accor.com

Curve right onto Rue de Gare and go under the rail tracks at the **station**. Veer right to follow Chemin du Vallon (café) and continue under a highway **bridge**, forking left to follow a road on the other side. Continue until you come to a bridge, and just before, turn left onto the **Sentier de la Venoge trail**, which will take you all the way to Lac Léman. Watch for signs carefully along the way, particularly when overhead auto and train bridges distract from the trail.

Pass a distinctive **orange pedestrian bridge** on the wooded path, as well as an **equestrian center** before crossing under the **Route Cantonale** and heading downhill

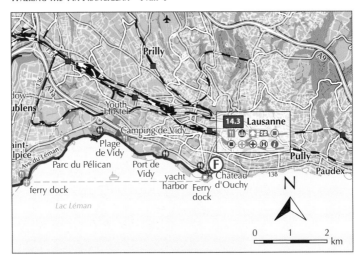

The wide sandy beach at Parc du Pélican at Lac Léman

on wide paths to the **lake**. Turn left to walk on the lakeside path, which continues through Lausanne and in fits and starts all the way to the mouth of the Rhône at Villeneuve. Coming to the first beach, **Plage de Saint-Sulpice**, you may choose to pause and reflect, in this beautiful spot beside the lake at the foot of the Alps, on your journey thus far and still ahead.

Continue along the lakeside path into the village of **Saint-Sulpice (8.0km)**, with its Romanesque church and hotel-restaurant set at a lakeside park. Continue now on lakeside paths and roads into first **Parc du Pélican**, then Parc des Pierrettes. Take a bridge to cross into the **Plage de Vidy** (WC) and pass a series of skate parks, beach volleyball courts, a carousel, and the bars and shops of the **Port de Vidy** marina. Continue through the park to the Port Lausanne-Ouchy, and come to the **Château d'Ouchy**, at the foot of **Lausanne (6.2km)**.

The Château d'Ouchy is the Via Francigena's terminus in Lausanne

(14.3KM) LAUSANNE (ELEV 377M, POP 139,111) 🚉 ⊕ △ 🅵 ⊙ ⊙ ⊕ ⊕ Ⓗ 𝒊
(1136.5KM)

Lausanne is capital of the Swiss Canton of Vaud and part of the Arc lémanique, a densely populated crescent around the west shore of Lac Léman that includes the city of Geneva. Although its population ranks behind Reims as the largest on the Via Francigena, its metropolitan area of 1.3 million residents is larger than any city until Rome.

The city enters history as a Roman fort named '*Lousanna*,' built over a Celtic settlement on the shores of Lac Léman between present-day Ouchy and Vichy. Roman foundations can be toured in an **archaeological park** above Vidy. After the fall of Rome, residents found it easier to defend the hills above the Roman settlement and the town was moved to the current location of its center city, clustered around the Lausanne Cathedral. The city prospered beginning in the 11th century and its cathedral, dedicated in 1275 by Pope Gregory X in the presence of King Rudolf I of Germany, capped a period of increasing influence. With the Reformation, the Cathedral became a Protestant church, and Lausanne became a training capital for Reformed clergy in Switzerland and France. First established in 1537 for this purpose, the **University of Lausanne** is one of the oldest universities in the world in continuous operation.

Lausanne's location on the shores of Lac Léman made it a stopover for luminaries including Shelley and Byron, then in later times people like TS Eliot, Ernest Hemingway, and Edward Gibbon. Since 1914 Lausanne has hosted the headquarters of the International Olympic Committee which also maintains a **museum** just 400 meters from Château d'Ouchy (CHF20, closed Mondays, https://olympics.com/muse).

The city is spread uphill from the lakeshore, with the **Château d'Ouchy** at the waterfront, the **cathedral** at the summit, and the train station roughly halfway up the steep hillside. A Via Francigena stop at Lausanne should include a stamp from the Cathedral, and footsore pilgrims may want to use the metro system that connects the city together and saves a climb. Walking downhill can allow full enjoyment of charming squares like the **Place du Palud** with its Renaissance fountain of Justice and the animated scenes of its **clock tower**. Narrow streets packed with shops continue downhill to **Place Saint-François**, capping an afternoon enjoying a spotless urban city of history and charm. (Bus: www.postauto.ch; train: www.sbb.ch)

🏠 **Auberge de Jeunesse de Lausanne** Ⓞ 🅿︎ Ⓓⓞ Ⓡ Ⓑⓡ Ⓓⓡ Ⓖⓣ Ⓦ Ⓢ Ⓩ 113/310, CHFcontact, Chemin du Bois-de-Vaux 36, lausanne@youthhostel.ch, tel +41 (0)21 626 02 22

▲ 🏠 **Camping de Vidy** Ⓞ 🅿︎ Ⓡ Ⓚ Ⓑⓡ Ⓓⓡ Ⓖⓣ Ⓦ Ⓢ Ⓩ 6/12, CHF -/40/40/60, bungalows, Chemin du Camping 3, info@clv.ch, tel +41 21 622 50 00, www.campinglausannevidy.ch, restaurant

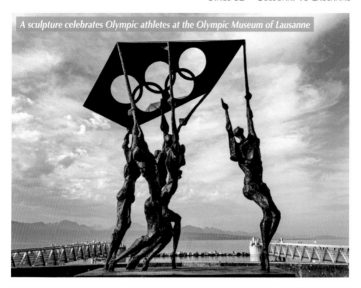

A sculpture celebrates Olympic athletes at the Olympic Museum of Lausanne

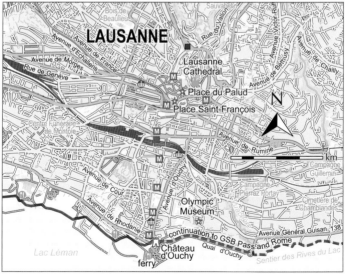

APPENDIX A
Stage planning table

Book stage	Location	Distance from start	Distance from previous point	Book stage distance	My itinerary
1	Canterbury Cathedral	0.0		17.2	
2	Shepherdswell	17.2	17.2	18.6	
	Dover	31.6	14.4		
	Dover ferry	34.4	2.8		
	Calais	35.9	1.5		
3	Sangatte	43.7	7.9	20.2	
	Wissant	56.1	12.4		
4	Landrethun-le-Nord	69.5	13.5	23.4	
	Caffiers	71.8	2.3		
	Guînes	79.4	7.6		
5	Licques	95.7	16.3	16.3	
6	Audenfort	98.7	3.0	15.0	
	Tournehem-sur-la-Hem	110.8	12.0		
7	Leulinghem	127.9	17.2	19.8	
	Wisques	130.6	2.7		
8	Delettes	148.5	18.0	18.0	
9	Thérouanne	152.8	4.2	22.8	
	Liettres	160.7	8.0		
	Auchy-au-Bois	167.8	7.1		
	Amettes	171.3	3.5		
10	Burbure	179.8	8.5	21.1	
	Bruay-la-Buissière	192.4	12.7		
11	D341 Houdain	195.1	2.6	24.7	
	Albain-Saint-Nazaire	217.1	22.1		
12	Souchez	219.9	2.8	22.5	
	Mont-St-Éloi	227.0	7.2		
	Maroeuil	231.3	4.3		
	Arras	239.6	8.3		

Book stage	Location	Distance from start	Distance from previous point	Book stage distance	My itinerary
13	D35 Boisleux Saint-Marc	249.0	9.4	26.4	
	Bapaume	266.1	17.1		
14	Péronne	294.7	28.7	28.7	
15	Vraignes-en-Vermandois	306.5	11.8		
	Trefcon	312.4	5.9	17.7	
16	Attily	318.2	5.8	28.2	
	Saint-Quentin	329.2	11.0		
	Seraucourt-le-Grand	340.6	11.3		
17	Tergnier	359.3	18.8	18.8	
18	La Fère	365.5	6.2	39.5	
	Bertaucourt-Epourdon	370.9	5.3		
	Cessières-Suzy	387.5	16.6		
	Laon (Rue Chatelain)	398.8	11.3		
19	Corbeny	428.4	29.6	29.6	
20	Berry-au-Bac	439.6	11.1	11.1	
21	Hermonville	451.8	12.2	28.5	
	Reims	468.1	16.4		
22	Verzenay	485.8	17.7	20.1	
	Verzy	488.2	2.4		
23	Condé-sur-Marne	508.1	19.9	19.9	
24	Châlons-en-Champagne	525.0	17.0	17.0	
25	Saint-Germain-la-Ville	537.5	12.4	12.4	
26	Chaussée	546.4	9.0	17.1	
	Saint-Amand-sur-Fion	554.5	8.1		
27	Vitry-le-François	569.4	14.9	14.9	
28	Courdemanges	576.9	7.4	21.1	
	Blaise-sous-Arzillières	582.6	5.8		
	Saint-Remy-en-Bouzemont	590.5	7.9		
29	Outines	602.5	11.9	11.9	
30	Lentilles	614.9	12.5	16.5	
	Montmorency-Beaufort	618.9	4.0		

Book stage	Location	Distance from start	Distance from previous point	Book stage distance	My itinerary
31	Rosnay l'Hôpital	627.2	8.3	20.6	
	Précy-Saint-Martin	639.5	12.3		
32	Saint-Lèger-sous-Brienne	643.8	4.3	13.4	
	Brienne-le-Château	646.3	2.5		
	Dienville	652.9	6.6		
33	Unienville	657.1	4.1	20.4	
	Amance	661.1	4.0		
	Dolancourt	673.4	12.3		
34	Bar-sur-Aube	685.5	12.2	18.5	
	Baroville	691.9	6.3		
35	Clairvaux/Ville-Sous-la-Ferté	700.5	8.6	26.9	
	Cirfontaines-en-Azois	711.1	10.6		
	Orges	718.7	7.7		
36	Châteauvillain	724.1	5.4	18.8	
	Richebourg	737.5	13.4		
37	Abbaye de Mormont	744.3	6.8	17.8	
	Leffonds	747.9	3.6		
	Faverolles	755.2	7.3		
38	Saint-Ciergues	767.2	12.0	21.0	
	Perrancey	770.0	2.8		
	Langres	776.2	6.2		
39	Culmont	799.7	23.4	24.8	
	Chalindrey	801.1	1.4		
40	Coublanc	824.7	23.7	23.7	
41	Leffond	828.6	3.8	11.7	
	Champlitte	836.4	7.9		
42	Dampierre-sur-Salon	855.9	19.5	19.5	
43	Seveux	864.6	8.7	33.9	
	Bucey-lès-Gy	889.9	25.2		
44	Montboillon	900.3	10.4	14.6	
	Cussey-sur-l'Ognon	904.5	4.2		

Book stage	Location	Distance from start	Distance from previous point	Book stage distance	My itinerary
45	Besançon	922.2	17.8	17.8	
46	Saône	936.2	14.0	25.7	
	Mamirolle	941.4	5.2		
	Foucherans	947.9	6.5		
47	Ornans	959.4	11.5	25.5	
	Montgesoye	963.6	4.2		
	Vuillafans	967.0	3.4		
	Lods	971.0	4.1		
	Mouthier-Haute-Pierre	973.4	2.4		
48	Ouhans D41 turnoff	981.5	8.1	23.7	
	Pontarlier	997.1	15.6		
49	La Cluse-et-Mijoux	1003.5	6.4	23.1	
	Les Fourgs	1009.6	6.0		
	Les Hôpitaux-Vieux	1016.1	6.5		
	Jougne	1020.2	4.2		
50	Orbe	1039.2	19.0	19.0	
51	Romainmôtier	1048.3	9.1	25.6	
	Éclépens	1057.6	9.3		
	Cossonay	1064.9	7.3		
52	Bussigny	1075.5	10.7	24.9	
	Lausanne	1089.8	14.3		
			Average distance/day	21.0	

APPENDIX B
Useful contacts

Emergency numbers

Service	England	France	Switzerland
General emergency	999, 112	112, 17	112
Police	101	17	117
Fire department	999, 112	18	
Medical emergencies	999, 112	15	
Non-emergency medical	111	15, 116, 117	144
Fires, wildfires		18	118
Wilderness rescue			1414, 1415

Tourist information centers

Canterbury
18 High St, tel +44 (0)1227 862162,
https://canterburymuseums.co.uk/the-beaney/visitor-information

Calais
12 Bd Georges Clemenceau, tel +33 (0)3 21 96 62 40, www.calais-cotedopale.com

Wissant
Pl de la Mairie, tel +33 (0)3 21 82 48 00, www.terredes2capstourisme.fr

Guînes
9 Av de la Libération, tel +33 (0)3 21 35 73 73

Arras
Hôtel de Ville, Pl des Héros, tel +33 (0)3 21 51 26 95, www.arraspaysdartois.com

Bapaume
10 Pl Faidherbe, tel +33 (0)3 21 59 89 84

Péronne
1 Rue Louis XI, tel +33 (0)3 22 84 42 38, www.hautesomme-tourisme.com

Saint-Quentin
3 Rue Emile Zola, tel +33 (0)3 23 67 05 00, www.destination-saintquentin.fr

Laon
Pl du Parv. Gaultier de Mortagne, tel +33 (0)3 23 20 28 62,
www.tourisme-paysdelaon.com

Reims
6 Rue Rockefeller, tel +33 (0)3 26 77 45 00, www.reims-tourisme.com

Châlons-en-Champagne
3 Quai des Arts, tel +33 (0)3 26 65 17 89, www.chalons-tourisme.com

Vitry-le-François
8 Esplanade de Strasbourg, tel +33 (0)3 26 74 45 30, www.lacduder.com

Brienne-le-Château
1 Rue Emile Zola, tel +33 (0)3 25 92 82 41, www.grandslacsdechampagne.fr

Bar-sur-Aube
4 Blvd du 14 Juillet, tel +33 (0)3 25 27 24 25, www.tourisme-cotedesbar.com

Châteauvillain
Rue de Penthièvre, tel +33 (0)6 70 14 17 38, www.tourisme-arc-chateauvillain.com

Langres
Place Olivier Lahalle, tel +33 (0)3 25 87 67 67, www.tourisme-langres.com

Champlitte
2 All. Du Sainfoin, tel +33 (0)3 84 67 67 19, www.entresaoneetsalon.fr

Dampierre-sur-Salon
2 bis Rue Jean Mourey, tel +33 (0)3 84 67 67 19, www.entresaoneetsalon.fr

Besançon
52 Grande Rue, tel +33 (0)3 81 80 92 55, www.besancon-tourisme.com

Ornans
7 Rue Pierre Vernier, tel +33 (0)3 81 62 21 50, www.destinationlouelison.com

Pontarlier
14 bis Rue de la Gare, tel +33 (0)3 81, 46 48 33, www.pontarlier.org

Les Fourgs
Locality La Coupe, tel +33 (0)3 81 69 44 91, www.les-fourgs.com

Orbe
Rue du Château 2, tel +41 (0)24 442 92 37, www.yverdonlesbainsregion.ch

Sainte-Croix
Rue Neuve 10, tel +41 (0)24 423 03 23, www.yverdonlesbainsregion.ch

Romainmôtier
Chemin Derrière-l'Eglise 1, tel +41 (0)24 453 38 28, www.yverdonlesbainsregion.ch

Lausanne
Place de la Gare 9, tel +41 (0)21 613 73 73, www.lausanne-tourisme.ch/en/

Pilgrim credential distribution points

Canterbury

Beaney House of Art and Knowledge of Canterbury, Visitor Information desk, 18 High Street, tel +44 (0)1227 862 162, canterburyinformation@canterbury.gov.uk

Calais

Association pour la Mise en Valeur du Patrimoine Architectural du Calaisis (AMVPAC) of Calais, Musée des Beaux-Arts, 25 Rue Richelieu, tel +33 (0)6 72 10 16 56, contact@amvpac.com

Champlitte

Bureau Information Touristique de Champlitte, 2 Allée du Sainfoin, tel +33 (0)3 84 67 67 19, ot4rivieres@gmail.comBureau Via Francigena, 33 bis Rue de la République, tel +33 (0)6 88 33 23 29, viafrancigena.champlitte@gmail.com

Lausanne

Editions Favre Sa, 29 Rue de Bourg, tel +41 (0)21 312 17 17, lausanne@editionsfavre. com

APPENDIX C
Bibliography

Travelogues

Belloc, Hillare. *The Path to Rome*. New York: Wallachia, 1953.

Bucknall, Harry. *Like a Tramp, Like a Pilgrim: On Foot, Across Europe to Rome*. London: Bloomsbury Continuum, 2014.

Egan, Timothy. *A Pilgrimage to Eternity: From Canterbury to Rome in Search of a Faith*. New York: Viking, 2019.

Mooney, Brian. *A Long Way for a Piazza: On Foot to Rome*. London: Thorogood, 2012.

Muirhead, Robert. *The Long Walk: A Pilgrimage from Canterbury to Rome*. CreateSpace, 2015.

Warrender, Alice, *An Accidental Jubilee: A Pilgrimage on foot from Canterbury to Rome*. York: Stone Trough Books, 2011.

Historical – Via Francigena

Caselli, Giovanni. *Via Romea, Cammino di Dio*. Florence: Giunti Gruppo Editoriale, 1990.

Champ, J . *The English Pilgrimage to Rome*. Herfordshire, England: Gracewing, 2000.

Magoun, F.P. 'The Rome of Two Northern Pilgrims: Archbishop Sigeric of Canterbury and Abbot Nikolas of Munkathvera.' *The Harvard Theological Review*, 33(4), 267–289.

Ortenberg, Veronica. 'Archbishop Sigeric's Journey to Rome in 990.' In M. Lapidge, M. Godden, & S. Keyes (eds.) *Anglo-Saxon England* Vol 19. (pp.19–26) Cambridge, England: Cambridge University Press, 1990. Ortenberg studies the meaning of the 23 churches visited by Sigeric in Rome.

Historical – France, pilgrimage and general

Birch, Debra J. *Pilgrimage to Rome in the Middle Ages*. Woodbridge, Suffolk: Boydell Press, 1998.

Black, Jeremy. *France: A Short History*. London: Thames & Hudson, 2021.

Webb, Diana. *Pilgrims and Pilgrimage in the Medieval West*. London: I.B. Tauris, 2001.

APPENDIX D
Sigeric's journey – then and now

Stage no. from English Channel to Rome	Sigeric's stage no. from Rome to English Channel	Sigeric's place name	Modern place name	Guidebook stage no.
Via Francigena Part 1: Canterbury to Lausanne				
1	LXXX	Sumeran	Sombre (Wissant)	Stage 3
2	LXXIX	Unlisted by Sigeric		
3	LXXVIII	Gisne	Guînes	Stage 4
4	LXXVII	Teranburh	Thérouanne	Stage 9
5	LXXVI	Bruwaei	Bruay-la-Buissière	Stage 10
6	LXXV	Atherats	Arras	Stage 12
7	LXXIV	Duin	Doingt	
8	LXXIII	Martinwaeth	Séraucourt-le-Grand	Stage 16
9	LXXII	Mundlothuin	Laon	Stage 18
10	LXXI	Corbunei	Corbeny	Stage 19
11	LXX	Rems	Reims	Stage 21
12	LXIX	Chateluns	Châlons-sur-Marne	Stage 24
13	LXVIII	Funtaine	Fontaine-sur-Coole	Variant Stages 25–31
14	LXVII	Domaniant	Donnement	Variant Stages 25–31
15	LXVI	Breone	Brienne-la-Vieille	Stage 32
16	LXV	Bar	Bar-sur-Aube	Stage 34
17	LXIV	Blaecuile	Blessonville	Variant Stages 35–36
18	LXIII	Oisma	Humes-Jorquenay	-
19	LXII	Grenant	Grenant	-
20	LXI	Sefui	Seveux	Stage 43
21	LX	Cuscei	Cussey-sur-l'Ognon	Stage 44
22	LIX	Bysiceon	Besançon	Stage 45
23	LVIII	Nos	Nods	-

Stage no. from English Channel to Rome	Sigeric's stage no. from Rome to English Channel	Sigeric's place name	Modern place name	Guidebook stage no.
24	LVII	Punterlin	Pontarlier	Stage 48
25	LVI	Antifern	Jougne/Yverdon-les-Bains	Stage 49
26	LV	Urba	Orbe	Stage 50
27	LIV	Losanna	Lausanne	Stage 52
Via Francigena Part 2: Lausanne to Lucca				
28	LIII	Vivaec	Vevey	
29	LII	Burbulei	Aigle	
30	LI	Sancte Maurici	Saint-Maurice	
31	L	Ursiores	Orsières	
32	XLIX	Petrecastel	Bourg-Saint-Pierre	
33	XLVIII	Sancte Remei	Saint-Rhémy	
34	XLVII	Agusta	Aosta	
35	XLVI	Publei	Pont-Saint-Martin (Montjovet?)	
36	XLV	Everi	Ivrea	
37	XLIV	Sancte Agatha	Santhià	
38	XLIII	Vercel	Vercelli	
39	XLII	Tremel	Tromello	
40	XLI	Pamphica	Pavia	
41	XL	Sancte Cristine	Santa Cristina e Bissone	
42	XXXIX	Sancte Andrea	Corte San Andrea	
43	XXXVIII	Placentia	Piacenza	
44	XXXVII	Floricum	Fiorenzuola d'Arda	
45	XXXVI	Sanctae Domnine	Fidenza (previously called Borgo San Donino)	
46	XXXV	Metane	Costamezzana	
47	XXXIV	Philemangenur	Fornovo di Taro	
48	XXXIII	Sancte Moderanne	Berceto	
49	XXXII	Sancte Benedicte	Montelungo	
50	XXXI	Puntremel	Pontremoli	
51	XXX	Aguilla	Aulla	
52	XXIX	Sancte Stephane	Santo Stefano di Magra	

Stage no. from English Channel to Rome	Sigeric's stage no. from Rome to English Channel	Sigeric's place name	Modern place name	Guidebook stage no.
53	XXVIII	Luna	Sarzana (Luni)	
54	XXVII	Campmaior	Camaiore	
Via Francigena Part 3: Lucca to Rome				
55	XXVI	Luca	Lucca	
56	XXV	Forcri	Porcari	
57	XXIV	Aqua Nigra	Ponte a Cappiano	
58	XXIII	Arne Blanca	Fucecchio	
59	XXII	Sce Dionisii	San Genesio near San Miniato	
60	XXI	Sce Peter Currant	Coiano (Castelfiorentino)	
61	XX	Sce Maria Glan	Santa Maria a Chianni (near Gambassi Terme)	
62	XIX	Sce Gemiane	San Gimignano	
63	XVIII	Sce Martin in Fosse	San Martino Fosci (Molino d'Aiano)	
64	XVII	Aelse	Gracciano (Pieve d'Elsa)	
65	XVI	Burgenove	Badia an Isola (Abbadia d'Isola)	
66	XV	Seocine	Siena	
67	XIV	Arbia	Ponte d'Arbia	
68	XIII	Turreiner	Torrenieri	
69	XII	Sce Quiric	San Quirico d'Orcia	
70	XI	Abricula	Briccole di Sotto	
71	X	Sce Petir in Pail	San Pietro in Paglia (Voltole)	
72	IX	Aquapendente	Acquapendente	
73	VIII	Sca Cristina	Bolsena	
74	VII	Sce Flaviane	Montefiascone	
75	VI	Sce Valentine	Viterbo (Bullicame)	
76	V	Furcari	Vetralla (Forcassi)	
77	IV	Suteria	Sutri	
78	III	Bacane	Baccano (Campagnano di Roma)	
79	II	Johannis VIIII	San Giovanni in Nono (La Storta)	
80	I	Urbs Roma	Roma	

A ladder leads over the barbed-wire fence of a pasture before Foucherans (Stage 46)

A VIA FRANCIGENA GUIDE IN THREE PARTS

Certified by the Council of Europe as an official Cultural Route, the Via Francigena brings to the modern pilgrim the amazing cultural heritage of four nations – England, France, Switzerland and Italy – and highlights their immense natural beauty and deep, ancient heritage. This guidebook is one of a set of three volumes that covers the route.

Part 1 – From Canterbury to Lausanne
The Via Francigena officially begins at Canterbury Cathedral, crosses the English Channel, then makes its way along French canals, battlefields, farmlands and historic villages to arrive at Lake Geneva in Switzerland.

Part 2 – From Lausanne to Lucca
Beginning at easily accessible Lausanne, the Via Francigena climbs toward the headwaters of the mighty Rhône River before branching off to summit the historic Great Saint Bernard Pass. The route descends the Alps along the Aosta Valley, traveling through the Po River Valley and then crossing the scenic Passo della Cisa into Tuscany. After a few days near the coast, the trail swings inland to Lucca, one of Tuscany's medieval jewels.

Part 3 – From Lucca to Rome
From Lucca to Siena the Via Francigena is at its most evocative. As it passes through dazzling Tuscan towns like Lucca, San Gimignano and Siena, the route crosses the Orcia and Paglia Valleys into the volcanic tufa stone ridges and basins of Lazio where the centuries-long rule of the Popes is felt in every village. This amazing pilgrimage ends at one of the world's great treasures – the Eternal City of Rome.

St Peter's Basilica towers above the buildings of Rome and the Vatican

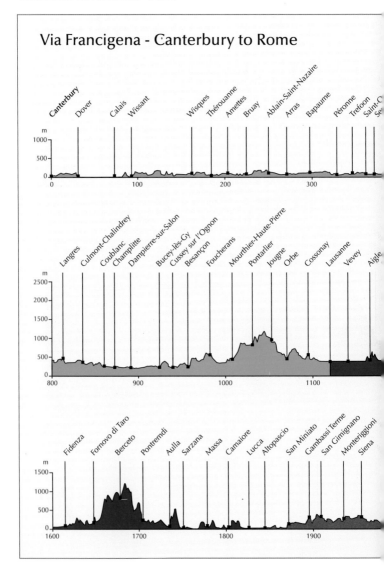

Via Francigena - Canterbury to Rome

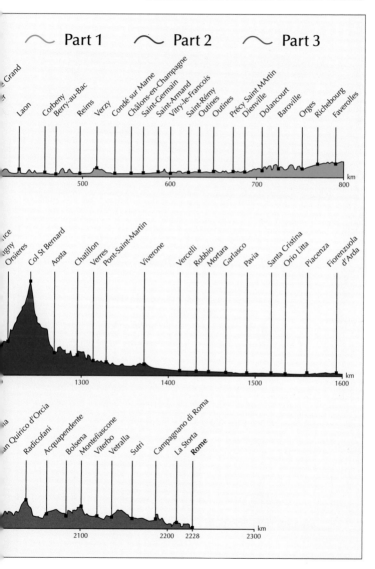

DOWNLOAD THE ROUTES
IN GPX FORMAT

All the routes in this guide are available for download from:

www.cicerone.co.uk/884/GPX

as standard format GPX files. You should be able to load them into most online GPX systems and mobile devices, whether GPS or smartphone. You may need to convert the file into your preferred format using a conversion programme such as gpsvisualizer.com or one of the many other such websites and programmes.

When you follow this link, you will be asked for your email address and where you purchased the guidebook, and have the option to subscribe to the Cicerone e-newsletter.

www.cicerone.co.uk

LISTING OF CICERONE GUIDES

Mountain Biking on the
North Downs
Mountain Biking on the
South Downs
Short Walks in the Surrey Hills
Suffolk Coast and Heath Walks
The Cotswold Way
The Cotswold Way Map Booklet
The Kennet and Avon Canal
The Lea Valley Walk
The North Downs Way
The North Downs Way Map Booklet
The Peddars Way and Norfolk
Coast Path
The Pilgrims' Way
The Ridgeway National Trail
The Ridgeway Map Booklet
The South Downs Way
The South Downs Way Map Booklet
The Thames Path
The Thames Path Map Booklet
The Two Moors Way
The Two Moors Way Map Booklet
Walking Hampshire's Test Way
Walking in Cornwall
Walking in Essex
Walking in Kent
Walking in London
Walking in Norfolk
Walking in the Chilterns
Walking in the Cotswolds
Walking in the Isles of Scilly
Walking in the New Forest
Walking in the North Wessex Downs
Walking on Guernsey
Walking on Jersey
Walking on the Isle of Wight
Walking the Jurassic Coast
Walking the South West Coast Path
Walking the South West Coast Path
Map Booklets:
Vol 1: Minehead to St Ives
Vol 2: St Ives to Plymouth
Vol 3: Plymouth to Poole
Walks in the South Downs
National Park

WALES AND WELSH BORDERS

Cycle Touring in Wales
Cycling Lon Las Cymru
Glyndwr's Way
Great Mountain Days in Snowdonia
Hillwalking in Shropshire
Hillwalking in Wales – Vols 1&2
Mountain Walking in Snowdonia
Offa's Dyke Path
Offa's Dyke Map Booklet
Ridges of Snowdonia
Scrambles in Snowdonia
Snowdonia: 30 Low-level and Easy
Walks – North
Snowdonia: 30 Low-level and Easy
Walks – South

The Cambrian Way
The Pembrokeshire Coast Path
The Pembrokeshire Coast Path
Map Booklet
The Severn Way
The Snowdonia Way
The Wye Valley Walk
Walking in Carmarthenshire
Walking in Pembrokeshire
Walking in the Brecon Beacons
Walking in the Forest of Dean
Walking in the Wye Valley
Walking on Gower
Walking the Shropshire Way
Walking the Wales Coast Path

INTERNATIONAL CHALLENGES, COLLECTIONS AND ACTIVITIES

Europe's High Points
Walking the Via Francigena Pilgrim
Route – Part 1

AFRICA

Kilimanjaro
Walks and Scrambles in the
Moroccan Anti-Atlas
Walking in the Drakensberg

ALPS CROSS-BORDER ROUTES

100 Hut Walks in the Alps
Alpine Ski Mountaineering
Vol 1 – Western Alps
Vol 2 – Central and Eastern Alps
The Karnischer Hohenweg
The Tour of the Bernina
Trail Running – Chamonix and the
Mont Blanc region
Trekking Chamonix to Zermatt
Trekking in the Alps
Trekking in the Silvretta and
Ratikon Alps
Trekking Munich to Venice
Trekking the Tour of Mont Blanc
Walking in the Alps

PYRENEES AND FRANCE/SPAIN CROSS-BORDER ROUTES

Shorter Treks in the Pyrenees
The GR10 Trail
The GR11 Trail
The Pyrenean Haute Route
The Pyrenees
Walks and Climbs in the Pyrenees

AUSTRIA

Innsbruck Mountain Adventures
Trekking in Austria's Hohe Tauern
Trekking in Austria's Zillertal Alps
Trekking in the Stubai Alps
Walking in Austria
Walking in the Salzkammergut:
the Austrian Lake District

EASTERN EUROPE

The Danube Cycleway Vol 2
The Elbe Cycle Route
The High Tatras
The Mountains of Romania
Walking in Bulgaria's National Parks
Walking in Hungary

FRANCE, BELGIUM AND LUXEMBOURG

Camino de Santiago – Via Podiensis
Chamonix Mountain Adventures
Cycle Touring in France
Cycling London to Paris
Cycling the Canal de la Garonne
Cycling the Canal du Midi
Cycling the Route des Grandes Alpes
Mont Blanc Walks
Mountain Adventures in the
Maurienne
Short Treks on Corsica
The GR5 Trail
The GR5 Trail – Benelux and
Lorraine
The GR5 Trail – Vosges and Jura
The Grand Traverse of the
Massif Central
The Moselle Cycle Route
The River Loire Cycle Route
The River Rhone Cycle Route
Trekking in the Vanoise
Trekking the Cathar Way
Trekking the GR20 Corsica
Trekking the Robert Louis
Stevenson Trail
Via Ferratas of the French Alps
Walking in Provence – East
Walking in Provence – West
Walking in the Ardennes
Walking in the Auvergne
Walking in the Briançonnais
Walking in the Dordogne
Walking in the Haute Savoie: North
Walking in the Haute Savoie: South
Walking on Corsica
Walking the Brittany Coast Path

GERMANY

Hiking and Cycling in the
Black Forest
The Danube Cycleway Vol 1
The Rhine Cycle Route
The Westweg
Walking in the Bavarian Alps

IRELAND

The Wild Atlantic Way and
Western Ireland
Walking the Wicklow Way

For full information on all our guides, books and eBooks,
visit our website:
www.cicerone.co.uk